Medical Secretary's Standard Reference Handbook

Medical Secretary's Standard Reference Handbook

Helen Norman Saputo
And
Nancy Gill Rutherford

Prentice-Hall, Inc.
Englewood Cliffs, New Jersey

Dedication

This book is dedicated to our husbands, children, and parents who encouraged and supported us in our efforts.

Prentice-Hall International, Inc., *London*
Prentice-Hall of Australia, Pty. Ltd., *Sydney*
Prentice-Hall of Canada, Ltd., *Toronto*
Prentice-Hall of India Private Ltd., *New Delhi*
Prentice-Hall of Japan, Inc., *Tokyo*
Prentice-Hall of Southeast Asia Pte. Ltd., *Singapore*
Whitehall Books, Ltd., *Wellington, New Zealand*

Library of Congress Cataloging in Publication Data

Saputo, Helen Norman
    Medical secretary's standard reference handbook.

    Includes index.
    1. Medical secretaries. 2. Medical offices—
Management. I. Rutherford, Nancy Gill,
joint author. II. Title. [DNLM: 1. Medical
secretaries—Handbooks. W80 S241m]
R728.8.S26 1980   651.3'741   80-13676
ISBN 0-13-572941-6

Printed in the United States of America

The Practical Value of This Handbook

This is a reference book written to provide you, the medical secretary, with the latest and most up-to-date medical office procedures and practices to increase your efficiency in the performance of your job.

You, as a medical secretary, are aware of the need for a handy up-to-date guide to help you handle the many diverse situations that arise in a medical office. This handbook is easy to read and understand and is focused on very *real* office practices. It covers a broad range of activities and furnishes practical, effective techniques and methods to aid you in your everyday work.

You will find the practical information and answers you need to arrive at a solution to almost *any* situation that may develop.

Here are just a few specific examples of how this standard handbook will help you in your everyday work.

Case studies are emphasized throughout the guide. It is unique in that there are many actual office situations—dealing with emergencies, difficult patients, or even people who want to take advantage of the doctor's time. This book will help you do an even better job of meeting such challenges.

Situations that every medical secretary handles are discussed. For example:

> *The doctor is generally very fair and even-tempered, but occasionally may act in a way that appears unfair. After he had given you quite a bit of dictation, and although you always check the spelling of difficult or unusual words, he made a point of spelling a word for you. When he checked the dictation, he called you into the office and was quite annoyed because you had spelled a medical term incorrectly. This happened to be the word he had spelled for you. Chapter 13 tells you how to handle situations of this type.*

Chapter 6, "Handling Correspondence More Effectively," provides you with many aids to help you increase your efficiency in the area of composing, transcribing, and typing letters. There are actual samples of tested, successful letters you will want to use frequently, such as referral letters to other doctors and letters to patients concerning their medication or results of tests.

5

You will also find help in all areas of medical secretarial activity including:

Making appointments

Making telephone calls and taking messages

Filling out forms

Opening files for new patients

Making hospital reservations

Making travel arrangements

Writing speeches

Composing letters

Greeting patients

Handling emergencies

Choosing office furniture

Choosing the color scheme for redecorating the reception room

Hiring a part-time assistant

This handbook provides the medical secretary with a handy reference book for fast answers to questions that occur daily. For easy readability throughout the book, we have referred to the medical secretary as "she" and the doctor as "he" but recognize that the opposite may also be true.

The *Medical Secretary's Standard Reference Handbook* has 15 chapters plus two appendices. One Appendix is a glossary of medical terminology, and the other is a list of commonly used medical abbreviations.

Each chapter provides paragraph headings which clearly identify the areas covered. The material is amply illustrated with photographs, drawings, and case studies which enable you to re-examine both the technical and the human aspects of medical secretarial work and update your knowledge.

The *Medical Secretary's Standard Reference Handbook* is *your* source book. From the very first page it will help to increase your effectiveness on the job. Because of the unique way it focuses on *you* and *your* job, *you* will find it invaluable as a reliable day-to-day guide.

H.N.S. and N.G.R.

Acknowledgments

Without the assistance and efforts of many consultants, this guide would not have come to fruition.

We would particularly like to acknowledge the help of the following:

Betty Doyle Campbell, who provided us with the excellent drawings and made-to-order illustrations which make our book so much more meaningful.

Margaret S. Kulgren, who faithfully read and commented in depth on all our chapters and whose comments, based on her years of experience as a medical secretary, have been incorporated into our guide.

Lynne Sondelski, I.C.T. (Infant Care Technician), who shared her experiences as a medical secretary with us and offered many helpful suggestions.

Per G. Stensland, Ph.D. who, during the early stages of this book, provided us with critical and invaluable assistance.

George Pepe, Supervisor, Customer Service Representatives, Flushing Main Branch of the United States Postal Service, who provided us with illustrations and information needed in the portion of our book dealing with the processing of mail.

A special thank you to our doctor friends who were always ready to answer questions that we very often had:

Richard A. Broderick, M.D.
Helen Claire Stopford, M.D.
Robert L. Ward, M.D.
Walter F. Watton, M.D.

Thank you to Clinton H. Rutherford, Ph.D for his advice and understanding.

And finally, to Vito Saputo, M.B.A., C.P.A., for his patience in reading and re-reading our manuscript, offering encouragement, suggestions, advice, and helpful criticism, thank you.

Helen Norman Saputo
Nancy Gill Rutherford

Contents

The Practical Value of This Handbook   **5**

Chapter 1 - Scheduling Patient Appointments   **13**

Timing and Coordination Are Key Factors in Scheduling (13) Knowing the Patients Is Essential to Effective Communication (14) Note the Doctor's Preferences (14) Patience Is Basic to Handling All Mix-Ups, Emergencies, and Cancellations (15) Be Sensitive to Patient Needs (16) Checklist for Better Scheduling (16)

Chapter 2 - Improving Your Telephone Skills   **27**

Realizing the Increasing Importance of Good Telephone Communication in the Medical Office (27) Establish Rapport with Patients (28) Key Points to Keep in Mind—Voice, Diction, and Manners (28) Here are Some Suggestions for Ways to Handle Various Types of Calls (30) Doctor's Specialty Determines the Types of Calls (31) Suggested Ways of Dealing with Problem Calls (32) Calls from Other Doctors (33) Tips on Taking Messages (33) Increase the Effectiveness of Your Doctor's Answering Service (35) Key Points to Remember (36)

Chapter 3 - Increasing Your Effectiveness as Receptionist   **37**

Why First Impressions Are Important (37) Interviewing the Patient (38) Advice for Taking Care of the Waiting Patient (38) Be Sensitive to Patient Needs (41) Be Calm in Times of Stress (42) Greeting Other Callers (45) Ideas for Creating a Receptive Atmosphere (45)

Chapter 4 - Managing the Office More Effectively   **49**

Maintaining an Attractive Office (52) Ideas for a More Receptive Waiting Area (53) How to Have an Uncluttered Desk (55) Helping the Doctor Keep a Neat Office (56) Examining Room Checkup (56) Checklist to Help You Manage (56)

Chapter 5 - Guidelines for Purchasing and Operating Dictation Equipment   **59**

Transcription Equipment (59) Transcription Equipment Increases Your Efficiency (60) Where Transcription Equipment Is Used (61) Update Your Knowledge of Word Processing Equipment (63) Word Processing Results in Increased Efficiency (65) Photocopying Saves Time (67) Secretary Analyzes the Equipment (68) Hints for Using Transcribing Equipment (69)

Chapter 6 - Handling Correspondence More Effectively   **73**

Improving Your Processing of Incoming Mail (73) Practical Tips on Handling the Mail (74) When the Doctor Is Away (77) Your Responsibility for Outgoing Mail (77) Guidelines for Composing Letters (80) Improving Grammar Skills (84) Model Letters (88) Styles (91) Choosing the Stationery (96) Analyze the Dictation (98) Transcribing (98) Time-Savers (99)

Chapter 7 - Maintaining and Ordering Office Supplies and Equipment   **105**

Hints on Keeping Up with Supplies (105) Systematic Approach Makes Ordering Easier (106) Your Responsibility for Office Equipment and Supplies (107) Factors to Consider in Ordering Office Supplies (109) Overstocking Can Be a Problem (109) Practical Value of Keeping a Running Inventory (109) Tips on Storing Supplies and Drugs (110) Shortcuts Will Make the Job Easier (111) Tips for Keeping the Doctor's Bag Ready (112)

Chapter 8   -   **Assisting the Doctor as Author and Speaker 115**

How You Can Assist the Doctor with Writing (115) Choosing Your Own Reference Books (116) Knowing Where to Find Information (118) Preparing Manuscripts (119) Become Familiar with Format (Quoted Material, Footnotes, Table of Contents, Title Page) (124)

Chapter 9   -   **Matching the Filing to the Doctor's Needs   127**

Analyze the Various Systems (131) Helpful Hints in Preparing Materials (132) Choosing the Right Supplies and Equipment (135) Influence of Automation (136)

Chapter 10 -   **Practical Tips on Keeping Patients' Permanent Records   137**

Chapter 11 -   **Techniques for Speedy Handling of Medical Insurance Forms   159**

How to Find Out About Health Insurance (159) Have a Better Understanding of the Secretary's Responsibilities (168) Streamlining the Processing of Forms (168)

Chapter 12 -   **Keeping Better Financial Records   175**

Selecting the Right Bookkeeping System (176) Advantages of a Billing Service (177) Keeping Accurate Records of Payments and Charges (192) Finding the Time to Do the Bookkeeping (195) Practical Tips on Collecting Fees (195) Planning Is the Key to More Efficient Record Keeping (196) Guidelines to Using Time More Effectively (197) Itemizing Statements Is Good Human Relations (203) Guidelines for Determining and Quoting Fees (204) Determining the Fee (204) Helpful Hints on Quoting Fees to Patients (205) Knowing the Patient's Ability to Pay (205) Arrangements for Patients to Pay Fees (206)

Chapter 13 - **Building Human Relations Through a Practical Approach**   **207**

How to Increase Your Knowledge and Understanding (207) Project an Attitude of Concerned Graciousness (208) Tips on How to Achieve Good Human Relations (209) Tips on Greeting the Patient (210) Tips on Dealing with the Unexpected (210) Scheduling More Efficiently (211) Maximizing Telephone Effectiveness (211) Discussing Fees (212)

Chapter 14 - **Outlining Your Legal and Ethical Responsibilities**   **213**

Guidelines for the Secretary's Ethical Responsibilities (213) How to Maintain Professional Confidentiality (217) Maintaining Professional Courtesy (218) Tips on Keeping Up with the Doctor's Legal Responsibilities (218) Key to Protecting the Doctor from Malpractice Proceedings (219) Informed Consent (220) How the Law Affects the Medical Secretary (220)

Chapter 15 - **Checklist of Key Factors**   **223**

Organization Is the Key to Efficiency (223) Effective Communication Is Vital (224) Become a Better Office Manager (225) Evaluate Your Personal Qualities (225) Update Your Knowledge of Medical Specialties (226) Expand Your Medical Vocabulary (227) Looking to the Future (230) Growing Professionally (231) Certifying Examination (233)

Appendix I   **237**

Appendix II   **247**

Index   **251**

Chapter 1

Scheduling Patient Appointments

As any medical secretary knows, scheduling appointments is one of the basic but most significant operations of the doctor's office. The medical secretary is the most important person when it comes to arranging and setting up the doctor's daily appointment schedule. You can increase your effectiveness in scheduling appointments through experience. Remember that the doctor's preference is the major, most important consideration. It is his/her time that is being scheduled.

TIMING AND COORDINATION ARE KEY FACTORS IN SCHEDULING

Too often because of poor scheduling, patients spend long periods of time waiting for the doctor. Studies have shown that patients leave one doctor for another more often because of prolonged waiting rather than high fees or other causes. You can learn quickly how to make more effective use of the doctor's day by observing the approximate routine, organizing the office in the best possible way, and getting to know the patients.

Often the doctor also schedules appointments. This can present a difficult situation if the secretary is unaware and then schedules conflicting appointments. Many medical secretaries are faced with this situation. *You* must find a way to deal with it.

Analyze *your* situation. If this only occurs occasionally, all that may be necessary is an apology to the patient; but if you see that this occurs frequently, determine a policy to follow. For example, some doctors have specified "call hours" when patients may telephone the doctor and be sure of reaching him. At that time he may tell a patient to come into the office during the day. You would have to check with him to see what appointments to add to your book. You may realize from experience that more catch-up time is necessary in this case. Or, you may have a doctor who says, "Come in around eleven" to several patients who call. Then you know that you had better not schedule appointments at that time.

Perhaps your doctor keeps the appointment book with him overnight, and you do not see it until he arrives in the office. When this is the case, make tentative appointments and explain to the patients that the doctor has the appointment book and you will have to confirm it when he comes in.

KNOWING THE PATIENTS IS ESSENTIAL TO EFFECTIVE COMMUNICATION

Knowing who your patients are, their backgrounds, their problems and idiosyncrasies, will help you to schedule more effectively. When you expect that Mrs. Jones will rush in ten minutes late with some excuse about her car or not being able to find her glasses, at least this will not disrupt your day completely.

Certain people who are very businesslike will be in and out in fifteen minutes, but there are those who will talk with the doctor as long as he will listen. When you get to know the patients, you can adjust for such irregularities. For instance, you could schedule the "always late" Mrs. Jones ten to fifteen minutes later than stated on her appointment card. While patients who are always on time are no problem, the secretary might try to work out with the doctor what to do about patients who always take longer than the scheduled time. A prearranged interruption to subtly remind the doctor to keep on schedule might work; or perhaps the doctor may wish to allow a longer time for such a person.

NOTE THE DOCTOR'S PREFERENCES

The key factor in scheduling is to find out the doctor's preferences and see how you can best implement them. If you have the right attitude and are open for suggestions from others you can make it work. Note that each patient is different and the time allotments will vary according to needs.

Although most doctors see patients by specific appointments, there are still those who have "office hours." If this is the case, the patients are seen on a first-come, first-served basis. But even if the doctor does not have specific appointments, you must be alert to the same problems that exist with scheduled appointments; otherwise office hours will extend indefinitely. For example, one doctor may need only ten minutes for a checkup of a returning patient's condition while another needs at least twenty minutes. Another preference is length of time for history and physical examination of a new patient. Another is simply how fast your doctor works, as in applying a cast or doing minor surgery or dressing change. The procedure will determine the time allotted.

You should consult with the doctor for his preferences. For instance, a doctor may have several patients come in for allergy shots and see them between other appointments as it only takes a moment to give a shot. They may then wait for a while and will be checked before they leave for any reaction to the shot. Or, you can have the doctor see another patient while waiting for lab results or when other delays occur.

PATIENCE IS BASIC TO HANDLING ALL MIX-UPS, EMERGENCIES, AND CANCELLATIONS

Keep in mind that regulating appointments carefully can enhance the doctor's opportunities to build his practice. Do not become upset should the schedule fall behind. Schedules fall behind for many reasons. For instance, in a pediatrician's office it is inevitable that some mother will make an appointment for one of her children for a shot and while there ask the doctor "if he can just look at Susie's ear and can he check the wart on Margaret's finger." Such predicaments will occur and the alert secretary should expect them. Handle them with firmness and tact without showing anger or aggravation. Very often there is no real way of preventing additional requests, so the wise assistant, who knows her patients, will probably allow extra time for this mother's appointment so that the schedule will not fall too far behind. Maintain an outward calm and resolve to straighten things out as soon as possible. Remember that problems can usually be resolved.

It is very important to be aware of the patient's feelings and need for privacy. Giving what appears to be *undivided* attention and *real* concern is the magic key to good patient relationships. The patient must feel that she/he is the most important concern, and is the only one being cared for at that moment.

Emergencies may occur in any specialty, but some medical offices are apt to have more than others—such as a pediatrician's office or the office of an obstetrician. So the wise secretary will recognize this fact; and though it is not possible to schedule emergencies, many medical secretaries allow extra time (catch-up time) for every two or three patients in order to maintain an approximate schedule.

The use of the examining rooms can be made more efficient. A patient can be ushered into one room while another patient is being examined in one of the other rooms. Efficient utilization of examining rooms speeds up the processing of patients.

BE SENSITIVE TO PATIENT NEEDS

Remember: Be very careful that in your desire to be efficient you do not dehumanize your relationship with the patient. Even though there are several examining rooms in use at a time, the patient must always feel that he has the doctor's and the medical secretary's undivided attention at that time. Patients should not feel that they are being processed in an assembly-line fashion.

Continually be aware of the feelings of your patients. In a busy office, it often becomes difficult to keep up with things. Do not get so involved with the efficient running of the office that you forget to be sensitive to the patient's feelings. For example, because you know that Mrs. Jones is very anxious for privacy, be careful not to usher her into an examining room at a time when she may encounter another patient entering another room. Also, if you have a patient who speaks very loudly, it would be better not to have Mrs. Jones in an examining room near him or she may feel that she also can be overheard when speaking with the doctor.

CHECKLIST FOR BETTER SCHEDULING

1. An appointment book is a necessity. The type used will be determined by the doctor's need or preference. There are appointment books for the single practice, the practice with more than one doctor, and others.

Analyze your needs; if you do not have the kind of appointment book that suits the situation, contact a firm that prints medical forms and discuss possible solutions with them. They may have just what you want. If not, they will be able to print forms for you.

Appointment books usually are broken down into 15-minute intervals. This is generally the best setup as it allows for many combinations. (See Figures 1-1, 1-2, 1-3, 1-4.) Some things to look for are: a separate page for each day, space for date, time, name, and the reason for seeing the doctor. (See Figure 1-1.)

The pegboard type bookkeeping systems are designed to be all-inclusive, with the appointment book and the appointment card being part of the system itself instead of being a separate book. There are multiple part forms on which the appointment, the service rendered, the fee charged, and the cash received can be entered. A portion of the form also can be torn off and given to the

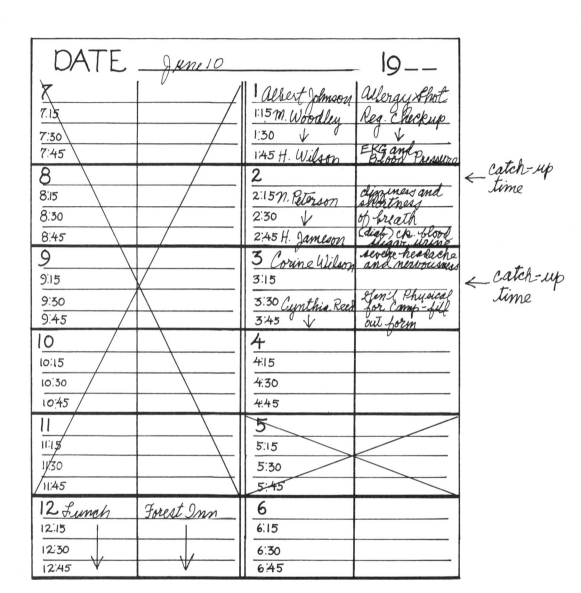

FIGURE 1-1
APPOINTMENT BOOK PAGE SHOWING APPOINTMENTS
AND CATCH-UP TIME

DATE			19__
7		**1**	
7.15		1:15	
7:30		1:30	
7:45		1:45	
8		**2**	
8:15		2:15	
8:30		2:30	
8:45		2:45	
9		**3**	
9:15		3:15	
9:30		3:30	
9:45		3:45	
10		**4**	
10:15		4:15	
10:30		4:30	
10:45		4:45	
11		**5**	
11:15		5:15	
11:30		5:30	
11:45		5:45	
12		**6**	
12:15		6:15	
12:30		6:30	
12:45		6:45	

FIGURE 1-2
GENERAL APPOINTMENT BOOK - SINGLE PRACTICE

DATE_____ 19____

DR._____   DR._____

7			
7:15			
7:30			
7:45			
8			
8:15			
8:30			
8:45			
9			
9:15			
9:30			
9:45			
10			
10:15			
10:30			
10:45			
11			
11:15			
11:30			
11:45			
12			
12:15			
12:30			
12:45			

FIGURE 1-3
GENERAL APPOINTMENT BOOK - TWO DOCTORS

JANUARY 6 MONDAY	JANUARY 7 TUESDAY	JANUARY 8 WEDNESDAY	JANUARY 9 THURSDAY	JANUARY 10 FRIDAY	JANUARY 11 SATURDAY
8	8	8	8	8	8
9	9	9	9	9	9
10	10	10	10	10	10
11	11	11	11	11	11
12	12	12	12	12	12
1	1	1	1	1	1
2	2	2	2	2	2
3	3	3	3	3	3
4	4	4	4	4	4
5	5	5	5	5	5
EVENING	EVENING	EVENING	EVENING	EVENING	EVENING

FIGURE 1-4
APPOINTMENT BOOK SHOWING A WEEK AT A TIME

patient as a reminder of the next appointment. (See Chapter 12—"Keeping Better Financial Records.")

But, no matter what style appointment book you use, remember to be careful to maintain confidentiality: shield the book from unauthorized eyes.

2. Appointments should be carefully recorded. Whether you use pencil or pen is your own preference. Some people prefer pen as the book is a permanent record. Others prefer pencil so that they may make corrections easily. Legibility (whether pencil or pen) is very important because other authorized personnel need to be able to interpret the appointment schedule. Care should be taken to spell the name correctly and the reason for the visit should be noted. Special care should be taken not to confuse names that have a similar sound or spelling. If there is any doubt as to the name, always ask the person to spell it and then you repeat it to make certain.

The appointment book could become a document of legal evidence, to prove in court that a patient had an appointment and failed to keep it, or that a patient was seen at a particular time or for a particular reason.

3. The time should be double-checked before giving the patient an appointment card as a reminder. There are many types of appointment cards. Some are for single appointments and others have two sides and are in booklet form with room for more than one appointment. These are handy when a person has a series of treatments such as dental or allergy appointments.

When a person calls in for an appointment, you may or may not mail them a card. You may find that, for some forgetful patients, it is a good idea to send them a reminder card if an apointment has been made far in advance. (See Figures 1-5, 1-6, 1-7, 1-8, 1-9.)

TELEPHONE 421-1200

ALVIN MYLES JONES, M. D.

OFFICE HOURS
1-2 AND 7-8 P.M.
AND BY APPOINTMENT

965 WALT WHITMAN ROAD
MELVILLE, N. Y. 11746

Courtesy of Histacount Corporation Subsidiary of SCM Corporation. Used by permission.

FIGURE 1-5
PROFESSIONAL CARD

HAmilton 1-1200

ALVIN MYLES JONES, M. D.

965 WALT WHITMAN ROAD   MELVILLE, N. Y. 11749

FIGURE 1-6
COMBINATION PROFESSIONAL CARD WITH
APPOINTMENT CARD ON REVERSE SIDE

M _____

HAS AN APPOINTMENT ON

☐ MON.   ☐ TUE.   ☐ WED.   ☐ THUR.   ☐ FRI.   ☐ SAT.

A.M.
DATE_____ AT_____P.M.

IF UNABLE TO KEEP APPOINTMENT, KINDLY GIVE 24 HRS. NOTICE.

FIGURE 1-7
COMBINATION PROFESSIONAL CARD WITH
APPOINTMENT CARD — REVERSE SIDE

ALVIN MYLES JONES, M. D.
965 WALT WHITMAN ROAD
MELVILLE, N. Y. 11749
—
HAmilton 1-1200

M_____

HAS AN APPOINTMENT ON

_____
DAY   MONTH   DATE

AT_____A. M. _____P. M.

IF UNABLE TO KEEP APPOINTMENT, KINDLY GIVE 24 HRS. NOTICE.

Courtesy of Histacount Corporation Subsidiary of
SCM Corporation. Used by permission.

FIGURE 1-8
APPOINTMENT CARD

M_____

HAS AN APPOINTMENT ON

☐ MON.   ☐ TUE.   ☐ WED.   ☐ THUR.   ☐ FRI.   ☐ SAT.

DATE _____   AT _____ A. M.
                                              P. M.

ALVIN MYLES JONES, M. D.
965 WALT WHITMAN ROAD
HAMILTON 1-1200   MELVILLE, N. Y. 11749

IF UNABLE TO KEEP APPOINTMENT, KINDLY GIVE 24 HRS. NOTICE.

*Courtesy of Histacount Corporation Subsidiary of
SCM Corporation. Used by permission.*

FIGURE 1-9
APPOINTMENT CARD

4. Always have a telephone number where the patient can be reached in case a cancellation should be necessary.

5. Cancellations should be carefully noted. One common method is to draw a line through the name and note when the appointment is rescheduled. This provides a record of the fact that the appointment has been rescheduled rather than erasing the prior appointment. (See Figure 1-10.)

6. The patient's preference for appointment time should always be considered. If the time requested is not available, then you should offer a choice of times; for example, "Would you like to come in Friday at 3 p.m. or Tuesday at 10 a.m.?"

7. The secretary allows time for each appointment according to the needs of the individual. A checkup may require only 15 or 20 minutes whereas a complete physical examination will require more time. A new patient is not given a complete examination unless requested, but more time is allowed a new patient because of the necessity of taking the medical history and setting up a new file. The secretary always knows how best to utilize the doctor's time by observing how smoothly the office is running and how rapidly the doctor is able to see the patients. Be flexible and ready to make changes in your office procedure if you find that what you are doing is not working well.

8. Allow some free time in the day's schedule. This provides time for making phone calls, doing catch-up work, or seeing walk-ins. If possible, a buffer time of 15 minutes between every three or four patients is ideal. This leaves time, too, for emergencies and for those appointments that run overtime. For example, these include returning the calls of anxious patients, making hospital arrangements, and talking with other physicians. The doctor will need to do this between patients, during lunch, or after office hours whenever he can squeeze it in. No matter how carefully you schedule

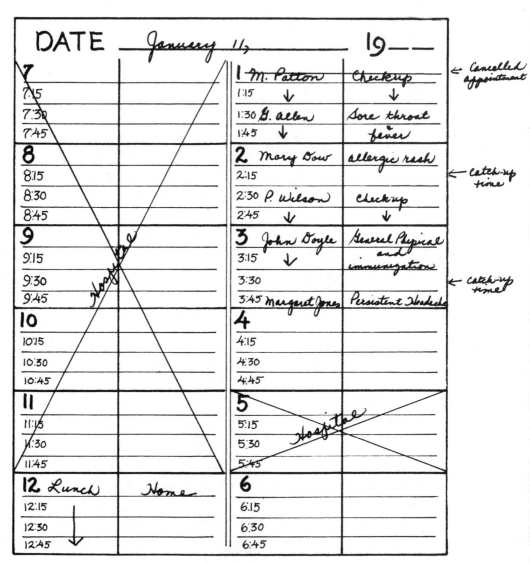

FIGURE 1-10
APPOINTMENT PAGE SHOWING CANCELLED APPOINTMENT

appointments, there will always be something to interfere. That is one reason why it is important not to schedule every available minute of the day.

9. Emergency cases are seen immediately. The reason for the delay should be explained in general terms to the waiting patients. For instance you could say:

"An emergency has occurred that will cause a little delay. The doctor will be with you shortly."

Reveal no details that would violate confidentiality. If the delay extends longer than anticipated, keep the patients informed.

10. Care should be taken to record all the doctor's appointments whether in the office or outside. Always make a note of telephone numbers where the doctor can be reached at all times. Make every effort to answer any questions or handle emergencies that might arise.

11. If the doctor must cancel an appointment, it should be noted in the appointment book immediately. The patient should be notified and given a reason. Treat the patient with courtesy and offer another appointment time.

12. If the doctor wants to see a patient again, the appointment should be made before the patient leaves the office. You should record the appointment immediately and give the patient a reminder card with the date and time on it.

Remember: Whatever the system used, the appointment book is very important. It helps the secretary to plan the day efficiently and also helps the doctor plan his day. It is an important permanent record of all patients seen by the doctor that can be used in a court of law to prove whether or not a person saw the doctor. (See Chapter 14.)

The foregoing suggestions will increase the efficient operation of your office. Of course, just following rules will not get the job done. In addition, you must employ a generous amount of common sense in the handling of all matters dealing with the public. This is always one of the most important considerations.

Chapter 2

Improving
Your Telephone Skills

As you know, effective use of the telephone is an integral part of every phase of business today, but perhaps nowhere is it more important than when dealing with people who are worried, upset, or confronted with an emergency situation.

Since the calls coming into a doctor's office are primarily from patients, you as a medical secretary are called upon to use the very best of telephone techniques in handling these calls. They range from the very ordinary call for an appointment for an annual checkup to a call from a relative concerned about a very ill patient of the doctor's or a sudden emergency situation which needs immediate handling.

REALIZING THE INCREASING IMPORTANCE OF GOOD TELEPHONE COMMUNICATION IN THE MEDICAL OFFICE

The first impression created on the caller is very important. The caller must know that the proper number has been reached.

The telephone could be answered as follows:

Secretary: *Doctor Freed's office, Miss Adams speaking.*

or: *Doctor's office, Miss Adams.*

Saying good morning or good afternoon is superfluous and, though pleasant, does not do anything to help create the proper impression. In fact, for the concerned patient it only adds an undue burden of response. A pleasant businesslike voice and manner that gives them the information they want is all that is necessary.

You must remain calm and collected at all times, answering the telephone with a very pleasant voice, never appearing hurried or harried or anxious to get to something else.

ESTABLISH RAPPORT WITH PATIENTS

Remember: Impressions given over the phone are very important. One medical secretary has said, "It can make or break the doctor." It is important in establishing rapport with patients to handle telephone problems pleasantly and intelligently. Many patients resent not being able to speak with the doctor personally. The *caring* medical secretary can help the patient realize that the doctor cannot speak with everyone and that is the reason he has an office assistant.

KEY POINTS TO KEEP IN MIND—VOICE, DICTION, AND MANNERS

The patient needs to feel certain that his message will be relayed to the doctor clearly and that the doctor's (instructions) reply will be relayed back to him exactly. Careless instructions or information could be detrimental, even disastrous, to the patient. The doctor needs to feel that he can have complete faith in his secretary to handle such situations.

Precious time should not be frittered away on the telephone, but it is equally important not to rush the patient. His problem, the manner in which it is handled, should be the prime consideration of the medical secretary. The patient should be made to feel this through the secretary's tone of voice and attitude.

If you are answering the telephone for more than one doctor, it is necessary to identify the doctor as follows:

Secretary: *Doctor Freed's office, Miss Adams speaking.*

A very important rule to remember and one that is often forgotten when we are under the stress of a busy office is:

The telephone should never be allowed to ring more than one or two times.
If possible it should be picked up on the first ring.

When speaking to another patient, excuse yourself and answer the telephone when it rings. As you know, it is impossible to concentrate on what you are saying to a patient while the telephone is ringing, so nothing is gained by trying to finish the conversation. It is also possible that the person calling may have an emergency situation in which every second counts.

Often, the telephone is ringing when you are talking to a patient. It is a very sensitive situation because each patient wants your and the doctor's undivided attention. You can handle this situation with ease if you are calm but firm. The patient will recognize the fact that if he were the party calling, he would also want to be answered immediately and not left waiting while you speak to someone else. After answering the phone, thank the patient for waiting, and resume the conversation.

Your attitude is the important one. *You* must remain calm, pleasant, efficient, and interested in both the patient to whom you are speaking and the caller.

Never appear harried, upset, or too busy to *listen* carefully. *You* remain in control of the situation. Be careful not to repeat anything that is confidential within hearing of another patient.

With these thoughts in mind you can then answer the telephone in a manner similar to the following:

Secretary: *Excuse me a moment, please (to the patient at the desk).*

or: *Would you mind waiting just a moment while I answer the phone.*

or: *(If you are already talking and another line is ringing, you can say:)*
Would you hold please while I answer the other phone.

Then you may say to the person on the phone:

Secretary: *Doctor's office—(Ask who it is or if it is an emergency and then say)—"Can you hold for a moment please, I'm on another line."*

(Then when you come back on the line) "Thank you for holding, may I help you?"

With the caller on hold, always check back with the waiting caller, never leaving the caller longer than two to three minutes. Even with the few words such as:

You are still on hold

or: *Sorry for the delay*

or: *Mrs. Jones, I'll get back to you in a moment,*

you won't lose your caller.

Remember: When you ask someone to hold a moment, it must be only a moment. Put yourself in the place of the caller. There is nothing more irritating than to be told to hold on a moment and then be left with a "dead" line for what seems (and may be) an endless time. Businesses lose many customers that way. Doctors would certainly hear about your inefficiency from their patients.

HERE ARE SOME SUGGESTIONS FOR WAYS TO HANDLE VARIOUS TYPES OF CALLS

Emergencies

If a telephone call turns out to be an emergency, the person calling will be very upset. It may be difficult to get all the information necessary such as name, address, telephone number (if you do not know the person) and nature of emergency situation. If the doctor is in the office, put him on the telephone immediately giving him the necessary information so that he does not have to waste time asking the same questions again. If the doctor is not in, you should know where he can be reached immediately. It may be that the doctor is not available at this time. Then, you as the secretary should be able to indicate to the patient the next type of action—either contacting another doctor or the emergency room of the hospital. The following is an example of the correct way to handle an emergency:

> Frantic Mother: *I must talk with the doctor right away. My daughter seems to be having a severe reaction to the medication. She is running a high fever and is breaking out. Should I bring her in or what should I do?*
>
> Secretary: *Mrs. Jones, tell me the details. I can call the doctor, find out what to do, and get back to you right away.*
>
> or: *Mrs. Jones, I'll have the doctor call you back in just a few moments. He's at the hospital right now.*

Do *not* say "Doctor isn't in his office right now." This gives the feeling of "Oh no, what'll I do!" Instead, immediately offer your help by saying;

"I can call him with the details if you'll just tell me who, what, etc."

Your doctor knows how he wants to handle emergency situations. He will very possibly have a prescribed course of action to be followed if he is not available immediately. This may involve your contacting another doctor for the patient or arranging for ambulance service to a hospital or whatever arrangements the doctor has.

Remember: A medical secretary is *not* to give any medical advice. You are not to take it upon yourself to determine whether or not this situation is serious enough to wait until later when the doctor comes in.

Drug Detail Men

Another type of call that will be received in a doctor's office is from salesmen more commonly known as "drug detail men." Be courteous to the salesmen as it is one of the ways in which the doctor keeps up to date on the new items in medicine and equipment. If the doctor is not busy, the salesman can be put through to the doctor, or if he wants an appointment, one can be made for him. It may be necessary to check with the doctor first and find out when he will be free to see the salesman. Tactful remarks such as

> *"The doctor is most anxious to speak with you but has a busy schedule this week; I could, however, squeeze you in for fifteen minutes on Wednesday afternoon if that would be all right."*

indicate to the salesman that the doctor would like to see him, but also limit his time so that he knows he cannot take any more time than that.

DOCTOR'S SPECIALTY DETERMINES THE TYPES OF CALLS

The kind of practice your doctor has determines the type of calls you get and the type of patients you have. As you know, in some offices there will not be too many emergency calls though, of course, some will come in. In other types of offices, there will be many. The pediatrician, for instance, will receive more emergency calls from people who are upset than the ophthalmologist or the dermatologist.

Some offices deal more with patients who are very ill than others and are more apt to get calls that require a great deal of understanding and sympathy. The doctor dealing with heart disease or cancer will probably have more to do with patients who are very ill and families who are upset than the podiatrist or allergist.

The nature of the specialty very often may determine the attitude of the patient and the medical secretary. For example, a general practitioner handles all types of patients, so you as the medical secretary are constantly being called upon to deal with all types of situations on the telephone from a case involving a 2-year old's sore throat to an 82-year old's complaints. This is what makes your job ever interesting, never dull.

Remember: The people with whom you deal over the telephone must have your careful and concerned attention. It does not matter how you feel that particular moment, nor how nasty or annoying a particular patient may be; *you* must always be polite, efficient, and effective in your telephone answering techniques.

SUGGESTED WAYS OF DEALING WITH PROBLEM CALLS

There is always the "annoyed" person. Again, take a breath, *put yourself in his place*. This always helps in dealing with people. Try to see things as they do. Also, *remember* it is easier for people to be difficult with others on the telephone because they are not making "eye contact" with the person with whom they are speaking, so someone who may be pleasant "face to face" may not be so over the telephone if he is the least bit upset over something.

Among the following situations, you will recognize some similar to those you have in your office:

Secretary: *Doctor's office, Miss Jones speaking.*

Patient: *Finally! I've been calling for the past two hours. What time do you people get to work? It's 10 o'clock.*

Secretary: *I'm sorry you were unable to reach us, but on Tuesday and Thursday, we don't come into the office until 10 o'clock. Are you a patient of the doctor's?*

Patient: *Yes, of course. Why do you think I'm calling? I'd like to speak with the doctor.*

Secretary: *The doctor is not in right now. May I have your name please.*

Patient: *Harry Sims.*

Secretary: *Mr. Sims, the doctor doesn't come into the office until two this afternoon. On Tuesday and Thursday, he comes in at two and on Monday, Wednesday, and Friday, he comes in at eleven. What can I do for you?*

or:

Secretary: *Perhaps, I can help you.*

or:

Secretary: *If you'll tell me your problem, maybe I can help.*

Patient: *No thanks. I want to speak with the doctor. This is personal.*

Secretary: *If you'll leave a telephone number where you can be reached this afternoon, I'll give the doctor your message.*

or:

Secretary: *I'll ask the doctor to return your call this afternoon.*

or:

Secretary: *Would you like to call back this afternoon around 3 o'clock?*

A very annoying problem is the patient who calls frequently and insists on talking with the doctor immediately even though nothing is seriously wrong.

Secretary: *Doctor's office.*

Patient: *I don't want to talk to you. I want to talk to the doctor.*

Secretary: *The doctor is very busy at the moment. Perhaps I can help you if you will explain the difficulty.*

Be tactful but firm with the patient and after a while the patient will begin to realize that the doctor cannot be disturbed for every little problem that arises.

CALLS FROM OTHER DOCTORS

Other doctors often call your doctor. These calls are important. They may be of a personal nature or they may have to do with a patient. Give these calls top priority. In the absence of instructions to the contrary, the doctor should be connected immediately if that is possible. If not, you should be certain that the doctor receives the message as soon as possible.

Keep a list of the doctors who frequently call. Familiarize yourself with their names and voices so that you will recognize them immediately and will not have to ask who they are.

Some examples of calls such as these are:

Other Doctor: *This is Paul Smith. Is Jim in?*

Secretary: *Oh yes, Dr. Smith, how are you? I'll put you through to Dr. Freed.*

      or:

Secretary: *The doctor isn't in, may I help you?*

Other Doctor: *This is Harvey Walden. Could you have Jim call me at the office?*

Secretary: *Is this Dr. Walden? Where can you be reached? I don't expect Dr. Freed back this afternoon. Is this urgent or can it wait until tomorrow?*

Families of other doctors may call for appointments. Give them every possible courtesy in making appointments as soon as possible. If it appears that the wait may be too long, your doctor should be advised so that he may instruct you how to handle this. You should get special instructions from your doctor on how to handle the families of other doctors. In an area where there are few doctors, there is little problem, but where there are many, your doctor may have determined a policy to follow.

TIPS ON TAKING MESSAGES

There are many different methods which you can use in taking telephone messages and recording them. One that is suggested for a doctor's office is

To_____

DATE_____ TIME_____ AM. P.M.

WHILE YOU WERE OUT

M_____
of_____
AREA CODE & EXCHANGE_____

TELEPHONED____	PLEASE CALL____
CALLED TO SEE YOU	WILL CALL AGAIN___
WANTS TO SEE YOU	URGENT____
RET. YOUR CALL___	

MESSAGE_____
_____
_____
_____
_____
_____

FIGURE 2-1
TELEPHONE MESSAGE FORM

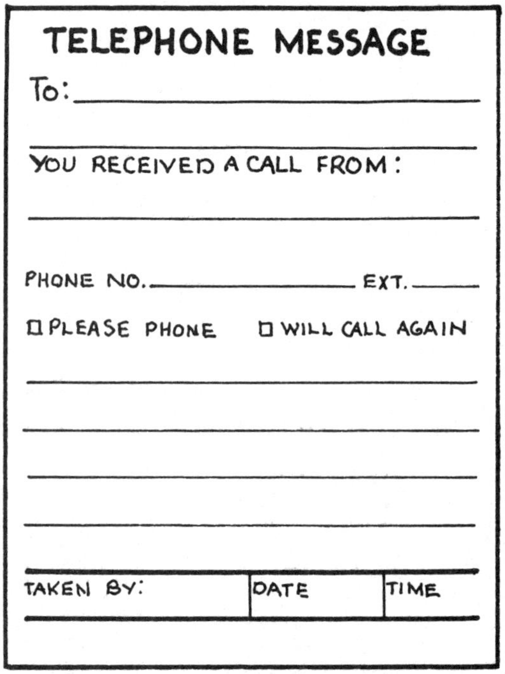

TELEPHONE MESSAGE
To:_____
_____
YOU RECEIVED A CALL FROM:
_____
_____
PHONE NO._____ EXT.____
□ PLEASE PHONE   □ WILL CALL AGAIN
_____
_____
_____
_____

| TAKEN BY: | DATE | TIME |

FIGURE 2-2
TELEPHONE MESSAGE FORM

```
┌──────────────────────────────────────────────────────────────┐
│          TELEPHONE CONVERSATION RECORD                         │
│  CONVERSATION WITH  Mrs. Craig                                 │
│                                          A.M. 9⁵⁵              │
│  ☐ I CALLED PARTY   ☒ PARTY CALLED ME   TIME P.M.___ DATE 1/15 │
│  SUBJECT DISCUSSED  Son James -- strep throat                  │
│  ────────────────────────────────────────────────────────────  │
│          WHAT I SAID         │      WHAT OTHER PARTY SAID       │
│  ────────────────────────────┼─────────────────────────────── │
│  Doctor will be in at        │  Checking in to advise          │
│  11¹⁵ a.m. and will          │  how James is doing             │
│  return call                 │  today -- fever down            │
│                              │  and feels much                 │
│                              │  better -- wants to             │
│                              │  know whether to                │
│                              │  continue medication.           │
│                              │                                 │
└──────────────────────────────────────────────────────────────┘
```

FIGURE 2-3
TELEPHONE MESSAGE FORM

writing out all telephone messages in duplicate, the secretary retaining one copy and giving the other copy to the doctor. If the message is from a patient, it is advisable to give the doctor that patient's file with the telephone message attached. The doctor should be prepared when talking to a patient with the background information on the patient. He cannot be expected to remember all the details of his patient's condition and treatment.

You should always have a record of telephone calls taken and follow-up action to make sure the doctor has called. Some secretaries keep a telephone log—stenographic notebooks work very well with their spiral bound pages and flat writing surface divided down the middle. You can then compose the message forms for the doctor from these notes. (See Figures 2-1, 2-2, 2-3.)

INCREASE THE EFFECTIVENESS OF YOUR DOCTOR'S ANSWERING SERVICE

Today most doctors have some form of telephone answering service. Be sure that messages are being picked up from them whenever you return to the office. These telephone messages should be followed through in the same manner as any telephone calls you have taken yourself. The telephone answering service is very important to the doctor. It is necessary that you be constantly aware of this and follow through on any complaint a patient may have which may indicate that his messages are not being received and transmitted properly.

The telephone answering service must be made aware of the doctor's wishes on various types of calls such as emergency calls or calls in which the patient wants the doctor to contact him as soon as possible. A patient does not want to be told on a Saturday that the doctor will call as soon as he can be reached and then not hear from the doctor until Monday morning. If this is going to be the situation, then the patient should be so advised.

Another common type of answering service is the automatic recording device. The caller is greeted with a taped message instructing him to leave his name, telephone number, and message. This can be very frustrating to a patient. For example, if an anxious patient calls and hears a recorded message saying that the doctor will not be in the office until tomorrow at two without indicating an alternate arrangement, he may become very upset.

The following is an example of an alternate arrangement:

Recorded Message: *The doctor is away from the office and will return your call after 2 p.m. tomorrow. If this is an emergency, call 631-7293 (the covering doctor OR the hospital) for help."*

or: *Doctor Stone is covering for Doctor Freed. Please call 631-6274.*

Remember: Tell the patient what time his call will be returned. Do not leave him waiting for a call to be returned if it will not be until the next afternoon.

KEY POINTS TO REMEMBER

In the medical office, special emphasis must be put on human relations, accuracy of written information, and careful follow-through in relaying complete information to the doctor.

Remember that the medical secretary follows all the correct telephone techniques set forth by the telephone company for all people engaged in answering the telephone. You must be even more careful, more accurate, and more helpful and understanding because you will be dealing in many instances with people who are upset, nervous, and who, themselves, are not employing good telephone techniques. Remember to *write, write, write* your telephone message to the doctor; do *not* trust your memory.

Chapter 3

Increasing
Your Effectiveness
as Receptionist

People coming to the doctor's office are usually either not feeling well or are apprehensive about their condition or that of a member of their family. They must be greeted with particular care and attention. How you handle your role as receptionist determines the mood and tone of the office. You must be constantly looking for ways to increase your effectiveness.

WHY FIRST IMPRESSIONS ARE IMPORTANT

You are the first person that the patient sees. The impression you make is very important. How the patient feels about the doctor may be influenced by the impression you make. Make the patient feel welcome. No matter how busy you are, do not appear so rushed or hurried that you give the patient the feeling of imposing upon you or that the doctor may be too busy to give proper attention. You reflect the doctor's attitude.

Put the patient at ease. Be sensitive to feelings. You can do this by being observant. You certainly do not want to be overly cheerful if the patient appears to be in distress. Make the patient feel welcome and secure in the fact that the doctor will provide the best possible attention.

As you know, it is easier to make a regular patient feel at ease than a new one. The old patient is familiar with the routine of the office and knows both you and the doctor. He may be worried about his condition, but he is usually not apprehensive about the care he will receive. A new patient, however, requires more attention at first and needs to understand the procedures to be followed. For example, he needs to know when the doctor will see him; which room he goes to first; does the doctor speak to him in his office first or directly in the examining room; and whatever else may be expected of him. Sometimes it is the simplest things that concern a patient and when he knows what to expect, many of his fears are allayed.

You may find that a patient does not know how to prepare himself for the examination. Don't assume that the patient knows that he must undress completely and put on the dressing gown with the opening in the back just because you have told him many times before. A new patient must have everything carefully explained to him.

INTERVIEWING THE PATIENT

You, as the secretary, interview the new patient and get all the personal data, such as name, address, telephone number, age, medical insurance plan and number. Whether or not you also take the medical history will depend on your doctor. Some doctors have special forms that are given to the patient to fill out himself prior to seeing the doctor (See Figures 3-1A and 3-1B). Whatever your practice is, you should explain it to the patient. Often, just sitting and filling out forms when he is anxious to see the doctor will be very upsetting so you should explain why this is done and also have him understand that it is a good way to utilize the time while he is waiting to see the doctor.

Be particularly careful while interviewing the patient. Be sure that you are doing so in an area from which you cannot be overheard by anyone else. No one likes to feel that others, for example maintenance staff or other personnel, are hearing his/her personal medical business. It is of grave importance to protect the patient's privacy. It is, in fact, the law that confidential medical information not be revealed to anyone without the patient's authorization. Also, make sure you are in an area in which you and the patient cannot overhear anyone else. If you can hear the doctor talking with a patient, the patient you are interviewing may feel that he can be overheard while he is with the doctor.

ADVICE FOR TAKING CARE OF THE WAITING PATIENT

After you have greeted the patient and completed whatever business is necessary, ask him to be seated and tell him the doctor will see him shortly. After telling a patient that the doctor will see him "shortly," make sure it is "shortly." If not, advise the patient why and indicate how much longer he will

PATIENT QUESTIONNAIRE

PATIENT'S NAME _____ BIRTH DATE _____ SEX _____ S. M. W. D.

ADDRESS _____ TEL. NO. _____

INSURANCE _____ REFERRED BY _____ OCCUPATION _____

INSTRUCTIONS: PUT ✓ IN THOSE BOXES APPLICABLE TO YOU AND IN THE "YES" OR "NO" SPACE. IF LINES ARE PROVIDED WRITE IN YOUR ANSWER.

FAMILY HISTORY

	FATHER	MOTHER	BROTHER 1	2	3	4	SISTER 1	2	3	4	SPOUSE	CHILDREN 1	2	3	4	5	6
AGE (IF LIVING)																	
HEALTH (G) GOOD (B) BAD																	
CANCER																	
TUBERCULOSIS																	
DIABETES																	
HEART TROUBLE																	
HIGH BLOOD PRESSURE																	
STROKE																	
EPILEPSY																	
NERVOUS BREAKDOWN																	
ASTHMA, HIVES, HAYFEVER																	
BLOOD DISEASE																	
AGE (AT DEATH)																	
CAUSE OF DEATH																	

PERSONAL HISTORY

HAVE YOU EVER HAD...	NO	YES	HAVE YOU EVER HAD...	NO	YES	HAVE YOU EVER HAD...	NO	YES
☐SCARLET FEVER ☐SCARLATINA			☐GONORRHEA ☐SYPHILIS			ANY ☐BROKEN ☐CRACKED BONES		
DIPHTHERIA			ANEMIA			RECURRENT DISLOCATIONS		
SMALLPOX			JAUNDICE			☐CONCUSSION ☐HEAD INJURY		
PNEUMONIA			EPILEPSY			EVER BEEN KNOCKED UNCONSCIOUS		
PLEURISY			MIGRAINE HEADACHES			☐FOOD ☐CHEMICAL ☐DRUG POISONING		
UNDULANT FEVER			TUBERCULOSIS			EXPLAIN		
☐RHEUMATIC FEVER ☐HEART DISEASE			DIABETES					
ST. VITUS DANCE			CANCER					
☐ARTHRITIS ☐RHEUMATISM			☐HIGH ☐LOW BLOOD PRESSURE			ANY OTHER DISEASE		
ANY ☐BONE ☐JOINT DISEASE			NERVOUS BREAKDOWN			EXPLAIN		
☐NEURITIS ☐NEURALGIA			☐HAY FEVER ☐ASTHMA					
☐BURSITIS ☐SCIATICA ☐LUMBAGO			☐HIVES ☐ECZEMA					
☐POLIO ☐MENINGITIS			FREQUENT ☐COLDS ☐SORE THROAT			WEIGHT: NOW ___ ONE YR. AGO ___		
BRIGHT'S DISEASE			FREQUENT ☐INFECTIONS ☐BOILS			MAXIMUM ___ WHEN ___		

ALLERGIES

ARE YOU ALLERGIC TO...	NO	YES	ARE YOU ALLERGIC TO...	NO	YES	ARE YOU ALLERGIC TO...	NO	YES
☐PENICILLIN ☐SULFA DRUGS			ANY OTHER DRUGS			ANY FOODS		
☐ASPIRIN ☐CODEINE ☐MORPHINE			EXPLAIN			EXPLAIN		
☐MYCINS ☐OTHER ANTIBIOTICS								
☐TETANUS ☐ANTITOXIN ☐SERUMS			ADHESIVE TAPE			☐NAIL POLISH ☐OTHER COSMETICS		

SURGERY

HAVE YOU HAD REMOVED...	NO	YES	HAVE YOU HAD REMOVED...	NO	YES	HAVE YOU...	NO	YES
TONSILS			☐OVARY ☐OVARIES			HAD HERNIA REPAIRED		
APPENDIX			HEMORRHOIDS			HAD ANY OTHER OPERATIONS		
GALL BLADDER			EVER HAVE A TRANSFUSION...			BEEN HOSPITALIZED FOR ANY ILLNESS		
UTERUS			☐BLOOD ☐PLASMA			EXPLAIN		

X-RAYS

EVER HAVE X-RAYS OF...	NO	YES	DATE	DISEASE PRESENT
CHEST				
☐STOMACH ☐COLON				
GALL BLADDER				
EXTREMITIES				
BACK				
OTHER				

FORM NO. 405   HISTACOUNT CORPORATION, MELVILLE, N. Y. 11746

Courtesy of Histacount Corporation Subsidiary of
SCM Corporation. Used by permission.

FIGURE 3-1A
PATIENT QUESTIONNAIRE (FRONT)

SYSTEMS

DO YOU NOW HAVE OR HAVE YOU EVER HAD . . .	NO	YES	DO YOU NOW HAVE OR HAVE YOU EVER HAD . . .	NO	YES
ANY ☐EYE DISEASE ☐EYE INJURY ☐IMPAIRED SIGHT			KIDNEY ☐DISEASE ☐STONES		
ANY ☐EAR DISEASE ☐EAR INJURY ☐IMPAIRED HEARING			BLADDER DISEASE		
ANY TROUBLE WITH ☐NOSE ☐SINUSES ☐MOUTH ☐THROAT			BLOOD IN URINE		
FAINTING SPELLS			☐ALBUMIN ☐SUGAR ☐PUS ☐ETC. IN URINE		
CONVULSIONS			DIFFICULTY IN URINATION		
PARALYSIS			NARROWED URINARY STREAM		
DIZZINESS			ABNORMAL THIRST		
HEADACHES: ☐FREQUENT ☐SEVERE			PROSTATE TROUBLE		
ENLARGED GLANDS			☐STOMACH TROUBLE ☐ULCER		
THYROID: ☐OVERACTIVE ☐UNDERACTIVE ☐ENLARGED			INDIGESTION		
ENLARGED GOITER			☐GAS ☐BELCHING		
SKIN DISEASE			APPENDICITIS		
COUGH: ☐FREQUENT ☐CHRONIC			☐LIVER DISEASE ☐GALL BLADDER DISEASE		
☐CHEST PAIN ☐ANGINA PECTORIS			☐COLITIS ☐OTHER BOWEL DISEASE		
SPITTING UP BLOOD			☐HEMORRHOIDS ☐RECTAL BLEEDING		
NIGHT SWEATS			BLACK TARRY STOOLS		
SHORTNESS OF BREATH ☐EXERTION ☐AT NIGHT			☐CONSTIPATION ☐DIARRHEA		
☐PALPITATION ☐FLUTTERING HEART			☐PARASITES ☐WORMS		
SWELLING OF ☐HANDS ☐FEET ☐ANKLES			☐ANY CHANGE IN APPETITE ☐EATING HABITS		
VARICOSE VEINS			☐ANY CHANGE IN BOWEL ACTION ☐STOOLS		
EXTREME ☐TIREDNESS ☐WEAKNESS			EXPLAIN		

IMMUNIZATION - EKG

HAVE YOU HAD . . .	NO	YES	HAVE YOU HAD . . .	NO	YES
SMALLPOX VACCINATION (WITHIN LAST 7 YEARS)			POLIO SHOTS (WITHIN LAST 2 YEARS)		
TETANUS SHOT (NOT ANTITOXIN)			AN ELECTROCARDIOGRAM WHEN		

HABITS

DO YOU . . .	NO	YES	DO YOU USE . . .	NEVER	OCC.	FREQ.	DAILY
EXERCISE ADEQUATELY			LAXATIVES				
HOW ?			VITAMINS				
AWAKEN RESTED			SEDATIVES				
SLEEP WELL			TRANQUILIZERS				
AVERAGE 8 HOURS SLEEP (PER NIGHT)			SLEEPING PILLS, ETC.				
HAVE REGULAR BOWEL MOVEMENTS			ASPIRINS, ETC.				
SEX - ENTIRELY SATISFACTORY			CORTISONE				
LIKE YOUR WORK (HOURS PER DAY) ☐INDOORS ☐OUTDOORS			ALCOHOLIC BEVERAGE				
WATCH TELEVISION (HOURS PER DAY)			COFFEE (CUPS PER DAY)				
READ (HOURS PER DAY)			TOBACCO: ☐CIGARETTES (PKS PER DAY)				
HAVE A VACATION (WEEKS PER YEAR)			☐CIGARS ☐PIPE ☐CHEWING TOBACCO				
HAVE YOU EVER BEEN TREATED FOR ALCOHOLISM			☐SNUFF				
HAVE YOU EVER BEEN TREATED FOR DRUG ABUSE			APPETITE DEPRESSANTS				
RECREATION: DO YOU PARTICIPATE IN SPORTS OR HAVE			THYROID MEDICATION: ☐NO ☐YES, IN PAST ☐NONE NOW NOW ON GR. DAILY				
HOBBIES WHICH GIVE YOU RELAXATION AT			HAVE YOU EVER TAKEN . . .				
LEAST 3 HOURS A WEEK.			☐INSULIN ☐TABLETS FOR DIABETES ☐HORMONE SHOTS ☐TABLETS ☐NO				

WOMEN ONLY

MENSTRUAL HISTORY . . .				NO	YES
AGE AT ONSET			ARE YOU REGULAR: ☐HEAVY ☐MEDIUM ☐LIGHT		
USUAL DURATION OF PERIOD DAYS			DO YOU HAVE ☐TENSON ☐DEPRESSION BEFORE PERIOD		
CYCLE (START TO START) DAYS			DO YOU HAVE ☐CRAMPS ☐PAIN WITH PERIOD		
DATE OF LAST PERIOD			DO YOU HAVE HOT FLASHES		

PREGNANCIES . . .	NO	YES		NO	YES
CHILDREN BORN ALIVE (HOW MANY)			STILL BORN (HOW MANY)		
CESAREAN SECTIONS (HOW MANY)			MISCARRIAGES (HOW MANY)		
PREMATURES (HOW MANY)			ANY COMPLICATIONS		

EMOTIONS

ARE YOU OFTEN . . .	NO	YES	ARE YOU OFTEN . . .	NO	YES
DEPRESSED			JUMPY		
ANXIOUS			JITTERY		
IRRITABLE			IS CONCENTRATION DIFFICULT		

Courtesy of Histacount Corporation Subsidiary of
SCM Corporation. Used by permission.

FIGURE 3-1B
PATIENT QUESTIONNAIRE (BACK)

have to wait. Remember, patients waiting to see the doctor are often nervous or apprehensive. They do not want to feel that they have been forgotten.

No patient who has an appointment should be kept waiting past his appointment time if at all possible. If he is, then something must be wrong—perhaps there is an emergency or the doctor is longer than expected with another patient. The waiting patient should be advised of this. If you find that appointments are always running late, perhaps you should re-examine your method of appointment scheduling. (See Chapter 1—"Scheduling Patient Appointments.")

If you do not have regular appointments, but patients come in on a first-come, first-served basis, you should try to keep the patients advised of the waiting time. Do not just seat them and go away. A word every now and again to them is very helpful. The patient does not know whether he must wait an hour or 20 minutes. Give him some idea. Also, be particularly aware of the sequence in which the doctor will see the patients. Do not take patients out of order without a word to the other patients. This does not mean that you explain anything personal to the other patients. Just make a remark such as, "Mr. Jones will go in before you Mr. Smith as he is only going to take a minute."

As you know from your own experience as a patient, there is nothing so frustrating as sitting in a doctor's office waiting to see him, wondering how much longer you will have to wait and then seeing someone who came in after you go in before you. You get the feeling that you have been forgotten. And if you can be forgotten in a waiting room, then it is entirely possible that something similar could happen when you get in to see the doctor.

BE SENSITIVE TO PATIENT NEEDS

The key to being sensitive to patient needs is to imagine yourself in a similar situation. For example, when ushering patients into examining rooms, make sure doors are closed and that privacy is insured. If you are not in the habit of accompanying patients into examining rooms, then it may be very embarrassing for them for you to enter. You must work with your own situation, being sensitive to all your patients' needs while maintaining efficiency.

New patients require more careful instruction than patients who have been coming to your doctor. Carefully explain what is necessary in preparation for the examination and inquire whether or not patients want assistance. Be particularly sensitive to a patient's feelings. Some will be happier if you stay with them and help; others prefer to be alone. Some patients are particularly sensitive about another person seeing their torn or inexpensive underclothing. Be aware of this and provide the patient with the opportunity for as much privacy as possible.

Be aware of small but important personal preferences. Women, for example, do not like to leave their handbags very far away from them. Provide an area where they can see the bag if necessary. Unthinking secretaries sometimes take a handbag away from a female patient saying "You won't need this; I'll put it away." A better approach would be, "Suppose I put your handbag over here on the table where it will be safe and out of your way."

You may be dealing with patients who speak languages other than English. You must be particularly careful in situations such as this to assure understanding on both sides. If this is only an occasional occurrence, usually the patient can be asked to bring someone with him to interpret, but if you are in a locality in which there are a great number of people speaking a particular language, it may be necessary to have someone on the staff who can speak the language.

Patients who do not speak the language that you or the doctor speak are often fearful and do not have confidence that they are able to communicate. *Remember*, the language spoken has no bearing on intelligence; so, if you are having difficulty communicating, be particularly careful that you do so in a manner that shows respect.

Elderly patients require more attention than others and you must be very patient and willing to assist. *Remember*, though, that elderly patients are *not* children, they are *adults* and should be treated as such. Just be a little more patient and a little more willing to assist. The tendency when a person is elderly and seems a bit feeble or disoriented is to be so over-willing to assist that we make a person feel unable to cope at all. You must be sensitive to the feelings of all patients but realize that certain situations put slightly different requirements on your abilities than others.

BE CALM IN TIMES OF STRESS

Even though a day may be very busy and you are extremely rushed, you must give an outward appearance of calm assurance. Patients must not get the impression that you are easily flustered or too busy to give them the time and attention they deserve.

Remember, patients in a doctor's office are generally very much concerned with themselves. You, as a medical secretary, personify the mood of the office. If you are harried or upset, if you do not feel well, if you are worried about a personal problem, you must learn not to show your concern or worry. Patients do not think in terms of their doctor or his secretary being sick or having any problems. For example, if you have a child at home ill and you are very worried, you must not communicate your worry to your patient. A patient who learns that you have a sick child at home will feel you are more concerned with the interests of your child than you are with doing your job as medical secretary.

Thus, mistakes can more easily be made and he may not get the proper treatment. If your doctor is not feeling well, there is no reason for the patient to know this. It might cause him to have less confidence in the doctor.

Plan your work so that things will go smoothly. You cannot completely plan everything in a doctor's office as there will often be emergencies or items that must be taken care of at once. (See Figure 3-2.)

In some offices emergency situations may occur more frequently than others. The obstetrician may be called away during office hours because of the imminent birth of a baby. The pediatrician often has to see young patients on an emergency basis because of a sudden high fever or a bad fall. Naturally, this affects the patients waiting to see the doctor. They will not be delighted to have to prolong their waiting time but will probably be understanding about it if you explain in general terms to them the cause of the delay. After all, any one of us

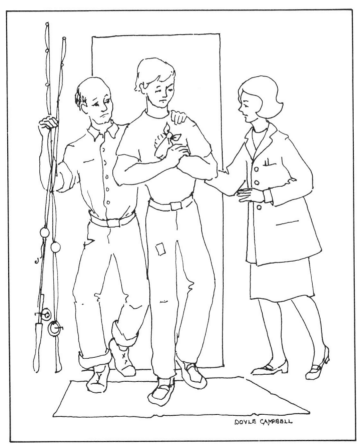

FIGURE 3-2
MEDICAL SECRETARY HANDLING EMERGENCY SITUATION

could have an emergency situation at any time and it is nice to know that the doctor will take care of us. For example, a patient has been waiting for some time and a mother comes in with a child who has fallen from a tree and she suspects a concussion. Your duties as receptionist are threefold. You must greet this woman and child properly, you must be sure that your other patients understand the delay, and you must advise the doctor in such a way that the patient he is now with is not affronted.

Get as much information from the woman and child as possible without making them feel they are being held back from seeing the doctor. Help them to see that getting the information beforehand will assist the doctor in caring for them more efficiently. Either usher them into a free examining room or seat them near you away from the other patients. Inform them that you are notifying the doctor and he will be right with them. Either call your doctor on the intercom or step into his office. Say for example, "Excuse me doctor, but there is an emergency. Could you come right away?" *Do not* mention names or the exact problem in the hearing of another patient, but make sure the patient who is with your doctor understands that he is only being temporarily inconvenienced and that the doctor will be right back. See to it that the patient is comfortable while waiting.

Naturally all doctors have different ways to handle these situations and you must examine your own and abide by it. If you think you can improve upon the method used, talk it over with the doctor before making any changes.

The patient who was waiting to see the doctor before the emergency occurred must be informed of the situation and told he will have to wait a little longer. Offer to get him a magazine or water or something to show your interest.

If the doctor is late in his schedule of appointments for any reason, be extra solicitous of the patients' comfort, reassuring them that the doctor will be with them soon. Sometimes the doctor is delayed at the hospital and patients will understand this. However, we are talking about unusual situations. If the doctor is generally delayed at the hospital and is not on time for his office hours, then you, as an alert assistant, should sit down with him and discuss the possibility of changing the time for the start of office hours. Perhaps his practice has increased to such an extent that the original time set aside is no longer enough. As you know, part of your job is to constantly be aware of situations and the possible solutions. The doctor has other things on his mind and may not notice purely mechanical problems. Running the office is *your* responsibility.

Remember, you must at all times be courteous and polite to patients while maintaining a warm, friendly, but impersonal relationship with both patients and callers. This may be difficult at times, because after you have worked with a doctor for a period of time you begin to know many of the patients fairly well. It is advisable, though, to avoid social engagements with any of the patients unless, of course, you make your doctor aware of the relationship.

Very often, patients who come to see the doctor are from all walks of life. Be particularly careful to show no distinction between your greeting to wealthy or prominent people and to less wealthy patients. A person who does not have much money may feel that his treatment from the doctor will not be the same as the wealthier person if the receptionist has shown a strong preference.

GREETING OTHER CALLERS

Your duties as receptionist are not confined only to greeting patients. There will always be the other callers such as drug salesmen (drug detail men — see Chapter 7), repairmen, delivery people, and any of the many people who perform a service. As you know, you must screen these callers and treat them all with tact and courtesy.

IDEAS FOR CREATING A RECEPTIVE ATMOSPHERE

Along with being sensitive to the needs of patients and other callers, a receptive atmosphere must be created. The physical setup of the office is discussed in Chapter 4 ("Managing the Office More Effectively"); but, remember that the person who is greeting callers and patients should be easily seen by them as they enter the office. It is very disconcerting for a patient to have to look around and see where he is to go. If you step away from your desk for a moment, make sure you check the waiting room to see if any patients have come in while you were away. Do not rely on their coming up to tell you. Show your interest by checking.

Your desk should always be neat and free from clutter. The patient who sees a sloppy desk may transfer this image in his mind to the type of treatment received. (See Chapter 4.)

You must always look pleasant and alert. A grumpy or sleepy receptionist will not inspire confidence. You must be clean and well groomed. If you wear a white uniform, it should be white, not dingy. Wear comfortable, attractive clothing. You may or may not wear a uniform depending on the doctor's preference, but there are so many attractive, colorful, easy-care uniforms available today that it will probably be to your advantage to decide on a uniform. (See Figure 3-3.)

Different practices require different images. You must look at your own and see what image you should be conveying. In some offices such as that of a psychiatrist or psychologist, it may be preferred that you do not wear a uniform, but rather dress more like a regular secretary in a business office.

DOYLE CAMPBELL

FIGURE 3-3
THREE STYLES OF DRESS FOR THE MEDICAL SECRETARY

Secretaries to pediatricians have found that because they usually choose to wear uniforms, the younger patients like to identify exactly who the doctor's "nurse" is. Generally, an attractive colorful uniform would be better than a stark white one.

Naturally, you must be well groomed and pleasant looking at all times. Sometimes when we are concentrating we tend to frown, or if we are tired we may yawn without realizing it. A very good practice would be to have a mirror installed opposite your desk. (See Figure 3-4.) This would not only be an addition to the decor of the office but could serve several purposes. We all have had the experience of catching a glimpse of ourselves in a store window or seeing our reflection as we sit on a bus. Suddenly, we are surprised to see that we are frowning. The mirror tends to keep us aware of our appearance and we would not be likely to "bite our lip" in concentration or frown or yawn. Be careful though; this mirror is not to be used to touch up your hair or face. No one likes to see a receptionist sitting at the desk combing her hair or putting on make-up.

If the mirror is situated properly, it not only keeps you aware of how others see you, but also can serve to reflect the waiting room. You can then be

FIGURE 3-4
MEDICAL SECRETARY WITH MIRROR OPPOSITE DESK

aware of restless patients or see if someone has arrived when you were not at your desk.

Examine your situation. There may be other physical aids that you can employ to increase your effectiveness. If you have young patients, perhaps you could provide lollipops, children's books or toys. Be sure all toys are safe for the children to play with. A table set up to "serve yourself" coffee may he helpful to older patients. (See Chapter 4.)

Listening to yourself on a tape recorder may help you improve the tone of your voice.

The key is to be constantly aware of the importance of good reception practices and to be sensitive to and aware of patient needs because the responsibility for greeting patients is a very important part of your job as medical secretary. Do not treat it lightly. *Remember*, you will be the first person the patient sees, not the doctor. The impression you make will be a reflection of the doctor. Be sensitive to the feelings of your patients in all matters within the scope of your position as medical secretary. An intelligent, poised, courteous secretary who shows kindness, friendliness, and tactfulness to the patients and callers will accomplish a great deal toward creating the proper climate in the doctor's office.

Chapter 4

Managing the Office More Effectively

Among the many and varied duties of the medical secretary falls the role of office manager. The medical secretary's responsibilities with regard to managing the operation of the doctor's office depend upon several factors. The job can be challenging, involving many different activities.

If the doctor has a staff including nurses, medical technicians, clerk typists, custodial employees, and so forth, you as medical secretary will allot more time to your role as office manager. Your role is expanded because you not only have to get along with the doctor and patients but also with the staff. You will be responsible for the smooth running of the office. Most doctors are too busy with the medical side of their practice to take time for business matters. The secretary who is willing and able to assume the job of office manager becomes a valuable asset in the medical office.

The medical secretary's duties are thus expanded because although there is still the responsibility for the regular duties, there is the added responsibility of overseeing the work of others.

In many instances temporary or part-time people must be instructed in the actual work of their positions. The secretary may have to schedule the working hours of the various employees so that they will be on hand when needed by the doctor.

It is a good idea to prepare a job description sheet for each of the positions in your office. This is helpful when hiring permanent personnel or vacation replacements. All the duties of the particular position should be listed and possibly who the immediate supervisor is. (See Figures 4-1 and 4-2.)

```
┌─────────────────────────────────────────────┐
│              JOB   DESCRIPTION                │
│                                               │
│   Name  _____ │
│                                               │
│   JobTitle_____ │
│                                               │
│   Training_____ │
│                                               │
│   Duties_____ │
│            _____  │
│            _____  │
│            _____  │
│            _____  │
│            _____  │
│            _____  │
│            _____  │
│            _____  │
│                                               │
│   Date _____ Signature_____ │
└─────────────────────────────────────────────┘
```

FIGURE 4-1
JOB DESCRIPTION FORM (BLANK)

Depending on the size of the office, it may or may not be necessary to designate the line of authority. For instance, the secretary who is also the office manager would report directly to the doctor. The part-time clerical help or the custodial staff would report to the secretary/office manager.

In your expanded role of office manager, you may no longer be personally responsible for preparing certain letters or charts, but it is still your responsibility to see that they are done correctly. Therefore, the medical secretary as an office manager has the responsibility to delegate some duties to others and see that they are done properly. Your responsibility may extend to checking up on the custodial staff to see that their jobs are being done properly, assigning vacations to the various members of the staff, arranging for coverage while they are away, preparing the payroll, seeing that equipment is maintained properly and repaired when necessary, ordering both medical and office supplies and equipment, and acting as liaison between the doctor and other professional associates.

J O B   D E S C R I P T I O N

Name: _____

Job Title: ___Medical Assistant/Secretary_____

Training: _____

Duties: ___1. Take electrocardiograms_____

2. Take and develop x-rays 3. Assist doctor in simple surgi-

cal procedures such as: Incision & Drainage, Proctoscope,

Arthrocentesis 4. Assist doctor in Pap smears, GC smears,

Fungus cultures, etc. 5. Irrigate ears 6. Administer

physiotherapy such as: neck traction, Whirlpool, Diathermy,

Hydrocollator 7. Sedimentary rate (blood test) 8. Urine

analysis 9. Check laboratory reports for abnormal results and

enter on patient's charts 10. Clean and change dressings,

bandages, etc. 11. Take dictation, type letters 12. Handle

phones, make hospital reservations, patient appointments

13. Make up Workmen's Compensation reports 14. Take patients

into examining rooms, weigh them, etc. 15. Collect money and

bill patients 16. Fill out insurance forms (Medicare, Blue

Shield, etc.) 17. Check and maintain medical and office supplies

_____

_____

_____

Immediate Supervisor: ___Doctor_____

FIGURE 4-2
COMPLETED JOB DESCRIPTION FORM

There are few jobs where one's duties are as diversified. The medical secretary is the receptionist, secretary, bookkeeper, insurance clerk, and doctor's assistant. Being the doctor's assistant may add several more duties such as assisting the doctor with patients in whatever capacity is required, whether it be draping a patient or assisting with minor surgery.

As mentioned before, the extent of the managerial function depends on several things, the size of the office, the type of office, the number of other assistants working *and*, importantly, the degree to which the doctor is willing to relinquish his own role as manager and delegate it to the secretary. Since doctors are generally not businessmen and since the business end of their work is becoming more and more complex, the trend is to allow the medical secretary more responsibility in this area.

MAINTAINING AN ATTRACTIVE OFFICE

The first impression that the patient has of a doctor's waiting room and reception area is extremely important. People form opinions very quickly; therefore, it is imperative that the reception area be clean, neat, and attractive. It sets the stage and influences people positively or negatively in their contact with the doctor. It is especially important if it is the patient's first visit that a favorable first impression is made.

Depending upon the doctor, decorating may be left entirely up to the secretary. A professional decorator may be called in to help select the furnishings. It is your responsibility as office manager to see that this is done properly.

For instance, if it is left up to you, keep in mind certain basic points reflecting good taste. Select a basic color scheme and do not stray too far. Select chairs that are attractive, comfortable, and durable. Select colors that do not show wear readily. Use color sparingly, but some color is necessary to give the room a bright and attractive appearance. Lighting is important, especially if there are few or no windows.

The furniture should be comfortable and easily cleaned and maintained. In selecting upholstery materials, choose synthetic fabrics that can be washed off regularly because they receive a great deal of wear. If the doctor treats young children, provision should be made for them either with a play area decorated appropriately or at least a few toys or several small chairs. (See Figure 4-3.)

The floor covering also would depend on the type of patients the doctor treats and again should be attractive, durable, and easily cleaned.

Manufacturers have many catalogs available and salesmen are more than willing to visit and advise on the proper type of furniture and floor covering for the doctor's needs. You will find that by glancing through the ads in the

FIGURE 4-3
PEDIATRICIAN'S WAITING ROOM

professional magazines to which your doctor subscribes that you will become quite knowledgeable about the various firms to contact when the doctor is ready to redecorate.

IDEAS FOR A MORE RECEPTIVE WAITING AREA

The doctor may or may not have definite preferences as to how the waiting room should appear. The care and maintenance of the waiting room is the responsibility of you as the secretary in your role as office manager.

If the doctor knows exactly what he wants the waiting room to look like, you must go along with this. If for some reason you feel that improvement could be made, this should be discussed with the doctor. You should be ready to give reasons for your suggestions.

For instance:

A medical secretary in a pediatrician's office feels that the addition of a corner bookcase with a small table and chairs would be very pleasing to the small patients and keep them or their young brothers and sisters occupied. The doctor should be presented with these reasons and catalog pictures and prices of furniture. Also, perhaps, the secretary may have read some articles in professional magazines concerning this.

On the other hand, you as the medical secretary may have a free hand in caring for the waiting room so you may not have to ask approval or "sell" your

FIGURE 4-4
A WELL-DECORATED WAITING ROOM

doctor on a new idea. Nevertheless, you should prepare a memorandum sheet for your employer concerning what you have done or are about to do.

Generally speaking, the waiting room should be pleasant, restful, clean, neat, comfortable, and decorated appropriately for the type of specialty the doctor practices. In the case of a general practitioner, provision should be made for the fact that there will be great diversity in age and degree of illness of patients. Perhaps an 80-year old man suffering from chronic arthritis will share the waiting room with a 2-year old crying with a sore throat or a 6-year old waiting impatiently for his allergy shots.

Current issues of magazines should be well displayed. Depending upon the interest of the patients, you may order magazines that are suitable; for example, in a pediatrician's office, magazines which appeal to children as well as those directed to parents are a welcome addition.

If smoking is permitted, ashtrays should be easily accessible and clean. If smoking is not permitted, this should be made clear by signs indicating that smoking is not allowed. Some doctors prefer to have signs made up thanking people for not smoking rather than simply "No Smoking." Even if smoking is not allowed, an ashtray should be provided for people to dispose of cigarettes which they may be smoking as they enter.

Plants do enhance the appearance of the waiting room. (See Figure 4-4.) Remember, though, that in order for a plant to have a cheerful influence, it must be alive and thriving. If you do not have a green thumb, another alternative is to employ a plant service that furnishes and cares for plants.

HOW TO HAVE AN UNCLUTTERED DESK

The reception desk usually is separated from the waiting room by a partition of some kind. However, this does not keep the area from being seen. The desk and the area around it should be kept in order, with things neatly arranged. Special care should be taken to see that clutter does not accumulate even though this appears to be next to impossible. Some doctors have more paper work than others. A medical secretary to a busy general practitioner may find that there is always a stack of charts on the desk to be posted (information such as lab reports, blood tests, x-ray reports attached to the patient's chart). Take care to have papers filed and cleared off each day before leaving; the secret is not to allow things to accumulate but to take care of them as they occur. This is sometimes impossible, but since it is imperative that the doctor's records be kept up-to-date, you must make sure to arrange the time to do this. Perhaps rearranging your hours with the doctor so as to come in earlier or leave later would be a solution if it is not possible to accomplish the paper work during office time. If this is not an adequate solution, there may be a need for a part-time clerical person. Doctors must have their clerical work up-to-date and it is a medical secretary's responsibility to see that it is.

HELPING THE DOCTOR KEEP A NEAT OFFICE

The general appearance of the office must be neat; the chairs should be facing the doctor's desk, the wall pictures should be straight and draperies or blinds neatly arranged.

The doctor's desk is of equal importance. Help keep it cleared of excess material every day. The impression a patient gets looking over a stack of papers at the doctor or when the doctor has to fumble through papers looking for some information is very poor. The feeling is that the doctor is too disorganized to be relied on to give a proper diagnosis or treatment.

EXAMINING ROOM CHECKUP

The examining rooms must be spotlessly clean. Check the rooms to see if they meet the doctor's standards, and if not, notify the custodial staff. It is necessary that the medical secretary follow through on this to see that the people doing the actual cleaning understand what is expected of them. The counter tops and floors must be clean, the blinds and shades dusted, bottles kept clean and the bathroom cleaned. You must develop an eye for detecting things that are not right. In addition, you may have to carry out some task that was not completed or was overlooked. These duties should not be considered as too menial because they are part of the responsibility of the office manager.

Most doctors prefer their secretaries, rather than the cleaning staff, to take care of tables and counters with medication and equipment on them. It doesn't take much to wipe a damp cloth over a few things each day or so and things do stay neat with daily or semi-daily checks.

The sample medicine shelves need frequent straightening out because the stock fluctuates rapidly. Drug company detail men (salesmen) provide samples for the doctor, but you should not permit them to place these on the shelves. You should handle this yourself; and, with the doctor's help, decide which products are used most frequently and accept only the amount needed from the detail men.

CHECKLIST TO HELP YOU MANAGE

You should develop a routine to be followed to see that the office is ready for the patients each day. This could be set up in a checklist fashion listing the various duties broken down to daily and periodic tasks for which you are responsible. This would be an aid to you because sometimes even though these duties become automatic, in a busy office they could easily be overlooked if you found yourself interrupted by several emergency calls just as you were performing one of these duties. Also, it is an invaluable aid to a new employee or to a temporary vacation replacement.

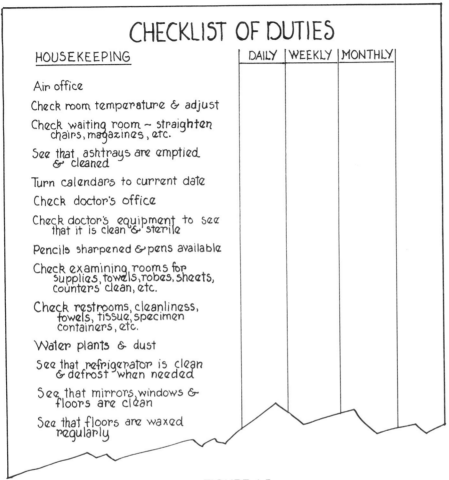

CHECKLIST OF DUTIES

HOUSEKEEPING

	DAILY	WEEKLY	MONTHLY
Air office			
Check room temperature & adjust			
Check waiting room ~ straighten chairs, magazines, etc.			
See that ashtrays are emptied & cleaned			
Turn calendars to current date			
Check doctor's office			
Check doctor's equipment to see that it is clean & sterile			
Pencils sharpened & pens available			
Check examining rooms for supplies, towels, robes, sheets, counters clean, etc.			
Check restrooms, cleanliness, towels, tissue, specimen containers, etc.			
Water plants & dust			
See that refrigerator is clean & defrost when needed			
See that mirrors, windows & floors are clean			
See that floors are waxed regularly			

FIGURE 4-5
CHECKLIST OF DUTIES

Many duties in a doctor's office are similar, so a checklist such as the one above or following, with additions or deletions, could be used (See Figures 4-5 and 4-6).

Remember, as medical secretary you often have the responsibility of managing the office staff. The degree and scope of your responsibility is determined by the size of the doctor's practice, whether it is a group practice, whether it is a partnership, whether there are other employees such as an x-ray technician, nurse, other office personnel, maintenance staff and so forth. A smooth-running office is dependent on workers who do their jobs properly. Without harmony among the staff this is not possible. Your role as office manager is a very exacting and challenging one.

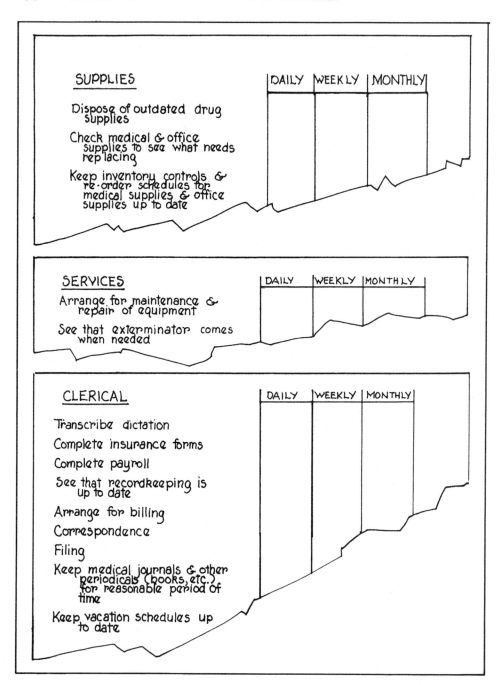

FIGURE 4-6
CHECKLIST OF DUTIES

Chapter 5

Guidelines for Purchasing and Operating Dictation Equipment

Because the secretarial and clerical work in medical offices is increasing so much, the introduction of dictating and transcribing equipment is helping to speed up the constant flow of records. This equipment increases the efficiency and accuracy of production and allows for more flexibility for the doctor and the secretary.

Saving time for both the doctor and the secretary is the major advantage. Greater efficiency occurs because the doctor can dictate at any time whether at home, in the car, on the plane, or after office hours. You as secretary are freed for other activities because the dictation can be transcribed when you are not faced with many interruptions.

TRANSCRIPTION EQUIPMENT

Transcription equipment refers to one or two pieces of equipment, usually purchased in sets—a dictating machine for the doctor and a matching transcriber for the secretary or one unit containing both the dictating and the transcribing function. The appearance (See Figure 5-1) is almost the same, but the transcriber permits the secretary to transcribe at her own rate—stopping,

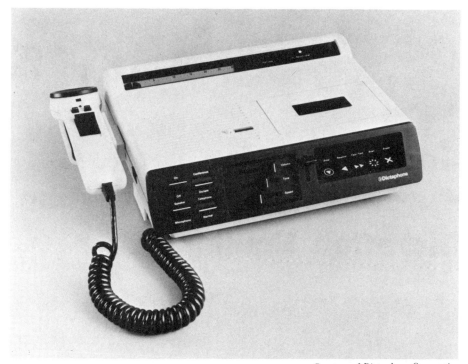

Courtesy of Dictaphone Corporation
Used by permission.

FIGURE 5-1
DICTATING/TRANSCRIBING UNIT WITH MICROPHONE

starting, or repeating whenever necessary. The transcriber is usually operated by a foot pedal leaving the hands free. Separate units for the dictator and the transcriber are more convenient and provide more flexibility. (See Figure 5-1.)

These units can be either stationary or portable depending on the needs of your office. Certainly the doctor would need to have a portable unit if dictation is done from various locations. (See Figure 5-2.)

TRANSCRIPTION EQUIPMENT INCREASES YOUR EFFICIENCY

As you know, accuracy is extremely important in the medical office. The operator of the transcriber should be a skilled typist and have a knowledge of medical terminology. Transcribing efficiency can be increased if you can find a time to transcribe when you are least likely to be interrupted by the telephone or by patients. (See Figure 5-3.) Try to find a "quiet" time early in the morning before the doctor arrives or late in the afternoon. Medical terms are easily

Courtesy of Dictaphone Corporation
Used by permission.

FIGURE 5-2
PORTABLE DICTATING UNIT

misunderstood or confused for other words, for example, "hypotension" (low blood pressure) for "hypertension" (high blood pressure). As you can see, this is the type of error you must be on the lookout for. Always keep a medical dictionary on hand to check spelling and meaning. If you find that you cannot figure out a word or phrase on your own, then you should certainly ask the doctor.

Usually the doctor will want to check your transcription before it is filed or mailed out, but often, because of a pressing schedule, he may skim over things lightly placing upon you the responsibility to proofread closely.

WHERE TRANSCRIPTION EQUIPMENT IS USED

Of course, not every medical office uses transcription equipment. For some offices, the volume of work may not be enough to make it worthwhile. It

Courtesy of Dictaphone Corporation.
Used by permission.

FIGURE 5-3
SECRETARY AT DESK TRANSCRIBING UNIT

can increase the efficient operation of many offices—from the private physician to the busy hospital. Specialists find transcription equipment a great time-saver because of the large amount of dictation usually required such as: detailed reports of physical examinations, progress reports, case histories, and referrals.

In large institutions such as hospitals, dictation and transcription equipment can be used most effectively because the flow of records is heavy and constant. (See Figure 5-4.) Records must be kept current and accurate. People are hired specifically for that purpose. Many hospitals have a separate Word Processing Department where a group of highly skilled transcribers (Word Processors) is required. A great deal of the skill is developed through the repetition of hearing the medical terms over and over again. The work consists of various types of reports such as: operative, progress, case histories, physicals, and autopsies. (See Figure 5-5.)

Benyas/Kaufman from Black, Starr—
Dictaphone Corporation. Used by permission.

FIGURE 5-4
DOCTOR DICTATING THROUGH TELEPHONE HOOKUP TO WORD
PROCESSING DEPARTMENT IN HOSPITAL

UPDATE YOUR KNOWLEDGE OF WORD PROCESSING EQUIPMENT

With the increase in the flow of information and trying to keep up with it, technology is constantly updating equipment. For example, in hospitals, clinics, laboratories, and group practices, where there is a large volume of dictation involving many people, dictation and transcription have been streamlined to and coordinated with the magnetic media typing equipment. This timesaving system that increases the efficiency of operation by cutting down on production time and greatly reduces costs is called Word Processing. The magnetic media, or power typewriter, is an electric typewriter with the

Courtesy of Don Rutledge from Black, Starr—
Dictaphone Corporation. Used by permission.

FIGURE 5-5
MEDICAL SECRETARIES TRANSCRIBING IN HOSPITAL MEDICAL RECORDS
DEPARTMENT

ability to record and store information that can be typed at rough draft speed because the typist can make corrections while copying by merely backing up and typing over the error. After the document is recorded, it can be played back at high speeds and stopped at any point for corrections, additions, or deletions. Many manufacturers produce this equipment and there are styles and models so versatile that they can easily be adapted to fit the needs of any situation.

The arrangement for setting up a Word Processing center usually involves special installation of equipment connecting the dictation equipment to the transcribing units that are located in one area where a group of skilled transcribers work either on standard electric typewriters or on magnetic media typing equipment. (See Figures 5-6, 5-7, 5-8.)

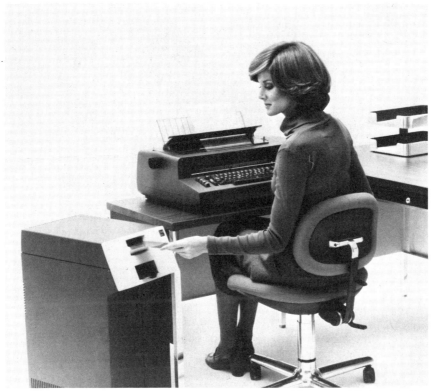

Courtesy of International Business Machines
Corporation Office Products Division. Used by permission.

FIGURE 5-6
IBM MAG CARD COMPOSER

WORD PROCESSING RESULTS IN INCREASED EFFICIENCY

For instance, this equipment can be used in a hospital for producing many reports such as pathology reports. The reports that are used most often are prerecorded on magnetic tape, cassettes, or cards leaving blank spaces for insertion of the pathologist's findings. Rather than having to dictate the entire report, the pathologist simply specifies which form is to be used and dictates only the data that has to be filled in. The transcriptionist then listens to the dictator's instructions, inserts the appropriate card or tape, automatically plays out the prerecorded error-free dictation up to the insertions, stops the machine for each insertion, types in the information, and continues the

Courtesy of International Business Machines
Corporation Office Products Division. Used by permission.

FIGURE 5-7
IBM DESK-TOP MEMORY TYPEWRITER
WITH 100-PAGE BUILT-IN ACTION FILE

Courtesy of Wang Laboratories, Inc.
Used by permission.

FIGURE 5-8
WORD PROCESSOR 10A (VIDEO SCREEN)

automatic playback. The result is a complete error-free report done in a fraction of the time it would have taken to type the entire report from beginning to end. Another advantage is that once it is recorded, as many error-free copies as needed can be produced at speeds of 200 words per minute or more.

There are other ways in which Word Processing equipment can be utilized to increase the efficiency of operation. It can be used to store in its memory bank (magnetic cards, cassettes, or tapes) such documents as memos, form letters, and employment correspondence.

The companies that sell the equipment have trained specialists who will help you design a plan for the most efficient way of handling the flow of work from input (where the document originates) to the production of the document.

PHOTOCOPYING SAVES TIME

An additional piece of equipment used in the production of documents is the photocopier. It is fast, easy, and relatively inexpensive. There are many different types and models in use today depending on the volume of paper work handled, size of the office, and the number of people using it. The copier saves

Courtesy of Xerox Corporation. Used by permission.

FIGURE 5-9A
COPIER - 9400 DUPLICATOR

Courtesy of Xerox Corporation. Used by permission.

FIGURE 5-9B
COPIER - 3400 COPIER

the secretary valuable time spent in typing carbon copies, produces clear copies
for the files, and provides copies that can be distributed to various departments
or for whatever use they are needed. It is becoming increasingly important to
keep copies of all records, especially medical and insurance records.
Remember, though, that it is the medical secretary's legal obligation to protect
the confidentiality of medical records. Even such a move as dropping a poor
copy of a confidential medical record into a waste basket might be a mistake.
Medical information may not be revealed to others except with the patient's
written authorization. (See Figures 5-9A and 5-9B.)

SECRETARY ANALYZES THE EQUIPMENT

There are several different brands of dictation equipment available that
are of comparable quality. Before making a choice, examine several machines.
By reading articles and ads in the various professional magazines that come
into the doctor's office, you will get a good idea of the various companies
manufacturing dictating and transcribing equipment. Request a catalog and
demonstration from representatives of the various companies. Sales
representatives are usually willing and anxious to demonstrate their
equipment. This extra time will be well spent because it will be possible to see
how the transcribing unit will fit into the operation of the office. Company

representatives are usually most helpful in recommending machines that would best fit the needs of the particular office setup. It may be advantageous to look into a service contract when you purchase a new machine.

Comparison and choice are based on ease of operation, quality of sound, availability of service for repairs and maintenance, and the requirements of a particular office. Price should be of the least consideration because in an important purchase such as this, quality is the prime concern. Try to consult other professionals who have used the equipment in office situations similar to yours; find out their experiences with the equipment. Do not forget the importance of proper repair services.

HINTS FOR USING TRANSCRIBING EQUIPMENT

Each company manufacturing transcription equipment provides instruction for use. Illustrated is a reproduction of portions of Dictaphone Corporation's Instruction Manual for their Thought Master Series 260 Electronic Dictating/Transcribing System. (See Figure 5-10.)

Power On—When you move the On/Off switch to the ON position, the On/Record level lamp will indicate that the unit is ready for operation.

Cassette Loading—To open the cassette compartment, press the Eject lever on the front of the unit. Put a cassette on the raised cassette tray with the exposed tape facing forward, and side 1 facing upward. Closing the cassette door automatically positions the cassette for transcription. Do not rewind the cassette at this time.

Display Pointer—Slide the Display Pointer and Scale Reference Arm to the extreme right side of the display area. This will extinguish the electronic display from the previous cassette and properly position the mechanism for generating the Display for the next cassette.

Check Controls—Be sure the Telephone Record switch is in the bottom Normal position. The Microphone/Speaker switch must be in the Microphone position to permit playback through the headset.

Display Scan—To generate the electronic display of dictation, press the Scan button on the keyboard. The Thought Master 260 will rewind the cassette and automatically generate an electronic display of the dictation. The unit will pause briefly at each electronic index tone, and generate a light to indicate the end of each memo. An audible tone will also be generated. When the Scan cycle is completed, the unit will automatically stop. The electronic display will indicate the approximate length of each memo and the Indicator Scale will indicate total dictation time. (Note: Short memos of less than one minute may not be displayed.)

Special transcription instructions may also be indicated by an index tone. The Autoscan feature (explained in a later section) will permit you to automatically review this special instruction before you type the memo.

Display Memory—The electronic dictation display has a memory and is not affected by the On/Off switch. The Thought Master 260 can be turned off for extended periods or overnight without affecting the electronic display. The display will remain lighted until the Scale Reference Arm is moved to the extreme right side of the display area. This is done only when transcription is completed and another cassette is to be transcribed.

Digital Counter—Before you begin transcribing, reset the Digital Counter to the "000" position by pressing the Counter Reset button. The digital counter is helpful for transcription referencing, and in locating dictation to be transcribed out of sequence.

Playback—To begin transcribing, press the center of the Foot Control and adjust the Volume, Tone, and Speed slide controls on the front of the unit to your preference. To transcribe, listen ahead and type. To pause, release the pressure on the foot control. Continue in this start-and-stop method until the transcription is completed.

Transcribing Hints—The following suggestions should help you process work more efficiently:

1) Organize your work before you start.

2) Keep cassettes to be transcribed and any correspondence or attachments in individual Dictaphone cassette correspondence folders. This will allow you to refer to these materials if necessary as you transcribe the cassette.

3) Listen, then type. Scan ahead on each memo to determine if there are any special instructions before you begin transcribing.

4) Erase the cassette after transcription is completed.

Courtesy of Dictaphone Corporation.
Used by permission.

FIGURE 5-10
PORTIONS OF INSTRUCTION MANUAL
FOR THE THOUGHT MASTER SERIES 260
ELECTRONIC DICTATING/TRANSCRIBING SYSTEM

Remember, the dictating and transcribing equipment already widely used in hospitals and doctors' offices becomes even more effective when used in conjunction with power typing equipment. You as a medical secretary should be aware of what is happening in this area and become familiar with the latest equipment. There are many makes and models of transcribing equipment to fit every need and the manufacturers are usually very willing to send salesmen to demonstrate the advantages of their equipment and advise you as to the most efficient use in your office setting.

Due to the rising cost of health care, economy of operation has become a major concern. In most offices, the trend of the future is toward increasing efficiency of operations through the increased use of automated equipment that makes it possible to produce more in less time without the necessity of hiring additional personnel.

Chapter 6

Handling Correspondence More Effectively

Increasing your effectiveness in handling mail will save both you and the doctor valuable time that can be used to good advantage in other areas. Remember to handle all mail as soon as it arrives, dividing it according to importance. If you are in a new position, check with the doctor concerning his preferences. Possibly you can answer much of it yourself or attend to whatever has to be done. Much of the correspondence you should be able to follow up on without consulting the doctor. An easy-to-follow system for processing the mail should be established and followed so that the daily handling is done with speed and efficiency.

IMPROVING YOUR PROCESSING OF INCOMING MAIL

When handling the incoming mail, keep handy an envelope opener, stapler, paper clips, pencils, file folders, dater or time stamp, cellophane tape, and a mail register (a record of the date and name of the sender of all important mail received such as registered, certified, special delivery, insured, and items that contain important enclosures). This record is helpful for several reasons: (1) in case something is lost and you need to know when a piece of correspondence was received, (2) to see if all enclosures were included, and (3) because the date of receipt is important for verification. (See Figures 6-1 and 6-2.)

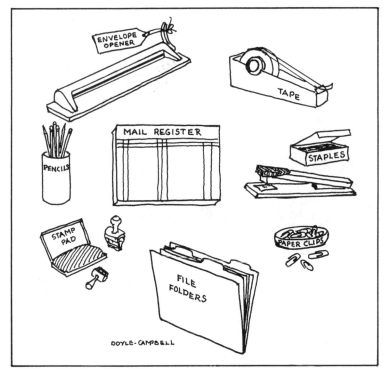

FIGURE 6-1
SUPPLIES NECESSARY FOR PROCESSING INCOMING MAIL

PRACTICAL TIPS ON HANDLING THE MAIL

Sort the mail into four general groups: correspondence, bills and statements, advertisements and circulars, and periodicals and professional publications. Go through the mail and first pull out all important looking business and personal mail. Never open anything marked "personal" without the doctor's permission. Put that on the doctor's desk first. The doctor may tell you to open *all* his mail whether marked personal or not. In deciding on the order of importance, look at the return address. Recognizing names of the correspondents becomes routine making it easy to determine what is most important. Business mail may be further sorted according to patients, other doctors, professional associates, and suppliers.

Hints on Handling the Contents

Before opening the envelopes, strike the lower edge of the stack of letters on the desk to lessen the possibility of cutting the contents with the letter opener. Be sure to empty all the envelopes and attach enclosures to each letter. Check to see that the address of the sender is on the letter and, if not, attach the

MAIL REGISTER							
RECEIVED :		FROM		ADDRESSED	DESCRIPTION :	REFERRED	
DATE	TIME	NAME / ADDRESS	DATED	TO	(Type of Mail)	TO	DATE

FIGURE 6-2
MAIL REGISTER

envelope to the letter. If a letter is not dated, the postmark date should be recorded in the register.

Each piece of mail is dated with today's date; envelopes may or may not be saved; certain things may be underlined and notations made in the margin. A letter referring to a patient or to previous correspondence calls for the secretary to go to the files and pull the patient's chart or piece of correspondence referred to in the letter and attach it to the letter before giving it to the doctor.

Note letters requiring follow-up or some future action in a special place such as a follow-up folder or on the secretary's calendar. Make a separate stack of those items that you can handle yourself. (See Figure 6-3.)

Personal Mail

The doctor's personal mail consists of anything other than matters directly related to his practice such as personal friends or relatives, clubs, civic

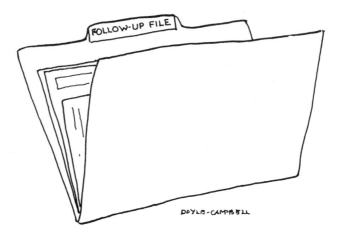

FIGURE 6-3
FOLLOW-UP FILE

organizations, and any correspondence relating to finances. The secretary should not open any of this mail unless the doctor authorizes it.

Professional Mail

Professional mail involves any correspondence relating to the doctor's practice including mail from patients, other doctors, or pharmaceutical companies, referrals, supplies, and any writing for professional magazines, speeches, lectures, or papers reporting on research.

Bills and Statements

Open these after you have finished with the other mail. Depending on the doctor's preference, either pay the bills and record that the bill has been paid or stack the bills on his desk so that he can attend to them. He may want to see them before having you pay them. (See Chapter 12.)

Advertisements and Circulars

Go through these and add your comments to any that you feel may be of particular interest to the doctor. Put those saved in a folder along with order blanks in case the doctor wants to order something.

Periodicals and Professional Publications

Choose the ones the doctor likes to read and put them in a folder or wherever it is most convenient for him. Save the doctor time by looking through the table of contents and noting for him various articles of special interest. He can immediately see whether or not it is important to read the magazine now or whether it can wait until he has more time. If he happens to be writing an article or giving a talk, he will want to be up to date on everything concerning his topic.

Before the doctor arrives at the office each day, arrange his mail on his desk in order of importance with the most important on top. It may be better not to put it all on his desk at once, saving the less important mail for later.

WHEN THE DOCTOR IS AWAY

The doctor may not come into the office every day. If this is the case, read through the correspondence to determine if anything needs his immediate attention so that you can call him or tell him when he calls the office. Write down the information from that correspondence that requires his immediate action so that you can tell him quickly what it is about. Acknowledge as many of the letters as possible yourself. If the doctor is away for several days, sort the correspondence and put it in labeled folders indicating that which needs his attention, those that you have already acknowledged, and miscellaneous items that he may just want to read.

YOUR RESPONSIBILITY FOR OUTGOING MAIL

Correspondence that goes out of the doctor's office creates an impression that is a reflection on him. It should have a neat appearance and be correct in form, punctuation, and spelling. Increasing your effectiveness in preparing outgoing correspondence will make you more valuable to your employer because correspondence makes a lasting impression upon the person who receives it.

The impression created can be either a good one or a poor one. Once a patient gets a bad impression, even if it is only by a poor letter, he may lose confidence in the doctor, which once lost is very difficult to rebuild.

For example, you are out of the office and the part-time assistant is covering your desk. A patient received the following letter prescribing medication. There were several uncorrected errors and an erasure in the name of the medication. The patient was upset and questioned the doctor whether or not the dosage and name were correct. (See Figures 6-4A and 6-4B.)

Fortunately, this was one of the doctor's regular patients. Had it been a new patient though, he may never have had a chance to apologize and reassure the patient.

ALVIN MYLES JONES, M. D.
965 WALT WHITMAN ROAD
MELVILLE, N. Y. 11746

TELEPHONE 421-1200

Jan. 10, 19--

Dear Mrs. Daniel,

Dr. Jones would like you to start taking Feasol Spansules
tow times a day. You can buy them at any drug store.
Glad to hear you are feeling well.

Sincerley

Margaret Black, secy.

Courtesy of Histacount Corporation Subsidiary of
SCM Corporation. Used by permission.

FIGURE 6-4A
INCORRECT LETTER SENT IN DOCTOR'S ABSENCE

ALVIN M. JONES, M. D.
965 WALT WHITMAN ROAD
MELVILLE, N. Y. 11746
—
HAMILTON 1-1200

January 10, 19--

Mrs. Thomas P. Daniel
17 Bluff Road
Northport, NY   11768

Dear Mrs. Daniel:

    Doctor Jones would like you to begin taking Feosol
Spansules two times a day. You can purchase them at any
pharmacy.

    Glad to hear that you are feeling well.

                        Sincerely,

                        Margaret Black
                        Secretary to Doctor Jones

*Courtesy of Histacount Corporation Subsidiary of
SCM Corporation. Used by permission.*

FIGURE 6-4B
CORRECTED LETTER

GUIDELINES FOR COMPOSING LETTERS

When you compose letters, the important thing to keep in mind is to say only what is necessary. Express yourself clearly and in as few words as possible. For example:

A student needs a letter from the doctor because he has been absent from school. A simple letter such as the one in Figure 6-5 is all that is required.

```
                    ALVIN MYLES JONES, M. D.
                    965 WALT WHITMAN ROAD
                    MELVILLE, N. Y. 11746
                    ——
                    TELEPHONE 421-1200




                                        January 10, 19--




           Professor Marvin Jenks
           Franklin High School
           601 Highgate Road
           Great Neck, NY 11020

           Dear Professor Jenks:

               James Jones has been under my care since
           January 4 for treatment of severe cold and con-
           gestion.  He is now able to return to school.


                            Sincerely,




           ms
```

Courtesy of Histacount Corporation Subsidiary of
SCM Corporation. Used by permission.

FIGURE 6-5
LETTER EXCUSING ABSENCE FROM SCHOOL

Professional

The doctor is interested in building up his practice. He is in constant contact with other doctors. When a patient is referred to another doctor, usually a phone call is made to that doctor. This is followed by a letter about the patient's condition, diagnosis, and probable outcome (prognosis). There may be further correspondence between the doctors to keep up with the patient's progress.

When the doctor receives a referral from another doctor, it is correct to write a letter of thanks. After he has seen the patient, he may want to write to the referring doctor about his findings. Often, he will include in his letter of thanks the results of his examination. (For examples of letters to other doctors, Referral Letter, Thank you, see Figures 6-6 and 6-7.)

The results of a physical examination can be sent by letter. Test results that are not emergencies can be handled through correspondence. Often the doctor dictates the results to you and has you compose the letter.

The doctor will be in contact with other doctors to discuss unusual cases for which he may want another opinion. This is a very important part of his correspondence. If this is handled by telephone, it is imperative that a record be kept.

An effective way of doing this is to record the information on a special telephone memorandum sheet in duplicate. The original is attached to the patient's file and shown to the doctor. The duplicate is placed in a special file for telephone messages. Remember to record *all* information such as the date, time, name of person calling, and nature of conversation (include exact information if it concerns a patient or another doctor). The illustration shows one that the secretary could make up herself and reproduce on an office copier. (See Figure 6-8.) (See also Chapter 2.)

This is one way of handling this type of situation. Make sure you check with your doctor to see how he wants it handled.

Doctors who are engaged in research will correspond with one another. This type of correspondence may involve difficult medical terminology. Keep a medical dictionary close at hand.

Most doctors attend meetings and conventions in distant cities. You should be able to make all travel arrangements, including writing or calling to make arrangements and following up with a letter. A phone call to a good travel agency or service will provide all the arrangements the doctor needs without charge, and when tickets are purchased the itinerary will be provided. Hotel reservations, too, can easily be made by telephone, often using a toll-free number. In handling this part of the doctor's correspondence, it is necessary to know the doctor's preferences as to hotels, type of room, type of transportation and such things as car rental.

                                      January 10, 19--

Dr. Douglas P. Clinton
10 Hickman Road
Northport, NY 11768

Dear Doug:

     I have referred one of my patients, Mrs. Barbara
Jenkins, to you for treatment. While she is under your
care, it won't be necessary for me to see her.

     Please send me your diagnosis and let me know of
her progress.

                    Sincerely,

                    Robert Smith, M.D.

ms

FIGURE 6-6
REFERRAL LETTER

Personal

The doctor's personality, his practice, his involvement in professional
associations, clubs, and other outside activities all influence the amount of

ALVIN MYLES JONES, M. D.
965 WALT WHITMAN ROAD
MELVILLE, N. Y. 11746

TELEPHONE 421-1200

January 10, 19--

Dr. G. W. Burns
1805 Seaview Avenue
Islip, NY 12211

Dear Dr. Burns:

Examination of Rudy Smith shows the following:

    Examination of the chest shows the
    lungs to be clear. There is no evi-
    dence of pulmonary infiltration.
    Both costo-phrenic sinuses are clear.
    The cardio-vascular silhouette is
    normal. The trachea is normal and
    in the midline. The mediastinum is
    normal. The bony thorax is normal.

    Impression: Normal heart and lungs.

Thank you for this reference.

       Sincerely,

ms

Courtesy of Histacount Corporation Subsidiary of
SCM Corporation. Used by permission.

FIGURE 6-7
THANK YOU FOR REFERRAL

personal correspondence he will have. A well-known doctor has many obligations through his professional associations such as being an officer in a medical organization which calls for even more involvement and communication with people.

The doctor has all the standard personal correspondence that anyone would have. There are letters to friends, to schools about his children, to department stores, and any number of others. You should be able to write some of these. (See Figure 6-9.)

```
                         TELEPHONE--MEMO

    Date _____  Time _____ a.m./p.m.
    For _____
    From _____

    Message _____
    _____
    _____
    _____
    _____
    _____
    _____
    _____

                         Secretary _____
```

FIGURE 6-8
TELEPHONE MEMO FORM

IMPROVING GRAMMAR SKILLS

You are called upon to punctuate, spell, and capitalize while transcribing the doctor's dictation. The doctor is too busy to be concerned with such details. A good secretarial handbook on English usage is a valuable aid, which every secretary should have. The following basic rules will be helpful.

Comma Usage

Parenthetical words or phrases are usually set off with commas. These words or phrases, which are not necessary for the meaning of the sentence, are used to enhance, to add interest, or to make the sentence more readable. Examples of parenthetical words or phrases are:

Perhaps	*In the event that*
Therefore	*Whenever necessary*
However	*As you know*

Introductory clauses are clauses used at the beginning of the sentence and should usually be set off with commas. However, if the sentence is very short,

ALVIN MYLES JONES, M. D.
965 WALT WHITMAN ROAD
MELVILLE, N. Y. 11746
——
TELEPHONE 421-1200

January 10, 19--

Dr. John T. Martin
55 Seneca Road
Amarillo, TX 77990

Dear John:

Joan and I often reminisce about the good times we had when we were in med school together in Houston. Since then we have seen so little of you and Helen.

I assume that you are planning to attend the medical convention here next month. Joan and I want to invite you and Helen to be our guests while you are attending the convention.

Let us know right away so that we can get tickets for a play while you are in town. We look forward to seeing you.

Regards,

ms

Courtesy of Histacount Corporation Subsidiary of
SCM Corporation. Used by permission.

FIGURE 6-9
PERSONAL LETTER

it may not be necessary to use commas. Such clauses usually begin with words
like:

> *As*
> *If*   *In case you haven't heard*
> *When*

Apposition occurs when a word or words are used in reference to a person,
name of a group, a company, or to describe more clearly who that person,
group, or company is. The added explanation is usually set off with commas.
For example:

> "*Dr. Jones, the head surgeon at Hickory Medical Center in
> Oceanview, will be the guest speaker at the annual meeting of the Cancer
> Society.*"

Dependent clauses are used to clarify the sentence to make it more
meaningful with the result that the sentence becomes longer and slightly
awkward. These clauses must be set off with commas to make the meaning of
the sentence clear; for example:

> "*Although the blood test was normal and all the other laboratory
> tests were negative, the patient continued to lose weight, which caused the
> doctor to insist on the patient entering the hospital for further tests.*"

A compound sentence consists of two independent clauses connected by a
conjunction (i.e. and, but, or, for). An independent clause is one that could be
a complete sentence alone. When there are two such clauses used in the same
sentence, they must be connected in some way. This is usually done by a
conjunction such as "and" preceded by a comma. For example:

> "*The secretary escorted the patient into the examining room, and
> she explained in detail the procedure to follow in undressing and
> preparing for the examination.*"

The conjunction may be omitted between two short clauses and a
semicolon may be used instead. For example:

> "*Miss Jones walked into the empty office; the telephone was ringing
> and the buzzer was buzzing.*"

Spelling and Word Division

A medical dictionary as well as a regular dictionary are *musts* for every
medical secretary. Keep these easily accessible on or near your desk. Many
people find it extremely helpful to also keep a small 3 x 5 card taped to the desk
listing the correct spelling of those words which they always find difficult.
Time is wasted by constantly checking the spelling of the same words.

Many people have trouble dividing words. The following rules will be helpful.

Divide words only at syllables as the dictionary indicates *remembering* certain basic rules which apply to typed copy:

Divide in the middle or at appropriate points, i.e.,

> appoint-ment
> metabo-lism
> tempera-ture

Divide after a single letter syllable in the middle of a word, i.e.,

> tempera-ture

Do not divide words of less than five letters such as

> into
> also
> ever

Do not divide words of one syllable

> chyme
> blood
> birth

Always carry at least three letters to next line

> microscopically (do not divide for *ly*)
> *Do*　　micro-scop-ically

Try *not* to divide words at the end of a page.

Divide before suffixes such as

> ed-ible

Divide after prefixes such as

> re-generate
> con-cussion

A hyphenated word should only be divided at the point of the hyphen.

> post-thrombotic syndrome
> cross-matching test

Try to divide as little as possible. A letter making a good impression does *not* have words divided on consecutive lines.

Do *not* separate a single letter syllable from the beginning of a word.

> amenorrhea　　*not*　a-menorrhea
> aphasia　　　 *not*　a-phasia

If possible, do not divide proper names.

> Bernheim's syndrome
> *Not* Bern-heim's syndrome

Divide *between* double consonants.

gul-let

hal-lux

MODEL LETTERS

The doctor welcomes any assistance with routine correspondence. Keep a looseleaf book of model letters. Check your files to see what styles and types of letters are used most frequently. Compose model letters for recurring

---

ALVIN M. JONES, M. D.
965 WALT WHITMAN ROAD
MELVILLE, N. Y. 11746
—
HAMILTON 1-1200

January 10, 19--

National Insurance Company
55 Forty-eighth Road
Chicago, IL 50114

Gentlemen:

Charles M. Smith was in for a physical examination on January 8. Enclosed is the report you requested.

I hope this is satisfactory.

Sincerely,

ms

Enclosure

Courtesy of Histacount Corporation Subsidiary of SCM Corporation. Used by permission.

FIGURE 6-10
MODEL LETTER TO INSURANCE COMPANY

correspondence such as referrals, test results, and letters to insurance companies. (See Figure 6-10.)

Certain points to emphasize in composing letters are:

1. Keep in mind the person to whom you are writing.
2. Be sure of what you want to say (the message).
3. Verify addresses and double-check dates.
4. Use appropriate style and placement of letters.
5. Proofread carefully before removing from typewriter.

ALVIN M. JONES, M. D.
965 WALT WHITMAN ROAD
MELVILLE, N. Y. 11746
————
HAMILTON 1-1200

January 10, 19--

Miss Joan Hill
144 East Shore Road
Northport, NY 11768

Dear Miss Hill:

    I am happy to inform you that the Pap smears* which were taken in the office on your last visit have been reported as negative.

            Sincerely yours,

ms

*Moderate estrogen level

Courtesy of Histacount Corporation Subsidiary of SCM Corporation. Used by permission.

FIGURE 6-11
MODEL LETTER OF TRANSMITTAL

When answering correspondence, read the letter more than once and decide what information is asked for. Underline the information requested. Decide on the answer and verify before responding. Make a quick outline of what you want to say.

Remember, doctors *rely* on their secretaries for correspondence and may not fully read a letter. Make carbon copies or photocopies of all correspondence for the files.

If the letter is simply transmitting test results or informing the patient of something such as the name of medication, only a brief message is necessary. (See Figure 6-11.) This type of letter is easy to compose.

On the other hand, a collection letter (past due account) requires much more thought and attention. It is a routine letter in that it will recur periodically (monthly), but it should be composed with a great deal of thought as to what and how you get the message across. You definitely do not want to have the patient become angry or annoyed when reading the letter. Remember, be as positive as possible, be polite, and be firm. This is a sensitive area and must be handled with discretion.

Use such words and phrases as:

"If you have already mailed your check, please disregard..."

"Since we have received no response to our previous correspondence, we are wondering if you have overlooked the amount owed Dr. _____."

A positive approach brings better results than a negative one. For examples see Figures 6-12A and 6-12B.

A letter informing the patient of information should get right to the point—stating simply and clearly in one or two paragraphs the necessary information. The letter should have an appropriate closing paragraph that leaves the patient with the feeling that the doctor is interested and concerned about his well-being.

Have a folder of sample letters that can easily be adapted to almost every situation that might arise. The letters should reflect the doctor's personality and should be approved by him. Generally, a letter that has been composed after giving it some forethought will make a much better impression than one that the doctor hurriedly dictates.

To save time and aggravation, a collection of the most commonly used letters can be utilized to great advantage. You can even save copies of all the different types that you or the doctor write, and ones that are received. Being able to get a letter out in a hurry without having to consult the doctor, who is probably not available, is a tremendous help.

You can prepare sample letters in advance. Compose several letters or paragraphs that can be put together to make complete letters. Go over these

```
                        ALVIN  MYLES  JONES,  M. D.
                         965  WALT  WHITMAN  ROAD
                          MELVILLE,  N.  Y.  11746

                          TELEPHONE  421-1200


                    January  10,  19--




       Mr.  David  Smith
       148  Maple  Lane
       Bayside,  NY   11364

       Dear  Mr.  Smith:

            You  have  ignored  our  last  two  statements.
       Your  account  is  more  than  60  days  overdue.

            If  you  do  not  remit  immediately,  we  shall
       refer  your  account  to  our  attorney  for  action.


                    Yours  very  truly,




       ms
```

Courtesy of Histacount Corporation Subsidiary
of SCM Corporation. Used by permission.

FIGURE 6-12A
MODEL OF NEGATIVE LETTER

with the doctor to get his approval and then keep them on file to be used when the occasion arises.

STYLES

Have a basic letter style to be used for most correspondence. Show the doctor several styles and select one. This saves time in the long run, because

ALVIN MYLES JONES, M. D.
965 WALT WHITMAN ROAD
MELVILLE, N. Y. 11746

TELEPHONE 421-1200

January 10, 19--

Mr. David Smith
149 Maple Lane
Bayside, NY 11364

Dear Mr. Smith:

It has been some time since we have heard
from you. Your account is more than 60 days
past due. Dr. Jones is understandably concerned about your account.

If you have already sent a check in payment, please disregard this letter. We look
forward to hearing from you soon.

Yours very truly,

ms

Courtesy of Histacount Corporation Subsidiary
of SCM Corporation. Used by permission.

FIGURE 6-12B
MODEL OF POSITIVE LETTER

through repeated use you set up letters more quickly. For samples of common
letter styles, see Figures 6-13, 6-14, and 6-15.

Types of Salutations and Closings

Use appropriate salutations such as

Dear Ms. Henry

ALVIN MYLES JONES. M. D.
965 WALT WHITMAN ROAD
MELVILLE, N. Y. 11746

TELEPHONE 421-1200

January 10, 19--

Dr. Joseph Abrams
855 Second Street
Manhassett, NY 11030

Dear Joe:

I advised one of my patients, Jerry Adams, to
see you for x-rays and examination of an injured
left knee.

As soon as you have completed the x-rays and
examination, please send the results and your
diagnosis so that I can proceed with treatment.

Cordially,

ms

Courtesy of Histacount Corporation Subsidiary
of SCM Corporation. Used by permission.

FIGURE 6-13
MODEL LETTER - FULL BLOCK STYLE

Dear Miss Hankins

Dear Doctor Johnson
    (Use Doctor *when you do not use first names or initials and* Dr.
    when using first names or initials)

Dear Professor Smith

ALVIN MYLES JONES, M. D.
965 WALT WHITMAN ROAD
MELVILLE, N. Y. 11746
—
TELEPHONE 421-1200

January 10, 19

Dr. Joseph Abrams
855 Second Street
Manhassett, NY 11030

Dear Joe:

I advised one of my patients, Jerry Adams, to
see you for x-rays and examination of an injured
left knee.

As soon as you have completed the x-rays and
examination, please send the results and your
diagnosis so that I can proceed with treatment.

Cordially,

ms

*Courtesy of Histacount Corporation Subsidiary
of SCM Corporation. Used by permission.*

FIGURE 6-14
MODEL LETTER - BLOCK STYLE

Use appropriate closings such as

Sincerely
Cordially
Yours very truly (more formal)

```
                    ALVIN MYLES JONES, M. D.
                    965 WALT WHITMAN ROAD
                    MELVILLE, N. Y. 11746

                    TELEPHONE 421-1200




                                    January 10, 19--



    Dr. Joseph Abrams
    855 Second Street
    Manhassett, NY 11030

    Dear Joe:

        I advised one of my patients, Jerry Adams, to
    see you for x-rays and examination of an injured
    left knee.

        As soon as you have completed the x-rays and
    examination, please send the results and your
    diagnosis so that I can proceed with treatment.

                    Cordially,




    ms
```

*Courtesy of Histacount Corporation Subsidiary
of SCM Corporation. Used by permission.*

FIGURE 6-15
MODEL LETTER - SEMI-BLOCK STYLE

Doctors usually sign letters as follows:

Alvin Myles Jones, M.D., not *Dr. Alvin...*

Always indicate special notations such as enclosures, carbon copies, or blind carbon copies as follows:

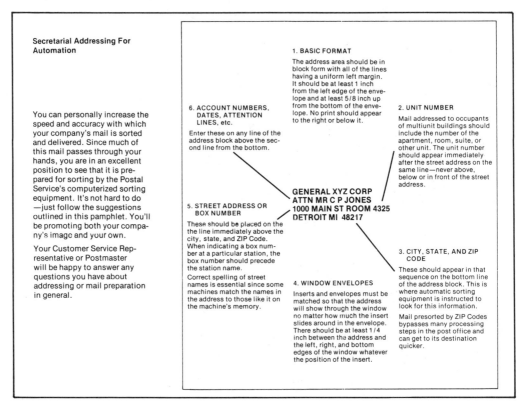

*Courtesy of the Flushing Main Branch of the United
States Postal Service. Used by permission.*

FIGURE 6-16
FORMAT FOR TYPING ENVELOPES

Enclosures

cc: *Professor S. Smith*
     Dr. Harry Stone

bcc: *(appears on the carbon copies only)*
     Mrs. Cynthia Russo
     Dr. Harry Stone

CHOOSING THE STATIONERY

Using the proper stationery is very important. Most doctors use a small letterhead for their medical correspondence to patients; however, this is not a requirement. Use whatever your doctor wants. If he has no particular preference, it is up to you to choose. Most medical supply houses are helpful in tailoring letterheads to your needs. Bear in mind that it is important to use the

SOME ADDITIONAL SUGGESTIONS TO KEEP IN MIND

7. Type addresses in upper case letters without punctuation.

8. Try to use type fonts other than italic, script, or proportionately-spaced fonts.

9. Be careful not to type the address at a slant.

10. Keep your typewriter keys clean to eliminate filled-in letters. Use a fresh, clean ribbon to get the best address impression possible.

11. Use rectangular envelopes that will provide good color contrast with the address impression. They should be no smaller than 3-1/2 by 5 inches and no larger than 6-1/8 by 11-1/2 inches.

12. Check to see that envelopes addressed back to your company have the correct address format and ZIP Code and that firms sending mail to your company have your correct ZIP Code.

13. If your firm wants to use a street location in its mailing address but wants its mail delivered to a post office box, the box number should be on the next-to-last line of the address. The ZIP Code

used should be the one for the box number, not the street address:

GENERAL XYZ CORP
1000 MAIN ST
PO BOX 3302 JEFFERSON STATION
DETROIT MI 48214

14. You can simplify addresses and increase the machinability of your mail by using two-letter abbreviations for state names:

TWO-LETTER STATE ABBREVIATIONS

Alabama	AL	Montana	MT
Alaska	AK	Nebraska	NE
American Samoa	AS	Nevada	NV
Arizona	AZ	New Hampshire	NH
Arkansas	AR	New Jersey	NJ
California	CA	New Mexico	NM
Canal Zone	CZ	New York	NY
Colorado	CO	North Carolina	NC
Connecticut	CT	North Dakota	ND
Delaware	DE	Ohio	OH
District of Columbia	DC	Oklahoma	OK
Florida	FL	Oregon	OR
Georgia	GA	Pennsylvania	PA
Guam	GU	Puerto Rico	PR
Hawaii	HI	Rhode Island	RI
Idaho	ID	South Carolina	SC
Illinois	IL	South Dakota	SD
Indiana	IN	Tennessee	TN
Iowa	IA	Texas	TX
Kansas	KS	Trust Territories	TT
Kentucky	KY	Utah	UT
Louisiana	LA	Vermont	VT
Maine	ME	Virginia	VA
Maryland	MD	Virgin Islands	VI
Massachusetts	MA	Washington	WA
Michigan	MI	West Virginia	WV
Minnesota	MN	Wisconsin	WI
Mississippi	MS	Wyoming	WY
Missouri	MO		

CUSTOMER SERVICES DEPT.
NOTICE 23-B/OCT. 1976

☆ U.S. GOVERNMENT PRINTING OFFICE 1976:721-439

Courtesy of the Flushing Main Branch of the United States Postal Service. Used by permission.

FIGURE 6-17
STATE ABBREVIATIONS AND SOME
ADDITIONAL SUGGESTIONS TO KEEP IN MIND

right size paper. A small letter looks better on small paper. If the letter is long, if should be on standard 8½ x 11 letterhead, not on several sheets of small paper. (See Chapter 7.)

The samples of stationery shown are the ones most commonly used. Envelopes should match the stationery. The quality should be good and take easily to correction materials so that the appearance will be attractive.

For copies, the proper grade and weight carbon paper and copy paper (onionskin) should be used. Many doctors prefer making photocopies. The skill and efficiency with which corrections are made require that the proper materials are readily available at all times. (See Chapter 7.)

Envelopes

There are certain rules prescribed by the United States Postal Service to be followed in preparing envelopes. In order for mail to be read by an optical scanner, the Post Office recommends that all addresses be typed in block style, single spaced, and consist of no more than four lines—always include the zip code and use the two-letter state abbreviations. (See Figures 6-16 and 6-17.)

ANALYZE THE DICTATION

Most correspondence is originated by the doctor either in answer to letters or initiating his own. Whether he dictates to you personally, writes in longhand, or uses a dictating machine depends upon many factors—personality, amount of time available, type of practice or specialty, and hours spent in the office.

Often the doctor's schedule is such that very little time is actually spent in the office except for seeing patients. If this is the case, the doctor may dictate at home in the evening, or in the office after regular office hours, or while traveling. There are many options with the use of the electronic dictating equipment now available. Analyze your situation to see which method of originating correspondence would be most effective and increase the efficiency of your office. Your doctor will welcome your suggestions.

TRANSCRIBING

Several belts or tapes may be dictated all at one time. If there is not a transcribing machine, you often are called in for an entire morning of dictation or you may have to compose much of the routine correspondence yourself. The test of how well you are handling this phase of your job is measured by how much responsibility you are given.

There is just no way for you to have things set up on a schedule that suits you completely. You must arrange your duties around the doctor's schedule. This is one of the things that makes working for a doctor interesting; one never knows exactly what to expect.

Whatever the policy, you may get the dictation or longhand copy the day after it is dictated. The important things to keep in mind are:

1. Check all dates.
2. Be accurate in transcribing from stenography notes or machine.
3. Be prompt in sending it out.
4. Organize time so that you will more or less have a schedule to follow.

There are many ways to accomplish the work. The most important consideration is to work *with* the doctor. Make your own schedule fit into the doctor's and always try to be as flexible as possible. Remember that *you* are working *for* the doctor and it is *your* responsibility to make things as convenient as possible for both of you.

When the correspondence is completed have everything ready in a folder for the doctor's signature. This folder is usually given to the doctor each day at a pre-determined time. The billing is usually the secretary's responsibility (See Chapter 12), since the doctor does not necessarily have time to check them.

When everything has been proofread and signed, check carefully to see that letters have been signed, enclosures included and that the contents of each envelope are correct. When an envelope contains more than one item, it is preferable to use staples rather than paper clips to attach papers.

TIME-SAVERS

For large offices where the outgoing mail is heavy, a postage meter can be acquired. The meter itself cannot be bought, but is leased and serviced by the Post Office. Have a small postage scale, use rubber stamps for special types of mail, and include the zip code in the address. Before mailing, sort the local mail from out-of-town mail into bundles. Speed up mail service by getting it out in the morning rather than waiting until the end of the day. You should definitely become acquainted with all the services available through the Post Office.

Remember these points: Handle all items with speed and efficiency; organize your work; free the doctor for more pressing responsibilities.

Much can be said about the importance of correspondence. You as the medical secretary help the doctor keep up with his responsibilities through his correspondence. Many doctors prefer using pre-printed form letters and notes to save time. The scope and content depend upon the doctor's own needs. (See Figures 6-18, 6-19, 6-20, 6-21, 6-22, 6-23, 6-24.)

The degree of your responsibility depends largely upon you. Your increase in efficiency leads to your being given more responsibility which increases both your personal job satisfaction and effectiveness.

ALVIN MYLES JONES, M. D.
965 WALT WHITMAN ROAD
MELVILLE, N. Y. 11749
—
HAMILTON 1-1200

MEDICAL REPORT FORM

RE:_____AGE_____

DATE_____

Dear Dr._____

Thank you for referring your patient. The following is a summary of essential findings.

HISTORY:_____

_____

_____

_____

PHYSICAL FINDINGS:_____

_____

_____

DIAGNOSIS:_____

_____

_____

_____

TREATMENT OR DISPOSITION:_____

_____

_____

_____

REMARKS: ☐ NONE   ☐ MORE COMPLETE LETTER TO FOLLOW

☐_____

☐ SEE ATTACHED DIAGRAM, X-RAY, ETC.

MR   Signed_____

Courtesy of Histacount Corporation Subsidiary of SCM Corporation. Used by permission.

FIGURE 6-18
REFERRAL LETTER

ALVIN MYLES JONES, M. D.
965 WALT WHITMAN ROAD
MELVILLE, N. Y. 11749

HAMILTON 1-1200

DATE_____

TO: _____

_____

This will introduce my patient,

_____

For the following: ☐ Diagnosis   ☐ Treatment

☐ Case history is enclosed with this introduction.

☐ Case history is being sent under separate cover.

Remarks:_____

_____

_____

_____

_____

_____

_____

_____

_____

_____

RS   Signed_____

Courtesy of Histacount Corporation Subsidiary of
SCM Corporation. Used by Permission.

FIGURE 6-19
REFERRAL LETTER

ALVIN MYLES JONES, M. D.
965 WALT WHITMAN ROAD
MELVILLE, N. Y. 11749
—
HAmilton 1-1200

CERTIFICATE OF HEALTH

_____19___

This is to certify that

_____

is free of any contagious or infectious disease and
has my permission to attend school.

Signed_____

116P

FIGURE 6-20
CERTIFICATE OF HEALTH

INOCULATION CERTIFICATE

Date_____

This is to certify that

_____

has received the following inoculations and tests:

☐ Diphtheria . . Dates:_____
☐ Tetanus . . . . .Dates:_____
☐ Pertussis . . . .Dates:_____
☐ Polio . . . . . . .Dates:_____
☐ Measles . . . . .Dates:_____
☐ Smallpox . . . .Date:_____
☐ Shick Test . . Date:_____Result_____
☐ T.B. Test . . . Date:_____Result_____
☐ Booster . . . . .Date:_____Type_____
Remarks:_____

_____
Dr._____

FORM NO. 117   PROFESSIONAL PRINTING CO., INC., MELVILLE, L. I., N. Y.

FIGURE 6-21
INOCULATION CERTIFICATE

Date_____

This is to certify that

_____

Is under my care for the following:

Dr._____

FORM No. 118   HISTACOUNT CORPORATION MELVILLE, NEW YORK 11746

Courtesy of Histacount Corporation Subsidiary of
SCM Corporation. Used by Permission.

FIGURE 6-22
SCHOOL NOTE

FROM:

ALVIN M. JONES, M. D.
965 WALT WHITMAN ROAD
MELVILLE, N. Y. 11746

HAMILTON 1-1200

DATE:

ATTENTION:

TO:

SUBJECT:

MESSAGE

SIGNED:

REPLY

DATE: SIGNED:

HISTACOUNT CORP., MELVILLE, N.Y. 11746 FORM NO. SK-1

THIS COPY FOR PERSON ADDRESSED

Courtesy of Histacount Corporation Subsidiary of SCM Corporation. Used by Permission.

FIGURE 6-23
SHORT-KUT NOTE

ALVIN MYLES JONES, M. D.
965 WALT WHITMAN ROAD
MELVILLE, N. Y. 11749
—
HAMILTON 1-1200

NAME————————————————————————DATE——————————

INSTRUCTIONS

Courtesy of Histacount Corporation Subsidiary of
SCM Corporation. Used by Permission.

FIGURE 6-24
INSTRUCTION SLIP

Chapter 7

Maintaining
and Ordering Office
Supplies and Equipment

Handling medical office supplies and equipment for the doctor's office is your responsibility. It is important that this operation be supervised closely. To properly maintain office and medical supplies and equipment, your duties consist of keeping up with what is on hand and reordering. You must know how and what to order.

HINTS ON KEEPING UP WITH SUPPLIES

A general knowledge of what supplies are needed is necessary. Further instruction from the doctor will guide you along. While working closely with the doctor, you must develop your own system of ordering, receiving and storing supplies, and making them readily available to the doctor when he needs them. It is important periodically to check what is on hand, paying strict attention to proper labeling, storing, and retention and disposal procedures. In purchasing supplies and equipment, factors such as quality, quantity, convenience, ease of disposability, reusability, and life span of product, are important. Basically, ordering supplies in the doctor's office is the same as in other offices. However, handling drugs, keeping an inventory of items used every day, and caring for medical equipment places additional demands on the secretary's time. The manner in which the buying, care and servicing, and inventory records are kept can save the doctor money and time, and increase the efficiency of operation.

SYSTEMATIC APPROACH MAKES ORDERING EASIER

In ordering, there are certain steps to be followed. Keep a checklist of all items that might be needed; then check with the doctor and check the supply on hand. (See Figure 7-1.) The quality of the product and quantity used have to be considered. Before taking advantage of discounts for buying in quantity,

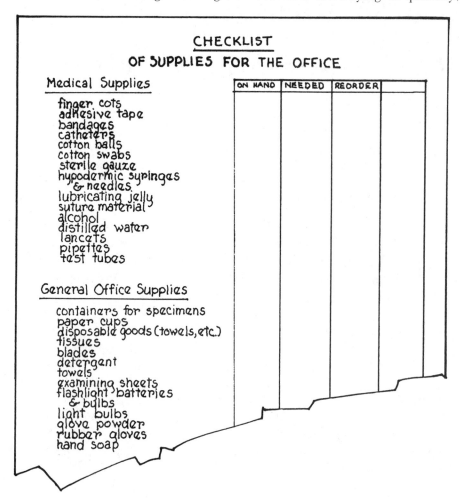

FIGURE 7-1
CHECKLIST OF SUPPLIES FOR OFFICE

determine whether or not the product can be used up before it deteriorates and whether adequate storage is available. Suggestions about such things as disposables should be thoroughly discussed with the doctor. Supply the doctor with information about time saved and the cost comparison of disposable and nondisposable items. Such items might include drape sheets, examination gowns, and hypodermics.

Certain items such as drugs and medicines must be authorized by the doctor, but it is your responsibility to see to it that the proper quantities are always on hand.

You should keep current catalogs and up-to-date information on medical supplies. Look through medical periodicals to see what new items are available that will increase efficiency and reduce costs. Make lists of items to be ordered, new products on the market, and suggestions for discussion with the doctor. Keep a list of salesmen who can be called when questions arise. Drug detail men call on the doctor regularly to keep him informed of the latest drugs on the market. Although he cannot see all of them, he will want to see some of them. Find out which ones he wants to see so that a time can be arranged. Keep the Physician's Desk Reference (PDR) easily accessible. (See Chapter 8.)

The doctor is given many samples by drug companies. Keep the ones the doctor wants in a place convenient for him. Store them according to the different types—antibiotics, tranquilizers, etc. Clean them out periodically, disposing of those that have been around too long. Keep drugs current by placing those with expiration dates soon to occur at the front of the shelf to be used first.

Be certain that drugs that are to be discarded are properly disposed of. They should not be just tossed into a wastebasket. This may be dangerous if they fall into the wrong hands. This is why you should first check with the doctor about the method of disposal.

YOUR RESPONSIBILITY FOR OFFICE EQUIPMENT AND SUPPLIES

The purchase of office equipment is authorized and approved by the doctor, but your opinion as to brand or model, or suggestions about new equipment that will increase the efficiency of running the office will be a definite factor in ordering equipment. For example, when the time comes to purchase a new typewriter, be aware of what is new in office equipment so that when asked you can offer your views. Types of equipment that will increase the efficiency of operation are: photocopying, dictation and transcription (See Chapter 5), and a postage meter (See Chapter 6). Estimate the amount of time saved as compared with the cost of the equipment before suggesting the purchase. If the doctor can see the advantages of these purchases, he will probably be most agreeable. Prepare a list of the advantages for the doctor to look at before making a decision.

You are responsible for ordering the supplies for office equipment such as forms, typewriter ribbons, paper for photocopying, and software for the dictating equipment. It will most likely be your responsibility to keep the equipment repaired and serviced. (See Figure 7-2.) Check with the company regarding availability and cost of service contracts. Be sure that equipment is always ready for use and that adequate supplies are on hand.

RECORD FOR SERVICING EQUIPMENT				
DATE	TYPE OF EQUIPMENT	NAME OF COMPANY	WHAT WAS DONE	NAME OF SERVICEMAN

FIGURE 7-2
RECORD FOR SERVICING EQUIPMENT

Those items used in a medical office are the same as in a business office except for the special forms that the doctor uses for such things as case histories, progress reports, and lab reports. The basic supplies consist of the following:

plain bond paper
letterheads
second sheets
carbon paper
file folders
labels
file cards
pencils, pens, and correction materials
envelopes
telephone memorandum pads
typewriter ribbons

forms such as:

printed blanks	charge slips
appointment books	bookkeeping forms
statements	appointment cards
tax and insurance forms	

FACTORS TO CONSIDER IN ORDERING OFFICE SUPPLIES

In purchasing office supplies, consider quality, price, and service rendered by the supplier. For instance: Will the supplier print your letterheads or forms in any manner you wish? Will they give you assistance in working up any new forms you may want? Maintain names and addresses of the suppliers of those items used and mark in the supply catalog the items ordered, so that when reordering it will be easy to copy the numbers of items and quantities. Refer also to previous purchase orders for item numbers and quantities.

OVERSTOCKING CAN BE A PROBLEM

Do not overstock supplies, because some things will age and deteriorate. Even though it is sometimes more economical to order in quantity, some supplies may not be used up fast enough to do so. For example: paper products such as letterheads will start to fade or turn yellow and you will not want to use them. If the letterhead is not crisp and new, it will appear that the office is run haphazardly.

PRACTICAL VALUE OF KEEPING A RUNNING INVENTORY

You must keep an account of all purchases to insure that the doctor has what he wants when he needs it. This necessitates some type of system by which you and the doctor can keep up with how much is on hand. If you are the only one in charge of handing out medical supplies or drugs, perhaps a running inventory chart could be kept indicating how much was ordered and any additions to the order. When something is removed from the shelves it could be entered on the chart. (See Figure 7-3.)

If, however, there are several people, including the doctor, with access to the supplies, it might be better to have a periodic check. If this is done frequently, it will be easier than if too much time elapses between checks. You must consider your own situation and work out the best system for you.

Careful records must be maintained on purchases. As supplies are received, they should be checked against the purchase order to see that all quantities, amounts, etc. are correct and to see that all items were received and that nothing was damaged or spoiled. Note that some bills paid within ten days are entitled to a discount. (See Figure 7-4.)

INVENTORY CHART OF SUPPLIES

DATE RECEIVED	DESCRIPTION OF ITEM	MAXIMUM QUANTITY	MINIMUM QUANTITY	REORDER

FIGURE 7-3
INVENTORY CHART OF SUPPLIES

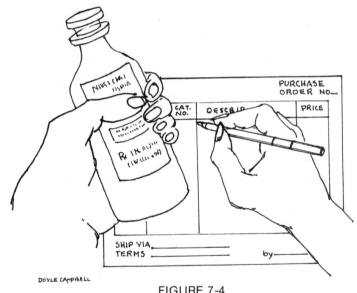

FIGURE 7-4
CHECKING SUPPLIES AGAINST PURCHASE ORDER

TIPS ON STORING SUPPLIES AND DRUGS

Supplies should be stored where they are easily accessible. Remember, drugs need special storage facilities. Many must be stored in a cool, dark, dry place. Some drugs may require refrigeration. Narcotics are kept in a separate place, under lock. Everything should be carefully labeled and grouped according to types of drugs and supplies. Many types of medications would be harmful if not used properly.

Everything should be stored in its proper place and should be checked often to see that it has not been moved or mixed in with other medication, labels are not missing, and to note what needs to be re-ordered. (See Figure 7-5.)

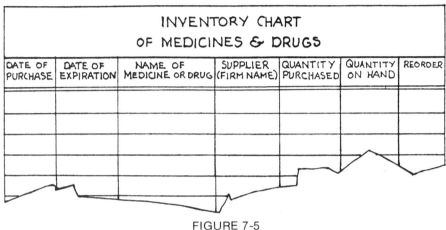

FIGURE 7-5
INVENTORY CHART OF MEDICINES AND DRUGS

SHORTCUTS WILL MAKE THE JOB EASIER

In some instances the doctor or a nurse may be the only one in charge of all medicines and drugs while other medical and office supplies are handled by the secretary. In other cases the secretary may handle all supplies. Although there may be more than one person involved with the ordering and dispensing of supplies, it is better to have final responsibility resting with one person. If the one in charge can devise ways of distributing and keeping count of supplies that will make the job easier, then by all means, do whatever reduces the workload and increases efficiency. For instance, a checklist is helpful. (See Figure 7-1.)

Distributing supplies to the examining rooms, bathrooms, x-ray room, and consultation rooms is time-consuming and has to be done daily. It should be scheduled at a regular time.

Managing supplies may seem to be a thankless job, but it is a very necessary part of running an efficient office. When a doctor needs particular supplies, they should be available immediately. To be sure that supplies are plentiful and distributed properly, separate supply lists should be kept for each room as a quick reminder and for those who are not accustomed to the regular procedure. It is helpful to attach a blank order form on the inside of the door of each cabinet so that whenever it is noticed that the inventory on a particular item is low, the information can be immediately noted on the form. (See Figure 7-6.)

FIGURE 7-6
SUPPLY CABINET SHOWING
CHECKLIST AND ORDER FORM ON DOORS

TIPS FOR KEEPING THE DOCTOR'S BAG READY

Your duties may or may not extend to checking the doctor's bag and keeping it orderly and well stocked. Knowing what to include and how to go about it is determined by the doctor's needs and preferences. The type of practice will also determine the types of instruments, medications, and any special instruments or diagnostic equipment required. Close consultation with the doctor is the best way to know how he wants you to care for the bag. It may be that he would rather take care of his own bag in which case you would be free to attend to other duties.

If this is one of your responsibilities, though, it would be wise to keep a checklist of items that he keeps in his bag so that each time you check it, you will be certain not to forget anything. Certain items have to be taken out and sterilized. Some things have to be replaced such as cotton, sterile gauze, bandages, needles. Duplicate sets of sterilized instruments and disposable materials should be kept ready so that they can be replaced at a moment's notice.

You can prepare a list of the items required and keep it in the desk drawer.

Daily, when you check the bag against the list, you should note any items that are running low.

Always check the medication to see if any need replacing and if there are any that are old (note the date on the label), dispose of them. Use the checklist as a guide in formulating a checklist tailored to the needs of your office. Discuss with the doctor to see what items should be added or deleted. (See Figure 7-7.)

Taking care of medical office supplies and equipment is a serious responsibility of the medical secretary. The doctor who does not have the proper equipment ready to give an injection, or cannot find his prescription pad when he needs it makes a poor impression on a patient.

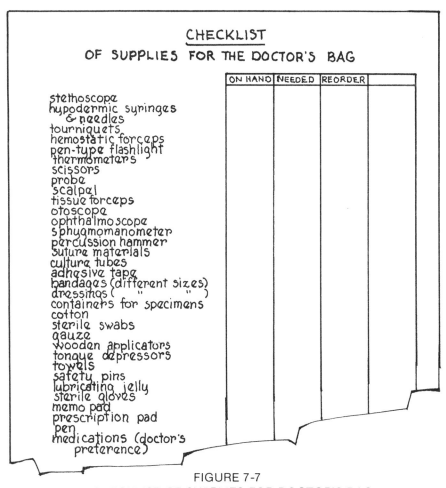

FIGURE 7-7
CHECKLIST OF SUPPLIES FOR DOCTOR'S BAG

Chapter 8

Assisting the Doctor as Author and Speaker

Greater emphasis than ever is being put on medical research and improved health care. New information is accumulating so rapidly that it is impossible for any one person to keep up with all the latest developments. A new discovery today may be a thing of the past tomorrow.

How does this affect you as the medical secretary? Does your employer depend on you for information sources? Is it an accepted part of your job to assist the doctor in searching out or gathering information to be used in the preparation of speeches and writing of all types, or just to help the doctor in keeping up with the current literature?

Whether or not you do any of these things will depend upon the job. However, should the doctor be engaged in any activities such as writing articles for medical periodicals, speaking or presenting papers, or participating actively in such organizations as medical societies, he will naturally need your help. If he is engaged in research, he will be writing reports on his findings. A knowledge of the preparation and production of manuscripts is needed.

HOW YOU CAN ASSIST THE DOCTOR WITH WRITING

In some offices, the secretary must be called upon to prepare abstracts or summaries of either the doctor's own article or articles that appear in professional magazines or a précis of part of an article. In order to do this, it would be necessary for the secretary to be familiar with the definitions of these terms.

115

The abstract and précis are similar, but the abstract deals with a whole article or book while the précis is involved only with a portion of the material. In each, only the essential ideas are extracted in the same order as presented in the original material. The emphasis is the same as the author indicated originally, but synonyms are used for many words and no comment is made.

A summary, however, differs in that the order and emphasis can be changed, the person summarizing may comment on a passage and may use the identical wording if necessary.

CHOOSING YOUR OWN REFERENCE BOOKS

Every office needs some reference books. The type and size of the office and the doctor's needs will determine the ones you will have. If you are asked what books you would like to have, those mentioned in the following paragraphs are suggested. Add to these any books that you or the doctor have found helpful. Keep close at hand those used most often, and those used less frequently should be easily accessible when needed.

The reference sources basic to any office are: a desk-sized dictionary, a secretarial handbook, and a telephone directory. Often a thesaurus and world almanac are added depending on the needs of the office. The medical secretary should also have a good medical dictionary, and the PDR (Physician's Desk Reference) should be easily accessible. To these basic source books, add any that would be particularly helpful in your situation—perhaps a dictionary of specialized terminology relating to your doctor's specialty.

When setting up your own personal library of reference books, the following should be taken into consideration.

Choose an up-to-date dictionary since dictionaries do become outdated. There are several excellent ones available.

The telephone directory is useful for finding things other than telephone numbers. You may need to refer to it for correct spelling of personal names, firm names, and addresses. Become familiar with the "Yellow Pages," which contain valuable information, useful when you order supplies or look for a dealer who handles a particular brand. The pages at the beginning of the directory contain a wealth of information such as where to call for telephone service and complaints, where and how to pay telephone bills, different types of calls and how to dial them, explanation of charges, area code and time zone map, area codes, long distance including international calls, zip code map and many other facts.

A secretarial handbook is a must for every secretary. Questions are constantly arising regarding items such as punctuation, capitalization, correct forms of address, abbreviations, and examples of letters. There are several excellent handbooks on the market.

An almanac is an annual publication containing a summary of facts both past and current. It gives a chronological record of recent events and statistics on government, labor, medicine, aviation, sports, education, literature, people, science, religion, and many other subjects.

For a medical secretary, a comprehensive medical dictionary is a necessity. There are many excellent ones to choose from. A thesaurus is also helpful if the doctor is engaged in writing of any kind such as research, reports, articles, speeches, or books. It is a collection of words and phrases arranged according to ideas, which can help in locating an appropriate word.

Be familiar with the major encyclopedias. Some include many volumes, but there are several one-volume encyclopedias that can be bought for office use.

It is very helpful to keep, for your own reference, current catalogs from manufacturers with whom you deal constantly.

There are various other useful reference books such as biographical and geographical dictionaries. Also, all published material is indexed. To locate a book, consult *The United States Catalog* published by H.W. Wilson Company. To locate a periodical, consult the *Reader's Guide to Periodical Literature*. For some information that is available only in pamphlet form, consult the *Vertical File Index*. For a specialist such as a medical secretary, there are available secretarial handbooks dealing specifically with that field.

You, as the medical secretary who fills out countless medical insurance forms, should keep on hand up-to-date manuals explaining the various insurance plans and how to fill out the forms. These are furnished upon request by the insurance companies and by the Social Security office for Medicare. (See Chapter 11.)

The doctor will probably subscribe to several medical periodicals such as the *Journal of the American Medical Association*, *Journal of American Hospital Association*, and *Journal of Medical Education*. There are many other medical magazines that come to the physician, some free, some on a subscription basis. Learn your doctor's preference for which to subscribe to and which to retain longer than a month or two. Have a special place to store them in chronological order for future reference. The doctor may call for a specific article in a back issue.

Most doctors keep on hand up-to-date reference books dealing with their particular field. You should be aware of the books the doctor keeps for his reference.

General Reference Books

In addition to the basic information sources, there are other books that should be easily accessible. Depending upon the type of office and your employer, you should have access to the *U.S. Postal Manual*, *Hotel Red Book*, (for making travel arrangements) a city directory, American Medical Directory, and possibly an atlas.

KNOWING WHERE TO FIND INFORMATION

Familiarize yourself with the public library, or if you work in a hospital or medical school learn what facilities are available to you. Ask the librarian for

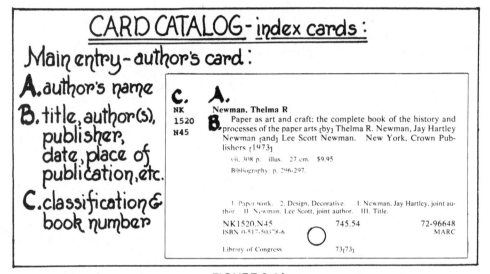

FIGURE 8-1A
AUTHOR'S CARD

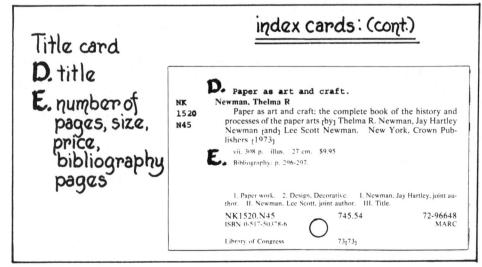

FIGURE 8-1B
TITLE CARD

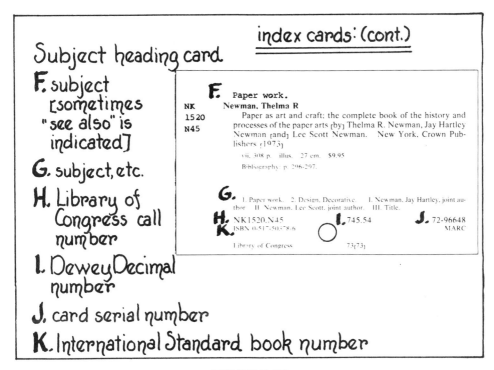

FIGURE 8-1C
SUBJECT CARD

help with your problems. Some public libraries have an information service that answers telephone requests.

The card catalog is the most important source of library information. All books are listed by author, title, and subject. (See Figures 8-1A, 8-1B and 8-1C.) If you have never used a library before, do not hesitate asking the librarian for assistance. Most libraries provide copying facilities for making exact copies of whatever material you need.

Special libraries deal with information relating to a specific field. You should locate the nearest medical library. The public library usually maintains a listing of special libraries in the area. Find out the location and the telephone number should you need it.

PREPARING MANUSCRIPTS

If your job includes the typing of manuscripts you must know the proper way of setting them up. Manuscripts are designed for the purpose of reporting what is happening or what is being done in a particular field. A manuscript can be in the form of an article, a book, a speech, a report of research findings, or a report of a medical meeting.

Preparation of manuscripts will be determined by the doctor for whom you are working. Some doctors are quite involved in writing for professional periodicals while others are constantly in demand as speakers. Whatever the need, the secretary should be aware of the particular needs of the doctor and try to be as much help as possible.

Gathering Information

The doctor usually prepares the manuscripts relying on the secretary mainly for help in editing, organizing, and in the end, typing up the final manuscript. In addition to knowing the mechanics of manuscript typing, the secretary should be aware of the importance of the work and the fact that the doctor probably needs a block of time (perhaps periodically) when work can go on uninterrupted.

Hints on Producing the Manuscript

You will probably be able to render the most assistance in typing the rough draft and in editing. (See Figure 8-2A.) Usually, several rough drafts are written before the final typing of the manuscript. (See Figure 8-2B.) For ease in revising, use wide margins with triple spacing so that changes and additions can be made easily. Use inexpensive paper and date each rough draft so that the drafts will not be confused during the revision process. Keep the old marked up drafts in a folder for reference until the final copy is typed.

Revising and editing the manuscript is where you as the secretary can prove the most helpful. The doctor will be concerned primarily with the subject and pertinent facts, whereas your concern should be with readability—the word usage, sentence structure, clarity of expression, consistency in thought, paragraphing, accuracy of spelling, punctuation, and capitalization. Standard proofreader's marks (See Figure 8-3.) should be used in the revision. During the revision, the secretary should have a reference book at hand to guide her— for example, a style manual and dictionary. Copies of other articles from the periodical for which the doctor is writing may be of help.

If copyrighted material is quoted, permission must be obtained from the owner of the copyright before quoting. The assistant is responsible for obtaining such permission. Consult a good secretarial handbook for an example of an appropriate letter requesting permission.

Final preparation of the manuscript requires that the assistant be familiar with the correct form, that it be arranged attractively, and that the typing be free of errors. The style is dictated by the type of manuscript and its purpose. Often for a magazine article or any published material, the format will be more and more important.

As the role of the professional nurse has become more specialized in its application to nursing and education, doctors in private practice have learned to depend more fully on the capabilities of that new invention, the medical assistant. Historically, this might have been a surprised medical secretary who suddenly found she needed to learn sterile techniques, or a technician who was asked if she wouldn't like to brush up on her typing and terminology, just to "fill in." Those of us who were frantically recruited to provide solution for the chaotic management problems in some offices know the uncertainities and frustrations of entering what was actually a brand new field.[1]

FLEXIBILITY

In supplying secretarial personnel in the health field

The need to be flexible and up to date became increasingly

apparent in almost every field in the 60's and will continue on

into the 80's. In order to meet the needs of increased specializa-

tion and technical innovation in an ever-changing society we must

be flexible, aware of situations, and willing to continue keeping

up to date in our chosen professions. *However,* A good general education

is basic to any job situation. Care must be taken to not over-

specialize because unless ~~the material learned~~ is used more would   *stet*

be forgotten than would be retained. And, with our changing

technology it is very possible that material learned may be

obsolete before it is used.

---

[1]Fortin, Nancy. "Are We A Collective Bargaining Agency?" North West Medicine, June, 1969, p. 589.

-3-

FIGURE 8-2A
EDITED ROUGH DRAFT WITH FOOTNOTE

more and more important.

> As the role of the professional nurse has become more
> specialized in its application to nursing and education,
> doctors in private practice have learned to depend more
> fully on the capabilities of that new invention, the
> medical assistant. Historically, this might have been
> a surprised medical secretary who suddenly found she
> needed to learn sterile techniques, or a technician
> who was asked if she wouldn't like to brush up on her
> typing and terminology, just to "fill in." Those of
> us who were frantically recruited to provide solution
> for the chaotic management problems in some offices know
> the uncertainties and frustrations of entering what was
> actually a brand new field. (Fortin)

FLEXIBILITY

In supplying secretarial personnel in the health field the
need to be flexible and up to date became increasingly apparent
in almost every field in the 60's and will continue on into the
80's.

In order to meet the needs of increased specialization and
technical innovation in an ever-changing society we must be
flexible, aware of situations, and willing to continue keeping
up to date in our chosen professions. However, a good general
education is basic to any job situation. Care must be taken
not to over-specialize because unless the material learned is
used more would be forgotten than would be retained. And, with
our changing technology, it is very possible that material
learned may be obsolete before it is used.

-3-

FIGURE 8-2B
MANUSCRIPT WITH MID-PAGE DOCUMENTATION

PROOFREADER'S MARKS

Capitalize	
Boldface type	
Use lowercase	
Delete	
Insert	
Change to italics	*ital*
Move to left	
Move to right	
Raise	
Lower	
Let type stand	...*stet*
Paragraph	
No paragraph	*No* ¶
Add horizontal space	#
Add vertical space	
Close up space (horizontal)	
Close up space (vertical)	
Spell out	*sp*
Transpose	*tr*
Verify or supply information	??
Wrong font	*wf*

FIGURE 8-3
PROOFREADERS' MARKS

supplied by the publisher. Again, the secretary should have at hand for reference a style manual or a secretarial handbook, or a copy of a previous article or speech.

In typing the report, use a good 8½- by 11-inch bond paper. Make at least one carbon copy. Manuscripts are usually double-spaced. Margins should remain uniform throughout except for the first page. The following table is a guide to generally accepted margins for manuscript typing:

Margins for Manuscripts

	Top-Bound	Side-Bound	Unbound
Top Margin			
First Page	2-2½″	2″	2″
Other Pages	1½″	1″	1″
Side Margins			
Left	1″	1½″	1″
Right	1″	1″	1″
Bottom Margins	1-1½″	1-1½″	1-1½″

To keep margins uniform on all pages, a guide sheet should be used. It is placed directly beneath the original copy so that the guide lines will show through clearly. (See Figure 8-4.) Prepare your own guide sheet using as a guide the sample shown here. The sample guide sheet shown is for a left-bound manuscript. The short numbered lines at the bottom left of the page are to be used as a guide in typing footnotes. The two lines at the top indicate a first page margin of 2-inches and succeeding pages of 1-inch. Page numbers may be placed either in the upper right hand corner one-half inch from the top edge of the paper even with the right margin or at the bottom of the page centered one-half inch from the bottom edge. The first page is not numbered, but succeeding pages are numbered beginning with page two. When a manuscript is to be bound at the top, it is better to number pages at the bottom.

BECOME FAMILIAR WITH FORMAT (QUOTED MATERIAL, FOOTNOTES, TABLE OF CONTENTS, TITLE PAGE)

Quoted material should be completely accurate and credit must be given in footnotes. When quoting less than four lines, the material can be enclosed in quotation marks, but if a longer quote is used, it should be indented from both margins and single spaced.

Footnotes give the source of quoted statements or ideas. They are identified by number of the statement or idea in the manuscript. Footnotes contain the names of authors, titles of complete works, publisher's names, places of publication, dates of publication, and page numbers where quoted material is cited. (See Figure 8-2a).

Often when material is submitted for publication the footnotes and

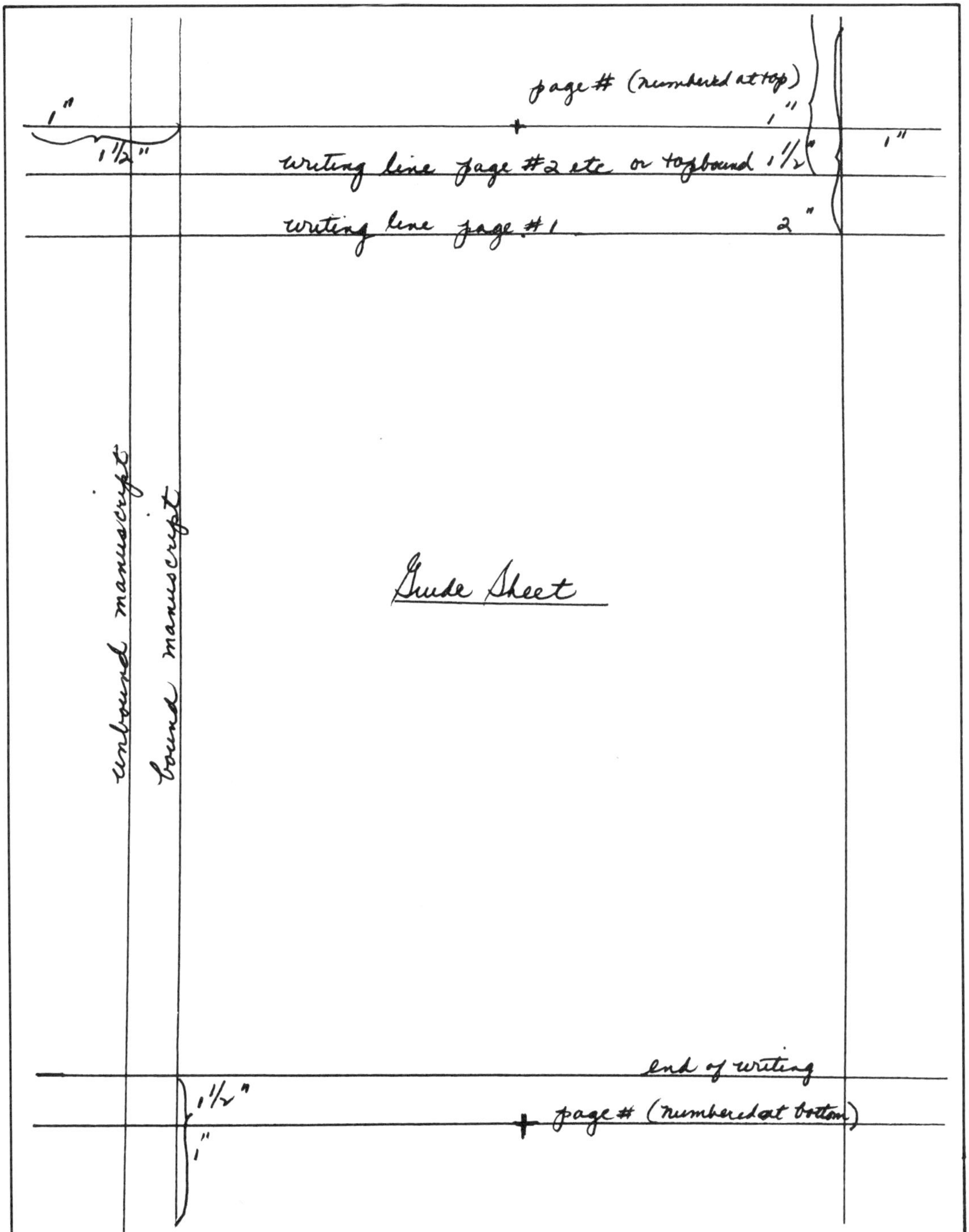

page # (numbered at top)

1"

1½"

writing line page #2 etc or topbound 1½"   1"

writing line page #1   2"

unbound manuscript

bound manuscript

Guide Sheet

end of writing

1½"

page # (numbered at bottom)

1"

FIGURE 8-4
MANUSCRIPT GUIDE SHEET

illustrations appear at the end of the paper. Another method of documentation is to include the reference wherever it occurs—mid-page or wherever—instead of at the bottom of the page. (See Figure 8-2B.) Ease for the reader is the object, and many medical research manuscripts are now done in this fashion. In the manuscript a reference section will appear containing the complete bibliographical reference. Consult a style manual prepared by an outstanding scholarly association in your field to determine the particular method to be used. If the material is for publication in a medical journal, follow the guidelines provided by that journal.

The bibliography is usually the last page of a manuscript, listing alphabetically by author the works consulted and cited in preparing the manuscript. The bibliography is listed on a separate page.

The table of contents is typed last because it lists all topics or divisions of the manuscript and their page numbers. It is included in a manuscript to provide quick reference to the various parts.

The title page is a covering page containing the title of the manuscript, the author, and the date. The arrangement should be simple but attractive. The secretary may want to experiment with the arrangement of the title so as to display it to the best advantage.

For more detailed information and examples of format on how to type quoted material, footnotes, a bibliography, table of contents, and a title page, consult a style manual. There are many good ones available.

In typing manuscripts and reports, keep in mind certain basic information concerning style and steps involved in the writing, editing and revising which have been covered. Most important is that one know what is available and where to look for the exact information needed to carry through a project. The significance of using reference books and their growing importance in a world undergoing constant change is quite evident in the medical profession where discoveries are made daily. It is a difficult task for a busy doctor to keep up with all the latest developments. Whatever you, the secretary, can do to help will be a worthwhile contribution.

Chapter 9

Matching the Filing
to the Doctor's Needs

The backbone of any business is its records. Without them a business would not know what has gone on before. For records to do their job in the building of a business, they must be available for use quickly. That is why filing is one of the most important jobs in any office, and especially in a medical office.

As you know, records must be quickly accessible and all the information on a particular subject must be there. So filing should not be considered a spare-time or fill-in job, but a very essential part of the day's activities. *Remember*, files must be kept up to date and care must be taken to see that all information on a particular subject is either filed together or can be readily found.

The size of the office determines the type of filing system used. Whether or not you work for one doctor, a group of doctors, a hospital, or a medical school, you must know some basic filing information. There are many filing reference books and most manufacturers of filing systems publish very helpful filing guides which can be obtained upon request. (See Figures 9-1 and 9-3.)

Remember, you as the medical secretary are responsible for seeing to it that the files in your office are up-to-date and in good order. In a small office you may do the filing yourself, while in a larger office there may be a file clerk. In a medical school or a hospital, there will probably be central files with a medical records librarian in charge. No matter what size or type of office though, you have the responsibility of seeing to it that all material is filed properly.

Losing records, misfiling, and sloppy filing systems cause terrible problems in any office because without records it is very difficult for a business to function. The damage to a patient in a medical office could be irreparable if the filing system is not effective and efficient. If something is misfiled, the doctor may not be aware of past treatment or diagnosis.

There are filing systems for every purpose and you must be aware of this and realize that setting up, reorganizing, or maintaining a filing system is a very important task. It is up to you to take a good look at your existing system and see if it is efficient, or if you are setting up a new system, do a little research in the area of filing to see how to do it best. Most manufacturers and distributors of filing equipment will be more than willing to give you some constructive advice in the form of printed information or a visit from a representative. Many of them have booklets containing filing rules such as those illustrated. (See Figure 9-1.)

Rule One—Alphabetize Last Names First

Arrange the *last* names in alphabetical order. If two or more last names are the same, it's the alphabetical order of the *first* names that counts. If both the first names and last names are the same, it's the alphabetical order of the *middle* names that counts.

> Irwin, Arthur
> Irwin, Fred
> Irwin, Theodore A.
> Irwin, Theodore P.
> Irwin, Theodore P., Jr..

Rule Two—Nothing Comes Before Something

A last name, when used alone, stands ahead of a last name with a first initial. This in turn precedes a last name with a full first name.

> Adair
> Adair, J.
> Adair, James
> Adair, James R.
> Adair, James R., Jr.
> Adamson, John
> Adamson, John, Jr.

Rule Three—Prefixes are Part of Names

Consider all prefixes as part of the name to which they are attached. Arrange them exactly as spelled.

Deems, A.
DeLuca, F.
Des Jardins, Charles
Fitzherbert, Mary
FitzPatrick, James
MacIntosh, L.B.J.
McDonald, Lewis
Sainforin, Roger
Saint John, Oliver
Saintjohn, Richard

Rule Four—Arrange Firm Names As Written

Center For Advanced Studies
Center Hardware Store
Cleveland Dancing School
Cleveland School of Printing
Consolidated Edison Company

Rule Five—Disregard "The" At the Beginning of a Name

"The National Cash Register Corporation"
    is indexed as
"National Cash Register Corporation (the)".
"The Center for Advanced Studies" is indexed as
    "Center for Advanced Studies (the)".
"Wick the Printer" is indexed as written, however.

Rule Six—Arrange Hyphenated Names As Written

Goldthwaite-Smythe, Lisa
Goldthwaite-Smythe Mortuary
Goldthwaite-Smythe, Norma

Rule Seven—One Word is Better Than Two

Any two words ordinarily written as one word should be treated as one word.

"Interstate" not "Inter State"
"Northeast" not "North East"

Rule Eight—Two-Word Geographical Names Are Considered One Word

> Des Moines
> New Haven
> New Jersey
> Rio de Janeiro
> Winston-Salem

—are all filed as though they were *one* word.

Rule Nine—Numbers Are Treated As Though Spelled Out

> "71st Street Garage" should be filed under "S" as if spelled out, "Seventy-First Street Garage."
> "1980 Broadway Building" should be filed under "N" as if "Nineteen Hundred Eighty Broadway Building"
> "40 and 8 Society" should be filed under "F" as if "Forty and Eight Society"

Rule Ten—Political Divisions Are Indexed With Major Name First

> "The Board of Estimate of New York City" is indexed as "New York City, Estimate (Board of)".
> "U.S. Department of Agriculture" is indexed as "United States Government, Agriculture (Dept. of)".
> "Highway Department, Village of Scarsdale" is indexed as "Scarsdale (Village of), Highway Dept."
> "Kingdom of Sweden Trade Commission" is indexed as "Sweden (Kingdom of), Trade Commission".

Courtesy of Oxford Pendaflex Corporation
Used by permission.

FIGURE 9-1
LIST OF FILING GUIDELINES FROM "THE OXFORD GUIDE
TO FILING EFFICIENCY" (PAGES 12 AND 13)

ANALYZE THE VARIOUS SYSTEMS

Alphabetic filing is basic to all types of filing. There are several different methods of filing, but alphabetic is the most common. An understanding of it will provide the background for learning the other types of filing systems. The most widely used filing systems are:

ALPHABETIC

NUMERIC

SUBJECT

GEOGRAPHIC

Alphabetic filing is simply putting records in order alphabetically by name beginning with A and going to Z. Certain rules basic to all alphabetic filing can be summed up in the ten basic rules outlined in Figure 9-1.

Indexing first is very important because there are many names that could create problems because of similar spelling, same initials, same last name, etc. There will always be exceptions to the basic rules, but if the basic rules are followed, then the exceptions can be worked out later. You should have an alphabetic filing manual handy for referral when a problem arises. These can be purchased very reasonably from a good book store.

Make sure you familiarize yourself with the other basic filing systems because they are usually used in combination with the alphabetic filing system. You must determine which suits your purposes best.

Numeric filing is simply assigning numbers to individual files and placing them in numeric order starting with the lowest number going to the highest. The advantages are that it is accurate and easy to understand. There are disadvantages—you cannot just open a drawer and find something right away. There must be a separate card index to explain what each number represents. In a doctor's office, hospital, or clinic, this requires a separate alphabetic card file on all patients, assigning a number to each one.

The numeric system is used very often in medical filing whether it be in a doctor's office or a hospital. As a new patient comes in, he or she is assigned the next number on the list, for example:

Yesterday, Ms. Linda Chase came for the first time to your doctor. She was Patient No. 6239. Today, Mr. Paul Jennings came in as a new patient and he became Patient No. 6240. File folders were set up for each of these patients and filed in the cabinet with the latest number first. (See Figure 9-1.)

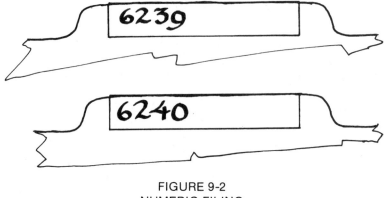

FIGURE 9-2
NUMERIC FILING

Along with the numeric filing, you will keep an alphabetical list of patients so that at any time you can look up Chase, Linda and see that her Patient No. is 6239. There are many ways to keep this alphabetic name file. One of them could be a card file which you would keep handy on your desk. This usually would include the name, address, and telephone number of a patient along with the patient number, and would be filed alphabetically by patient name. The information kept on this card and the manner of filing would differ depending on your individual needs, but basically it is an alphabetic file used in conjunction with the numeric filing system.

Subject filing is simply filing records in order according to what they are about rather than names of persons who sent them or persons to whom they are being sent. The advantage of subject filing is that all materials (correspondence, memos, pamphlets, etc.) on insurance, for example, can be filed in one folder and all the correspondence on office equipment can be filed in one folder. Once topics or subjects for folders are decided upon, it is very easy to set up such a system. In keeping the doctor's personal business records, this system would be especially suitable.

Geographic filing is based on location—city, state, county, or a particular section of a city or state. Each location is filed alphabetically. You may not have a need for geographic filing in a doctor's office, but in a larger facility such as a group of doctors or a large hospital, it might be necessary.

Color coding is used in the different filing systems for accuracy in filing and to speed up finding items. Colored tabs stand out and make it easier to go right to the proper folder. For example, in numeric filing, all the "2" folders could have yellow tabs.

HELPFUL HINTS IN PREPARING MATERIALS

When you have set up or re-examined your particular system, it is a good idea to write out some easily understandable directions for the maintenance of the files so that anyone would be able to file properly if you were not available. These written instructions can be kept either separately or in your personal secretarial manual.

Histacount Corporation includes in their catalog helpful suggestions for a doctor's filing system. (See Figure 9-3.)

HELPFUL FILING SUGGESTIONS

AN EFFICIENT DOCTOR'S FILING SYSTEM SHOULD PROVIDE FOR THE FOLLOWING BASIC RECORDS AND MATERIALS.

(1) The filing of patients' case history and financial account records.

(2) The filing of correspondence, reports, reprints, documents, etc.

(3) The storing of record books, office supplies, personal items, etc.

●

FOR EFFICIENT FILING & FINDING OF PATIENTS' RECORDS A DOCTOR'S FILING SYSTEM SHOULD CONTAIN 3 SECTIONS.

(1) **ACTIVE PATIENTS:** A file for patients who are currently under care & patients who owe money, whether under care or not.

(2) **INACTIVE PATIENTS:** A file for patients who are not currently under care and who do not owe money, but are likely to return.

(3) **FORMER PATIENTS:** A file for patients who are not under care, who owe no money and are not likely to return. This section should hold records of patients not heard from in two or more years.

●

AN EFFICIENT DOCTOR'S FILING SYSTEM SHOULD CONSIST OF TWO BASIC TOOLS IN ADDITION TO FILING CABINETS.

(1) GUIDES which divide the drawers into alphabetical sub-divisions.

(2) FOLDERS or POCKETS which hold all records of a patient or topic.

Arrange each file alphabetically with not more than 30 folders behind each guide. Standard 25 division guides will adequately care for most filing requirements. For extensive files however, we recommend 40 or 80 division guides with sub-divided letters, to make finding easier.

Courtesy of Histacount Corporation Subsidiary of
SCM Corporation. Used by permission.

FIGURE 9-3
HELPFUL FILING SUGGESTIONS

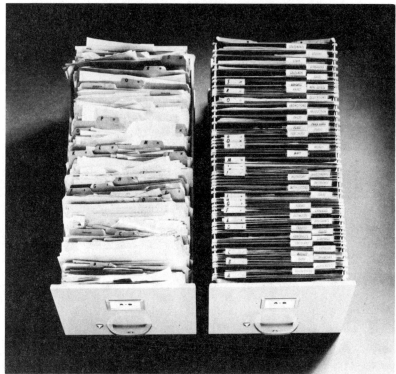

Courtesy of Oxford Pendaflex Corporation
Used by permission.

FIGURE 9-4
NEAT AND SLOPPY FILES

Remember that keeping neat, up-to-date files (See Figure 9-4) will make your job easier. All materials should be clearly visible. File drawers crammed too full with papers sticking out make it difficult to find things. You will need to set aside time, perhaps twice a year, when you can go through your files pulling out old files, opening new folders, and rearranging. Some folders will be put into inactive files while others will be stored because a patient has moved, changed doctors or died. For those folders that have become too full for easy handling, make another folder.

Cross-referencing is one method used to reduce the confusion over materials that could be filed under several captions. If material could be filed in several places, it would be cross-referenced to the various places. This could be done as in libraries with a card filed under "Equipment" indicating "See also Examining Room Equipment, Sterilizing Equipment, or Jones Furniture Company" and, of course, a similar card would be made up for each reference. Another way of cross-referencing is to put a file folder directly in the file for each area with a reference note. (See Figure 9-5.)

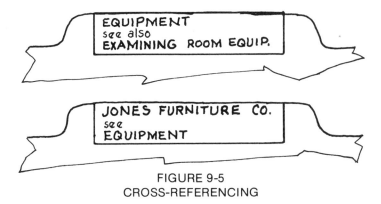

FIGURE 9-5
CROSS-REFERENCING

For files that are being used, some method should be devised to indicate that such is the case. One way is to use a charge card (out-guide) inserted in the empty folder space indicating the name, date, and location of the missing file. When it is returned, the charge card is removed and the name is crossed off. (See Figure 9-6.)

CHARGE CARD

File Number	Date Out	Out to (NAME)	Date Ret.

FIGURE 9-6
CHARGE CARD

After indexing the names, preparation for filing includes stapling material together or removing clips, and sorting them alphabetically. Then the actual filing is faster and more efficient.

CHOOSING THE RIGHT SUPPLIES AND EQUIPMENT

Whether or not you are setting up a new system or re-examining an existing one, you must determine what kind of records you are keeping—size, shape, and so forth—the length of time you need to keep your records, and the type of filing system you will use.

The size and style of file folders varies according to your needs. For example, expandable folders are available for files which contain bulky material or too many papers for an ordinary size folder.

It is possible to design your own forms. Some stationery supply companies will allow you to design the form according to your particular preference and will even furnish a kit describing how to do it.

Equipment should be studied so that the most efficient use can be made. Look through your files to see what types of forms are being used, and the size and types of folders. Then see what types of cabinets you have and what you could add or change to make the system more effective; for example, for ease and quick access, a small card file box on the secretary's desk containing all the patients' names with pertinent information on each patient. For larger records that must be kept in folders, a standard size, upright filing cabinet may be used. You might consider an altogether different type of cabinet such as the accessible file.

INFLUENCE OF AUTOMATION

Automation has penetrated every phase of office work and filing is no exception. This is especially true in large institutions, such as hospitals. For example, files can now be operated electronically, so that by pushing a button information can be retrieved immediately. Through the use of computers, information can be stored on magnetic tape for almost instant retrieval. This type of equipment is suitable for storing great quantities of data. Although you may not actually use the automated systems in your office, you should know that such systems are in use and how they affect the storing of data in general.

Filing properly is a top priority responsibility for you as a medical secretary. Whether or not you do the actual filing, you are responsible for seeing that it is done properly. Types of filing systems and equipment vary depending upon size, type, and needs of the office. Whatever system is used though, the important thing is that it be effective and efficient. Effectiveness and efficiency are measured by the quick accessibility and availability of all records on a given topic when required.

Remember: Using correct filing methods in a medical situation is of vital importance for several reasons.

1. Files should be immediately available in an emergency situation; it could mean life or death.

2. The patient's privacy should be protected. Only authorized personnel may have access to the files.

Chapter 10

Practical Tips on Keeping Patients' Permanent Records

Experienced medical secretaries know how important accurate, detailed, and up-to-date records are. The key to efficient handling of records is promptness. Make entries immediately. Waiting for a more convenient time leads to errors and incomplete records.

It is your responsibility as the medical secretary to see that all record keeping is done properly. Whether or not you actually do it yourself will depend on many factors such as size of the office, type of practice, number of people employed, doctor's preference, and types of equipment. But the fact remains that the responsibility rests with you.

Since all patient records are confidential, the patient's right to privacy must be protected. Handle records carefully so that they are not left where other patients can see them. Entries should be made promptly, accurately, and neatly, after which the material should be refiled immediately. Make sure that the person preparing material for the file always remembers to cover it when away from the desk.

There are various types of information that make up the patient's permanent record such as personal data, medical history, test results, x-rays, letters of referral, and reports from other doctors. The patient's basic statistics are obtained at the first appointment.

Courtesy of Memorial Sloan-Kettering Cancer Center
Used by permission.

FIGURE 10-1
PROCESSING RECORDS IN HOSPITAL

Usually the medical secretary is the first to interview the patient and open the file. The facts needed are:

Date of Visit
Name
Social Security Number
Home address and telephone
Occupation
Age
Sex
Marital Status
Person Responsible for Paying Bill
Medical Insurance
Policy Number
Nearest Relative

The secretary may sit down with the patient and question him. A more efficient method would be to provide him with a patient registration form. This method has become almost routine in many offices. The patient can fill this out and then give it to you. You should check it over carefully to see that it is complete. In some instances, these forms are mailed to the patient before his appointment so that he can bring it with him already filled in. Use the method that best fits the needs of the situation. (See Figure 10-1.)

Remember to keep records current. Check with patients from time to time to make sure you have up-to-date addresses and telephone numbers. This information is important for several reasons. For instance, the telephone number is probably the most important and should be taken down when the patient calls for the first appointment. Often you must contact a patient quickly. Having an incorrect telephone number will cause inconvenience to the patient, the doctor, and yourself. For example, in the event of an emergency in which the doctor is called away, you must notify the patients. Should a patient cancel an appointment, leaving an opening for someone else, there is always someone who wanted an earlier appointment; it is considered good policy to call that individual personally.

The doctor usually will take down the medical history. Many doctors will make notes, and, after seeing the patient, dictate the history either to you directly or by the use of dictating equipment for you to transcribe later. Most hospitals utilize dictating equipment and hire typists or medical transcriptionists to do the transcribing. (See Chapter 5—"Guidelines for Purchasing and Operating Dictation Equipment.") (See Figures 10-2, 10-3A, 10-3B, 10-4.)

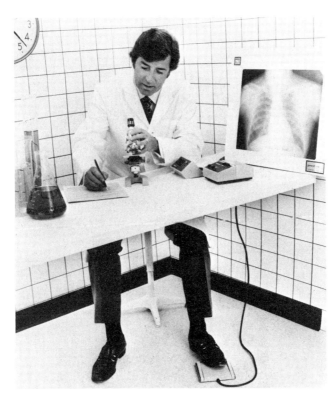

Courtesy of Dictaphone Corporation
Used by permission.

FIGURE 10-2
DOCTOR DICTATING THROUGH HANDS-FREE DICTATE STATION FOR
DICTAPHONE THOUGHT TANK SYSTEM 192

FIGURE 10-3A
DOCTOR
DICTATING
THROUGH
TELEPHONE
HOOKUP

Courtesy of Dictaphone Corporation
Used by permission.

FIGURE 10-3B
DOCTOR
DICTATING
THROUGH
TELEPHONE
HOOKUP

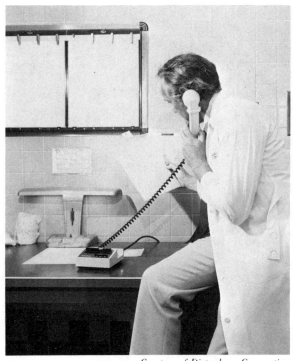

Courtesy of Dictaphone Corporation
Used by permission.

Courtesy of Dictaphone Corporation.
Used by permission.

FIGURE 10-4
SECRETARY TRANSCRIBING (TOUCH TRONIC SCAN FEATURE OF
DICTAPHONE'S THOUGHT MASTER ELIMINATES INDEXING SLIPS)

Remember: All entries on the patient's permanent record should be either written very clearly or typed so that they can be read easily. (See Figure 10-5.)

There are many preprinted forms available for making up the patient's permanent record. Whether or not the doctor chooses to use a printed form, plain paper, or a card, is determined by his own desires and the amount of detail required. Forms are readily obtainable through medical supply houses, commercial stationers, or companies that handle medical forms. Forms are available for a particular specialty or the doctor can have his own forms printed. If you cannot find a form that exactly suits your purposes, forms can be designed for the doctor's needs. They should be carefully planned so that information appears in the proper sequence. (See Figures 10-6A, B, C, D; 10-7A, B; 10-8A, B; 10-9A, B, C.)

Some doctors prefer to use blank paper or cards so that they can have complete freedom to record whatever they desire. An internist, for example, might prefer a blank form because it is important that his records be very detailed and he does not want to be limited by a form. A dermatologist, on the other hand, who sees some patients only once, may require only a small card. (See Figures 10A and 10B.)

One disadvantage of the printed form is that the doctor is limited by space and may not be able to write as much as he pleases.

6239
CASE NO.

Chase, Linda
PATIENT'S NAME

ADDRESS 23 Bluff Road, Northport, N.Y.   11768   INSURANCE _____   DATE 1/11/

TEL. NO. 272-6039   REFERRED BY M. Jones   OCCUPATION Secretary   AGE 32   SEX F   S. M. W. D.

CASE NO. 6239

FAMILY HISTORY: FATHER_____ MOTHER_____

BROTHERS_____ SISTERS_____

CANCER_____ TUBERCULOSIS_____ INSANITY_____ DIABETES_____ HEART DISEASE_____ RHEUMATISM_____

GOUT_____ GOITER_____ OBESITY_____ NEPHRITIS_____ EPILEPSY_____ OTHER_____

PAST HISTORY: DIPHTHERIA_____ MEASLES_____ MUMPS_____ CHICKEN-POX_____ SCARLET FEVER_____ SMALL POX_____

INFANTILE PARALYSIS_____ TYPHOID_____ MALARIA_____ PNEUMONIA_____ DYSENTERY_____ JAUNDICE_____ BOILS_____

RHEUMATIC FEVER_____ TUBERCULOSIS_____ ASTHMA_____ HEART DISEASE_____ HYPERTENSION_____ DIABETES_____

INFECTIONS_____ GONORRHEA_____ SYPHILIS_____ TONSILLITIS_____ NEPHRITIS_____ OPERATIONS_____

MENSTRUAL: ONSET_____ PERIODICITY_____ TYPE_____ DURATION_____ PAIN_____ L.M.P._____

MARITAL: MISCARRIAGES_____ ABORTIONS_____ CHILDREN_____ STERILITY_____

HABITS: ALCOHOL_____ TOBACCO_____ DRUGS_____ COFFEE_____ TEA_____ MEALS_____ WATER_____

SLEEP_____ BOWEL MOVEMENTS_____ EXERCISE_____ AMUSEMENTS_____

PRESENT AILMENT: _____

PHYSICAL EXAMINATION: TEMP._____ PULSE_____ RESP._____ B.P._____ HT._____ WT._____

GENERAL APPEARANCE _____

SKIN _____ MUCOUS MEMBRANE _____

EYES: VISION_____ PUPIL_____ FUNDUS_____

EARS: _____

NOSE: _____

THROAT: _____ PHARYNX_____ TONSILS_____

CHEST: _____ BREASTS_____

HEART: _____

LUNGS: _____

ABDOMEN: _____

GENITALIA: _____

RECTUM: _____

VAGINA: _____

EXTREMITIES: _____

LYMPH NODES: NECK_____ AXILLA_____ INGUINAL_____ ABDOMINAL_____

REFLEXES: _____

REMARKS: _____

LABORATORY FINDINGS:

(Urine · Blood · Sputum · Smears · Exudates Transudates · Feces · Gastric Contents · Wassermann Kahn · Chemistry · Pregnancy Tests · X-Ray Fluoroscopy · Schick · Dick · Etc.)

Date

PATIENT'S NAME CHASE, LINDA

DIAGNOSIS: _____

TREATMENT: _____

SYMBOLS: √ NORMAL, _____ ABNORMAL (UNDERLINE WORD)
DEGREE OF ABNORMALITY: X   XX   XXX

HISTACOUNT®   FORM NO. 4011   HISTACOUNT CORPORATION, MELVILLE, L. I., N. Y. 11746

Courtesy of Histacount Corporation Subsidiary of SCM Corporation. Used by permission.

FIGURE 10-5
PATIENT'S PERMANENT RECORD
PARTIALLY COMPLETED BY MEDICAL SECRETARY

OBSTETRICS (COMPLETE)

CASE NO. _____   PATIENT'S NAME _____

ADDRESS _____ TELEPHONE _____ LABOR EXPECTED _____ 19 _____

AGE _____ OCCUPATION _____ PREGNANCIES _____ NAT. OR RELIGION _____

INSURANCE _____

HUSB. NAME _____ AGE _____ OCCUP. _____

BUS. ADD. _____ BUS. PHONE _____

FAMILY HISTORY: _____

PERSONAL HISTORY: _____

PRESENT OBSTETRICAL HISTORY: _____

MENSTRUATION: FIRST AT AGE _____ DAYS INTERVENING _____ DAYS DURATION _____ AMOUNT _____ PAINS _____

LAST MENSTRUATION: FIRST DAY _____ 19 _____ DAYS DURATION. AMOUNT _____ QUICKENING _____ 19 ____

PREVIOUS PREGNANCIES

	DATE	AT TERM	MONTH			PREGNANCY COMPLICATED	DELIVERY OPERATIVE	MULTIPLE	MONTHS BREAST FED	WEIGHT AT BIRTH	REMARKS
			MIS-CARRIAGE	PRE-MATURE	STILL BORN						
1											
2											
3											
4											

PHYSICAL EXAMINATION: HEART _____ LUNGS _____ BREASTS _____

LIVER _____ SPLEEN _____

ABDOMEN _____

FUNDUS _____ IN.

PELVIC MEASUREMENTS: EXTERNAL CONJUGATE _____ IN. CM.; INTERNAL CONJUGATE _____ IN. CM.; TROCH. INTERSPINOUS _____ IN. CM

INTERTUBEROUS _____ IN. CM.; EXTERNAL OBLIQUE _____ IN. CM; COCCYX: FORWARD _____ BACKWARD _____ CREST _____ MOVABLE _____

SACRUM: FORWARD _____ BACKWARD _____; SYMPHYSIS PUBIS: HEIGHT _____ ARCH: WIDE _____ NARROW _____

FETUS: HEART, LOCATION _____ QUALITY _____ RATE _____

PRESENTATION AND POSITION _____

PERINEUM: FIRM _____ LACERATED _____ ANUS: HEMORRHOIDS _____ FISSURE _____

VULVA: URETHRAL ORIFICE, INFLAMED _____ RELAXED _____ LEAKAGE _____

VAGINA: SECRETION _____ RELAXED _____ CYSTOCELE _____ RECTOCELE _____

EXTERNAL OS-DILATATION _____ OBLITERATION _____ EDEMA _____

CERVIX: LENGTH _____ THICKNESS _____ LACERATIONS _____

UTERUS: POSITION _____ MOBILITY _____ CONSISTENCY _____

PRESENTATION OF FETUS _____ POSITION OF FETUS _____

PRESENT PREGNANCY: TEMP. _____ PULSE _____ RESP. _____ NIPPLES: ERECT _____ FLAT OR INVERTED _____ EDEMA: FACE _____ FEET _____ LEGS _____

VARICOSE VEINS _____ DYSPNOEA _____ SPOTS BEFORE EYES _____ NAUSEA OR VOMITING _____ A. M. _____ ALL DAY

HEADACHE _____ CONSTIPATION _____ DIARRHEA _____ VAGINAL DISCHARGE: WHITE _____ YELLOW _____ OR BLOODY _____

VAGINAL SORENESS _____ FETAL HEART RATE _____ URINALYSIS: SP. GR. _____ REACTION _____ ALBUMIN _____ SUGAR _____

QUANTITY IN 24 HOURS _____ NORMAL WEIGHT _____ PRESENT WEIGHT _____ BLOOD PRESSURE _____ DIASTOLIC _____ SYSTOLIC _____

CASE NO.

PATIENT'S NAME

Courtesy of Histacount Corporation Subsidiary of SCM Corporation. Used by permission.

FIGURE 10-6A
SAMPLE PERMANENT RECORD - OBSTETRICS (PAGE 1)

PROGRESS DURING PRESENT PREGNANCY

DATE	WT.	BLOOD PRESSURE	TEMP.	PULSE	RESP.	NIPPLES			EDEMA			VARICOSE VEINS	DYSPNOEA & SUFFOCATION	SPOTS BEFORE EYES	NAUSEA & VOMITING		HEADACHE	CONSTIPATION	DIARRHEA	VAGINAL DISCHARGE			VAGINAL SORENESS	CERVICAL SMEAR	FOETAL HEART RATE
						ERECT	FLAT	INVERTED	FACE	HANDS	FEET & LEGS				A. M.	ALL DAY				WHITE	YELLOW	BLOODY			

LABOR RECORD

LABOR NO._____MONTH OF PREGNANCY_____LABOR BEGAN_____LABOR ENDED_____

PREPARATORY EXAMINATION_____

_____SHOW_____

FETUS: MOVEMENTS_____HEART: LOCATION_____QUALITY_____RATE_____

FIRST STAGE: BEGAN_____ENDED_____EXAMINATION_____

PROGRESS_____

SECOND STAGE: BEGAN_____ENDED_____EXAMINATION_____

PROGRESS_____

DELIVERY_____

_____ANESTHETIC_____SEX OF CHILD_____

THIRD STAGE: BEGAN_____ENDED_____

PLACENTA: TIME_____METHOD OF DELIVERY_____

CONDITION:_____MEMBRANES:_____CORD:_____

HEMORRHAGE_____

LACERATIONS_____

MEDICATION_____SUTURES_____

CONDITION OF MOTHER_____

CONDITION OF CHILD_____

UNUSUAL FEATURES, OPERATIONS, SUMMARY OF LABOR, PROGRESS_____

Courtesy of Histacount Corporation Subsidiary of SCM Corporation. Used by permission.

FIGURE 10-6B
SAMPLE PERMANENT RECORD - OBSTETRICS (PAGE 2)

URINALYSIS							BACKACHE	INSTRUCTIONS FOLLOWED	BLOOD COUNT							TREATMENT AND REMARKS
SPECIFIC GRAVITY	REACTION	ALBUMIN	SUGAR	QUANTITY IN 24 HRS.	MICRO-SCOPIC				R. B. C.	W. B. C	HGB.	R.H. (MOTH)	R.H. (FATH)	WASSER-MAN	BLOOD TYPE	

POST-PARTUM RECORD

DATE	TEMPER-ATURE	PULSE	RESPIR-ATION	IN BED	FUNDUS		LOCHIA			SUTURES			NIPPLE CRACKED		BREASTS				URINE, AMOUNT IN 24 HOURS	STOOLS, NUMBER IN 24 HRS.	TREATMENT AND MEDICINE
					HEIGHT	Firm	Moder-ate	Pro-fuse	COLOR	In-tact	In-fam-ed	Heal-ed	R	L	Secret-ing	Pain-ful	Dis-tend-ed	Skin redden-ed			

CONDITION ON DISCHARGE _____

REMARKS: _____

POST-NATAL RECORD

DATE	TEMPER-ATURE	WEIGHT	CORD			STOOLS IN 24 HRS.	VOID-ING	EYES			SKIN			SNUFF-LES	FEEDING					TREATMENT AND MEDICINE
			OFF	Bleed-ing	Im-flam-ed			RED	Swoll-en	Dis-charg-ing	Rash	Dry	Scaly		Well Taken	Breast	Form-ula	Any-thing	INTERVAL	

CONDITION ON DISCHARGE: HEART _____ LUNGS _____ UMBILICUS _____ WEIGHT _____

EYES _____ NOSE _____ MOUTH _____ SKIN _____ FEEDING _____

REMARKS: _____

_____

_____

_____

_____

_____

Courtesy of Histacount Corporation Subsidiary of
SCM Corporation. Used by permission.

FIGURE 10-6C
SAMPLE PERMANENT RECORD - OBSTETRICS (PAGE 3)

Courtesy of Histacount Corporation Subsidiary of SCM Corporation. Used by permission.

FIGURE 10-6D
SAMPLE PERMANENT RECORD - OBSTETRICS (PAGE 4)

SURGICAL

CASE NO.

PATIENT'S NAME

ADDRESS _____ INSURANCE _____ DATE _____

TEL. NO. _____ REFERRED BY _____ OCCUPATION _____ AGE ____ SEX ____ S.M.W.D.

CASE NO.

PRESENT AILMENT: _____

PAST HISTORY _____

PHYSICAL EXAMINATION: TEMP. _____ PULSE _____ RESP. _____ B.P. _____ GENERAL CONDITION _____

PRE-OPERATIVE DIAGNOSIS: _____

POST-OPERATIVE DIAGNOSIS: _____

PATHOLOGICAL FINDINGS: _____

PATIENT'S NAME

OPERATION: DURATION _____ ANESTHETIC _____ ANESTHETIST _____

BY _____ ASSISTED BY _____ AT _____ DATE _____

DIAGNOSIS: _____

TREATMENT: _____

HISTACOUNT   FORM NO. 1701

HISTACOUNT CORPORATION, MELVILLE, L. I., N. Y. 11746

Courtesy of Histacount Corporation Subsidiary of
SCM Corporation. Used by permission.

FIGURE 10-7A
SAMPLE PERMANENT RECORD - SURGICAL (FRONT)

CASE No.	PATIENT'S NAME			

DATE			SUBSEQUENT VISITS AND FINDINGS	ACCOUNT RECORD		
MO.	DAY	YR.		CHARGE	PAID	BALANCE

CASE No.

PATIENT'S NAME

FIGURE 10-7B
SAMPLE PERMANENT RECORD - SURGICAL (BACK)

GYNECOLOGY

CASE NO.

PATIENT'S NAME

ADDRESS _____ INSURANCE _____ DATE _____

TEL. NO. _____ REFERRED BY _____ OCCUPATION _____ AGE _____ S.M.W.D.

FAMILY HISTORY _____

PERSONAL HISTORY _____

PRESENT AILMENT: _____

MENSTRUATION: FIRST AT AGE _____ DAYS INTERVENING _____ DAYS DURATION _____ AMOUNT _____ PAINS _____

LAST PERIOD _____ AMENORRHEA _____ MENORRHAGIA _____ DYSMENORRHEA _____ MENOPAUSE _____

VAGINAL DISCHARGE: COLOR _____ CHARACTER _____ AMOUNT _____

VESICLE SYMPTOMS: _____

GASTRO-INTESTINAL SYMPTOMS: _____

OBSTETRICAL RECORD

	DATE	AT TERM	MONTH MIS-CARRIAGE	MONTH PRE-MATURE	MONTH STILL BORN	PREGNANCY COMPLI-CATED	DELIVERY OPERATIVE	MULTIPLE	MONTHS BREAST FED	WEIGHT AT BIRTH	REMARKS
1											
2											
3											
4											

PHYSICAL EXAMINATION: TEMP. _____ PULSE _____ RESP _____ B. P. _____ WT. _____ HT _____

HEART _____ LUNGS _____ LIVER _____ SPLEEN _____

ABDOMEN _____

BREASTS: SECRETING _____ PAINFUL _____ DISTENDED _____ SKIN REDDENED _____

NIPPLES: CRACKED _____ ERECT _____ FLAT _____ INVERTED _____

LOWER EXTREMITIES _____ REFLEXES _____

PERINEUM: FIRM _____ LACERATED _____ ANUS: HEMORRHOIDS _____ FISSURE _____

VULVA: URETHRAL ORIFICE: INFLAMED _____ RELAXED _____ LEAKAGE _____

VAGINA: SECRETION _____ RELAXED _____ CYSTOCELE _____ RECTOCELE _____

CERVIX: LENGTH _____ THICKNESS _____ LACERATIONS _____ ENDOCERVICITIS _____

UTERUS: POSITION _____ MOBILITY _____ CONSISTENCY _____

SIZE _____ TUMORS _____

RIGHT ADNEXA _____ LEFT ADNEXA _____

UTERO-SACRAL LIGAMENTS _____

REMARKS: _____

LABORATORY: _____

DIAGNOSIS: _____

TREATMENT: _____

HISTACOUNT®   FORM NO. 1251
© 1956 HISTACOUNT CORPORATION, MELVILLE, L. I., N. Y.

SYMBOLS: V NORMAL. _____ ABNORMAL (UNDERLINE WORD)
DEGREE OF ABNORMALITY: X XX XXX

Courtesy of Histacount Corporation Subsidiary of SCM Corporation. Used by permission.

FIGURE 10-8A
SAMPLE PERMANENT RECORD - GYNECOLOGY (FRONT)

CASE No._____	PATIENT'S NAME_____			

DATE			SUBSEQUENT VISITS AND FINDINGS	ACCOUNT RECORD		
MO.	DAY	YR.		CHARGE	PAID	BALANCE

Courtesy of Histacount Corporation Subsidiary of
SCM Corporation. Used by permission.

FIGURE 10-8B
SAMPEL PERMANENT RECORD - GYNECOLOGY (BACK)

GENERAL PRACTICE

CASE NO.

PATIENT'S NAME

ADDRESS_____INSURANCE_____DATE_____

TEL. NO   REFERRED BY   OCCUPATION   AGE   SEX   S.M.W.D.

PRESENT AILMENT_____

_____

_____

_____

_____

PAST HISTORY_____

_____

_____

_____

_____

FAMILY HISTORY_____

_____

_____

_____

_____

PHYSICAL EXAMINATION

TEMP._____PULSE_____RESP._____B. P._____HT._____WT._____

SKIN_____MUCOUS MEMBRANE_____EYES_____EARS_____

NOSE_____MOUTH_____NECK_____CHEST_____

LUNGS_____HEART_____ABDOMEN_____RECTUM_____

VAGINA_____GENITALS_____EXTREMITIES_____

LABORATORY FINDINGS

REMARKS:_____

_____

_____

_____

_____

_____

_____

_____

_____

_____

_____

SYMBOLS √ NORMAL _____ABNORMAL (UNDERLINE WORD)
DEGREE OF ABNORMALITY: X   XX   XXX

HISTACOUNT® FORM NO. 150

HISTACOUNT CORPORATION, MELVILLE, L. I., N. Y. 11746

Courtesy of Histacount Corporation Subsidiary of
SCM Corporation. Used by permission.

FIGURE 10-9A
SAMPLE PERMANENT RECORD - GENERAL PRACTICE (PART 1)

DIAGNOSIS: _____

TREATMENT

DATE			SUBSEQUENT VISITS AND FINDINGS	ACCOUNT RECORD		
MO.	DAY	YR.		CHARGE	PAID	BALANCE

*Courtesy of Histacount Corporation Subsidiary of
SCM Corporation. Used by permission.*

FIGURE 10-9B
SAMPLE PERMANENT RECORD - GENERAL PRACTICE (PART 2)

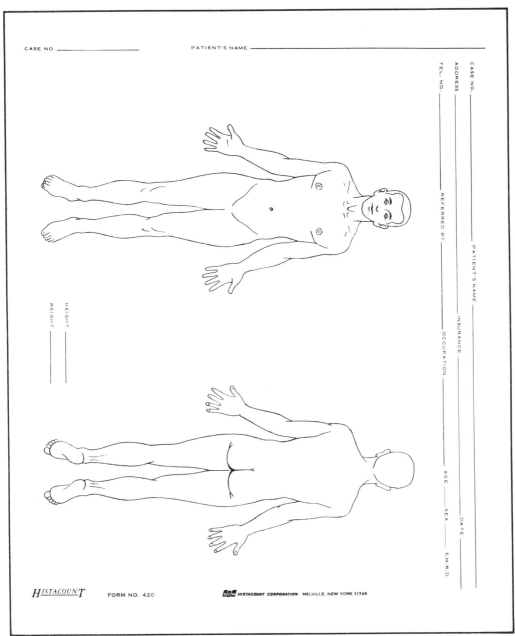

CASE NO. _____   PATIENT'S NAME _____

CASE NO. _____

PATIENT'S NAME _____

ADDRESS _____

TEL. NO. _____

REFERRED BY _____

INSURANCE _____

OCCUPATION _____

AGE _____ DATE _____

SEX _____ S.M.W.D. _____

WEIGHT _____

HEIGHT _____

*H*ISTACOUN*T*   FORM NO. 420   HISTACOUNT CORPORATION MELVILLE, NEW YORK 11746

Courtesy of Histacount Corporation Subsidiary of
SCM Corporation. Used by permission.

FIGURE 10-9C
SAMPLE PERMANENT RECORD - GENERAL PRACTICE (PART 3)

A general checklist of information that would be included in the patient's permanent records follows:

1. Basic statistics (name, age, date of birth, parents, husband, wife, children, telephone (home and business), addresses (home and business), type of work, social security number, medical insurance plan)

2. Patient's chief complaint and history of present illness

3. Patient's medical history

4. Patient's family history

5. Patient's psychiatric history

6. Results of examination

7. Diagnosis

8. Prognosis (opinion of the outcome of illness)

9. Treatment and medication prescribed

10. Discharge and final statement

Remember that a patient's record is only as good as what is entered on it. If it is not complete, it is worthless. In fact, it may do actual damage. Doctors rely on records because it would be impossible to remember everything that transpires with a patient. When the doctor looks at the record, he must feel sure that it is complete. If you have not gotten around to entering the results of the last laboratory tests or the latest medication, the doctor may duplicate prior treatment or give an incorrect diagnosis.

If you find that you cannot keep your records up-to-date and that the day is always being extended, then you must examine the method being used in your office. Are you utilizing your time efficiently? Do you have too much work? Are the methods used not adequate to meet the demands of the office? Perhaps the doctor is spending too much time dictating to you or writing out reports when it could be accomplished much faster with the use of dictating and transcribing equipment. (See Chapter 5.)

Be honest with yourself. Really investigate the situation. It may be possible that there is just too much work for one person. You may need help. Perhaps the answer is to have someone come in on a part-time basis to type reports. If this is the case, *remember*, usually it is better to have someone come in a few hours every day and keep work current rather than to save work for one day a week. The goal to always keep in mind is to have complete and up-to-date patient records while maintaining confidentiality.

Your responsibility for keeping the records is a very vital part of your job. Rather than looking at it as dull, routine, and time-consuming, always keep in mind the *urgent* importance of well-kept records. (See Figures 10-11A, 10-11B, 10-12, 10-13.)

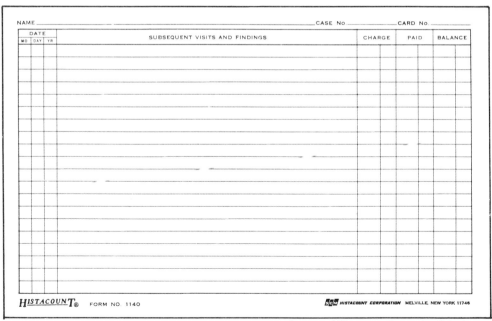

CASE NO._____ PATIENT'S NAME_____

ADDRESS_____ INSURANCE_____ DATE_____

TEL. NO._____ REFERRED BY_____ OCCUPATION_____ AGE_____ SEX_____ S. M. W. D.

FAMILY HISTORY_____

PAST HISTORY_____

PRESENT AILMENT_____

PHYSICAL EXAMINATION: TEMP._____ PULSE_____ RESP._____ B.P._____ HEIGHT_____ WEIGHT_____

SKIN_____ MUCOUS MEMBRANE_____ EYES_____ EARS_____ NOSE_____ MOUTH_____

NECK_____ CHEST_____ LUNGS_____ HEART_____ ABDOMEN_____ RECTUM_____

VAGINA_____ GENITALS_____ EXTREMITIES_____ OTHER_____

LABORATORY FINDINGS:_____

DIAGNOSIS:_____

TREATMENT:_____

REMARKS:_____

$H_{ISTACOUN}T$® GENERAL PRACTICE FORM NO. 1150   HISTACOUNT CORPORATION, MELVILLE, L. I., N. Y.

FIGURE 10-10A
PATIENT RECORD CARD (FRONT)

NAME_____ CASE No_____ CARD No_____

DATE			SUBSEQUENT VISITS AND FINDINGS	CHARGE	PAID	BALANCE
MO	DAY	YR				

$H_{ISTACOUN}T$® FORM NO. 1140   HISTACOUNT CORPORATION MELVILLE, NEW YORK 11746

Courtesy of Histacount Corporation Subsidiary of
SCM Corporation. Used by permission.

FIGURE 10-10B
PATIENT RECORD CARD (BACK)

ELECTROCARDIOGRAM

CASE NO. ________ DATE ________ PATIENT'S NAME ________

ADDRESS ________ TEL. NO. ________

INSURANCE ________ OCCUPATION ________

HT. ____ WT. ____ B.P. ____ AGE ____ SEX ____ S.M.W.D. REFERRED BY ________

MEDICATION ________

________ DATE OF LAST EKG ________ BY DR. ________

ADDRESS ________

GRAPHIC FINDINGS

RHYTHM ________

AURICULAR RATE ________ VENTRICULAR RATE ________ ELECTRIC AXIS ________

P - R INTERVAL ________ QRS DURATION ________ Q - T INTERVAL ________

P WAVE ________

QRS ________

____

S - T SEGMENT ________

T - WAVE ________

ATTACH RHYTHM STRIP HERE.

INTERPRETATION

____

____

____

____

____

____

____

____

____

____

____

SIGNED ________

CASE NO. ________

PATIENT'S NAME ________

FORM NO. 4564

SCM HISTACOUNT CORPORATION MELVILLE, NEW YORK 11746

Courtesy of Histacount Corporation Subsidiary of SCM Corporation. Used by permission.

FIGURE 10-11A
RECORD FOR ELECTROCARDIOGRAM (FRONT)

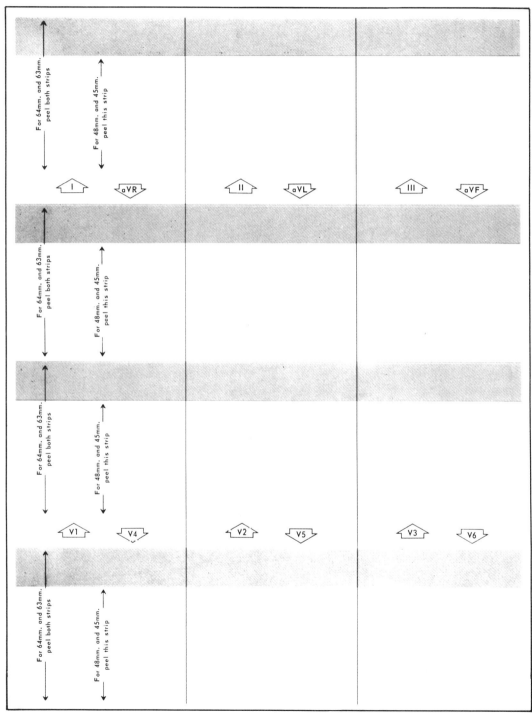

Courtesy of Histacount Corporation Subsidiary of
SCM Corporation. Used by permission.

FIGURE 10-11B
RECORD FOR ELECTROCARDIOGRAM (BACK)

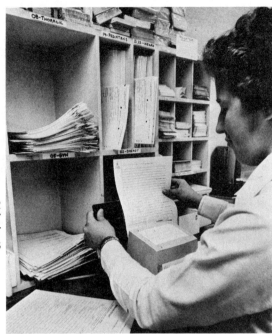

FIGURE 10-12
MEDICAL SECRETARY
PROCESSING PATIENT
RECORDS

*Courtesy of Memorial Sloan-Kettering Cancer
Center. Used by permission.*

FIGURE 10-13
MEDICAL SECRETARY
PROCESSING PATIENT
RECORDS

*Courtesy of Memorial Sloan-Kettering Cancer Center.
Photograph by Guy Gillette. Used by permission.*

Chapter 11

Techniques for
Speedy Handling of
Medical Insurance Forms

Practically speaking, medical insurance or some form of public assistance has become a necessity in this age of improved health care. Most large companies include health insurance as part of the employee fringe benefits. There are various forms of state and federal health care assistance. Many unions have some type of medical and dental insurance. The paper work created by the many and varied health care plans increases the secretary's workload as more and more of the medical secretary's time is spent filling out these forms.

HOW TO FIND OUT ABOUT HEALTH INSURANCE

The secretary must be familiar with the various types of insurance plans used by the doctor's patients. You are not expected to be an expert in the field of health insurance, but you should keep on hand a supply of the forms the doctor may need.

If information is desired, government agencies furnish data about qualifications for coverage, application procedures, and benefits. For example, the nearest Social Security Office can be contacted for an instruction booklet that explains how to apply for Medicare and how to make claims for benefits.

There are many medical plans. For information concerning welfare or Medicaid plans, contact your state, county, or local goverment office or agency. There are booklets available explaining the particular plans and giving information concerning who can apply, how, where, and so forth. If you have patients who may be eligible under a welfare plan or Medicaid you should have this information readily available.

There are many private hospital and medical insurance plans. You do not have to know them all, but you should become aware of the plans used by the patients with whom you deal and have available the necessary forms. A phone call or letter to the individual company will provide you with forms, instruction booklets and any information you might want. In a large company you would contact the manager of the customer service, provider relations, public relations, or educational department to obtain this information. In many cases you may deal with a local insurance agent. You may have to do a little research to discover the exact agency in your area but once you have made contact with the proper person, ask to be put on the mailing list to receive information about coverage, changes in procedure, and so forth. (See Figures 11-1A and B; 11-2; 11-3A and B.)

Some firms hold seminars for medical assistants to familiarize them with procedures in filling out insurance claims. Others publish a newsletter which can be sent to the doctor on a regular basis.

Insurance coverage rules and regulations keep changing—you cannot just consult one reference and feel that this is all you have to do. You must continually keep up-to-date on procedures. This will require a little work on your part to check with the insurance companies or government agencies and to read all current literature on the subject.

Remember, you are not expected to be an expert but you should be able to know where to find any information you may need.

If your employer treats worker's compensation cases (those where a worker has been injured while working or has become ill as a result of his job), it would be advisable for you to write to the State Department of Labor for information as to the doctor's responsibility in reporting claims.

There are many different types of health insurance plans such as Blue Cross, Blue Shield, Group Health Insurance, Inc., various plans obtained through school, job, or union with innumerable combinations of benefits. The patient must check his contract or insurance company to find out about his particular benefits, coverage for office visits, hospitalization, laboratory tests, special out-patient hospital care, medication, dental care, and optical care. There may be certain restrictions such as time limits that should be noted. For instance, some insurers say that a form must be submitted within 30 days after the doctor sees the patient. Some policies specify that certain claims are not covered until a person has been insured for six or nine months. Pregnancy, for example, may not be covered until one has been insured for several months. (See Figures 11-1A and B.)

REQUEST FOR MEDICARE PAYMENT

MEDICAL INSURANCE BENEFITS—SOCIAL SECURITY ACT (See Instructions on Back—**Type or Print Information**)

Form Approved
OMB No.
72–RO730

NOTICE—Anyone who misrepresents or falsifies essential information requested by this form may upon conviction be subject to fine and imprisonment under Federal Law.

PART I—PATIENT TO FILL IN ITEMS 1 THROUGH 6 ONLY

Copy from YOUR OWN HEALTH INSURANCE CARD (See example on back)

1 Name of patient (First name, Middle initial, Last name)

2 Health insurance claim number (Include all letters)   ☐ Male   ☐ Female

3 Patient's mailing address   City, State, ZIP code   Telephone Number

4 Describe the illness or injury for which you received treatment (Always fill in this item if your doctor does not complete Part II below)

Was your illness or injury connected with your employment? ☐ Yes ☐ No

5 If any of your medical expenses will be or could be paid by another insurance organization or government agency (including FEHB), show below.
Name and address of organization or agency   Policy or Identification Number

Note: If you **Do Not** want information about this Medicare claim released to the above upon its request, check (X) the following block ☐

6 I authorize any holder of medical or other information about me to release to the Social Security Administration or its intermediaries or carriers any information needed for this or a related Medicare claim. I permit a copy of this authorization to be used in place of the original, and request payment of medical insurance benefits either to myself or to the party who accepts assignment below.

Signature of patient (See instructions on reverse where patient is unable to sign)   Date signed
SIGN HERE ▶

PART II—PHYSICIAN OR SUPPLIER TO FILL IN 7 THROUGH 14

7 A. Date of each service	B. Place of service (*See Codes below)	C. Fully describe surgical or medical procedures and other services or supplies furnished for each date given / Procedure Code	D. Nature of illness or injury requiring services or supplies (diagnosis)	E. Charges (If related to unusual circumstances explain in 7C)	Leave Blank
				$	

8 Name and address of physician or supplier (Number and street, city, State, ZIP code)

Telephone No.

9 Total charges $

Physician or supplier code   **10** Amount paid $

11 Any unpaid balance due $

12 Assignment of patient's bill ☐ I accept assignment (See reverse) ☐ I do not accept assignment.

13 Show name and address of person or facility which furnished service (if other than your own office or patient's home)

14 Signature of physician or supplier (A physician's signature certifies that a physician's services were personally rendered by the physician or under the physician's personal direction)   Date signed

*O—Doctor's Office   H—Patient's Home (If portable X-ray services, identify the supplier)   SNF—Skilled Nursing Facility   OL—Other Locations
IL—Independent Laboratory   IH—Inpatient Hospital   OH—Outpatient Hospital   NH—Nursing Home

FORM SSA 1490 (11-75)

Department of Health, Education, and Welfare
Social Security Administration

Courtesy of United States Department of Health, Education and Welfare, Health Care Financing Administration. Used by permission.

FIGURE 11-1A
MEDICARE FORM (FRONT)

HOW TO FILL OUT YOUR MEDICARE FORM
There are two ways that Medicare can help pay your doctor bills

One way is for Medicare to pay your doctor.—If you and your doctor agree, Medicare will pay the doctor directly. This is the assignment method. You do not submit any claim; the doctor does. All you do is fill out Part I of this form and leave it with your doctor. Under this method the doctor agrees to accept the charge determination of the Medicare carrier as the full charge for covered services; you are responsible for the deductible, coinsurance, and non-covered services. Please read Your Medicare Handbook to help you understand about the deductible and coinsurance.

The other way is for Medicare to pay you.—Medicare can also pay you directly—before or after you have paid your doctor. If you submit the claim yourself, fill out Part I and ask your doctor to fill out Part II. If you have an itemized bill from the doctor, you may submit it rather than have the doctor complete Part II. (This form, with Part I completed by you, may be used to send in several itemized bills from different doctors and suppliers.) Bills should show who furnished the services, **the patient's name and number,** dates of services, where the services were furnished, a description of the services, and charges for each separate service. It is helpful if the diagnosis is also shown. Then mail itemized bills and this form to the address shown in the upper left-hand corner. If no address is shown there, use the address listed in Your Medicare Handbook—or get advice from any social security office.

Notice: It is important to keep a record of your claim in case you ever want to inquire about it. Before you send it in, write down the date you mailed it, the services you received, the date and charge for each, and the name of the doctor or supplier who performed the services. Have this information available when you inquire about a claim.

SOME THINGS TO NOTE IN FILLING OUT PART I
(Your doctor will fill out Part II.)

1 & 2 Copy the name and number and indicate your sex exactly as shown on your health insurance card. Include the letters at the end of the number.

3 Enter your mailing address and telephone number, if any.

4 Describe your illness or injury. Be sure to check one of the two boxes.

5 If you have other health insurance or expect a welfare agency to pay part of the expenses, complete item 5.

6 Be sure to sign your name. If you cannot write your name, sign by mark (X), and have the signature witnessed. The witness's signature and address must also be shown in item 6.

If you are filing the claim for a Medicare beneficiary, in item 6 enter the patient's name and write "By", sign your name and enter your address in this space, show your relationship to the patient, and explain why the patient cannot sign. (If the patient has died, the survivor should contact any social security office for information on what to do.)

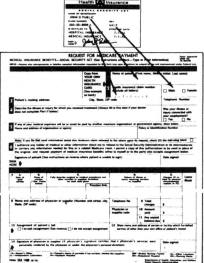

IMPORTANT NOTES FOR PHYSICIANS AND SUPPLIERS

Item 12: In assigned cases the patient is responsible only for the deductible, coinsurance, and non-covered services. Coinsurance and the deductible are based upon the charge determination of the carrier if this is less than the charge submitted.

This form may also be used by a supplier, or by the patient to claim reimbursement for charges by a supplier for services such as the use of an ambulance or medical appliances.

If the physician or supplier does not want Part II information released to the organization named in item 5, the physician or supplier should write "No further release" in item 7C following the description of services.

COLLECTION AND USE OF MEDICARE INFORMATION

We are authorized by the Social Security Administration to ask you for information needed in the administration of the Medicare program. Social Security's authority to collect information is in section 205(a), 1872 and 1875 of the Social Security Act. as amended.

The information we obtain to complete your Medicare claim is used to identify you and to determine your eligibility. It is also used to decide if the services and supplies you received are covered by Medicare and to insure that proper payment is made.

The information may also be given to other providers of services, carriers, intermediaries, medical review boards, and other organizations as necessary to administer the Medicare program. For example, it may be

necessary to disclose information about the Medicare benefits you have used to a hospital or doctor.

With one exception, which is discussed below, there are no penalties under social security law for refusing to supply information. However, failure to furnish information regarding the medical services rendered or the amount charged would prevent payment of the claim. Failure to furnish any other information, such as name or claim number, would delay payment of the claim.

It is mandatory that you tell us if you are being treated for a work related injury so we can determine whether workmen's compensation will pay for the treatment. Section 1877(a)(3) of the Social Security Act provides criminal penalties for withholding this information.

☆U. S. GPO:1976-0-211-071/68

Courtesy of United States Department of Health, Education and Welfare, Health Care Financing Administration. Used by permission.

FIGURE 11-1B
MEDICARE FORM (BACK)

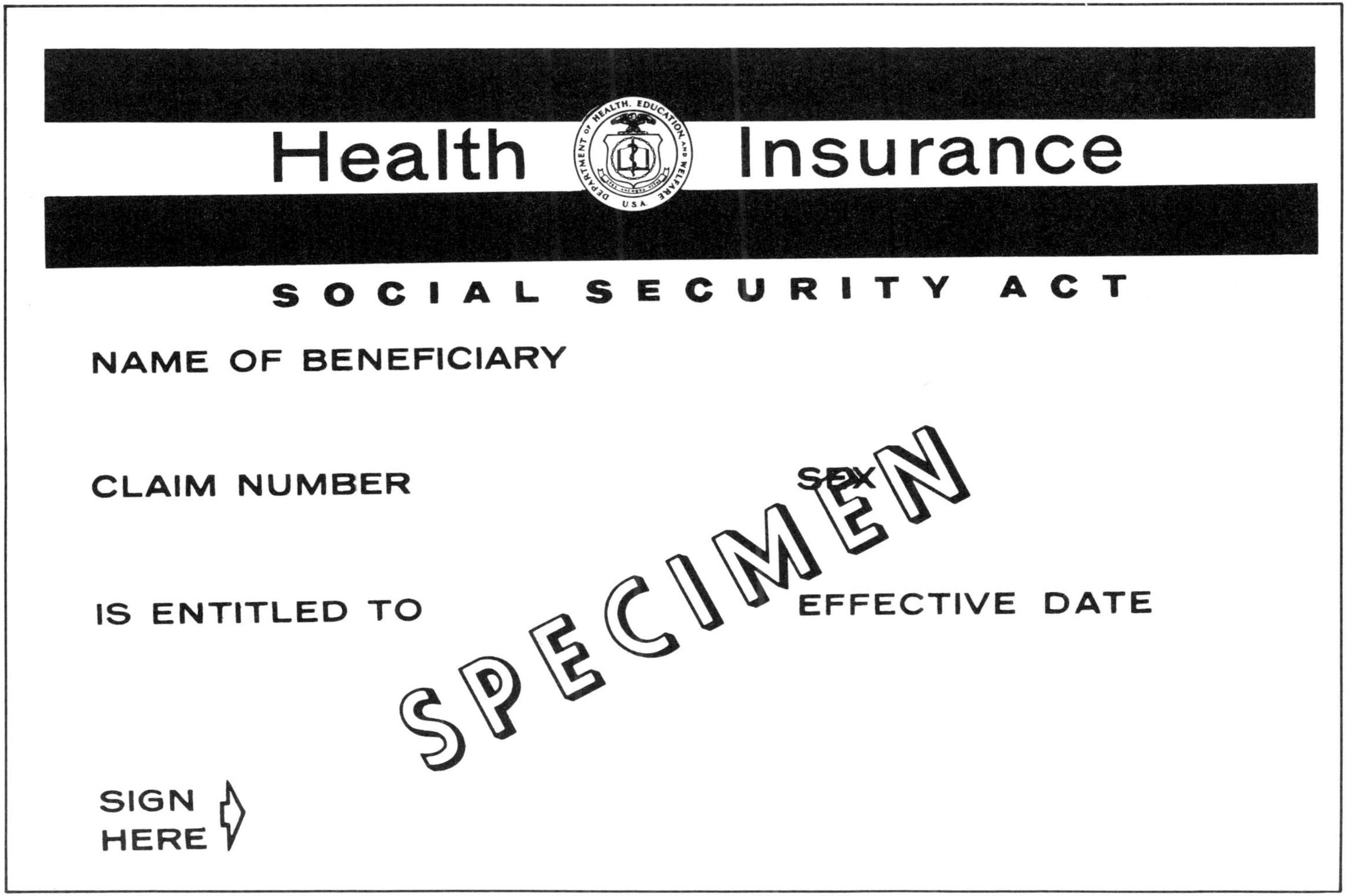

Health Insurance

SOCIAL SECURITY ACT

NAME OF BENEFICIARY

CLAIM NUMBER

IS ENTITLED TO

SEX

EFFECTIVE DATE

SPECIMEN

SIGN
HERE

FIGURE 11-2
IDENTIFICATION CARD

How to complete the Request for Medicare Payment

The *Request for Medicare Payment* (also called SSA–1490) is the form you or your doctor or supplier uses to claim Medicare medical insurance payments. The form is shown on the next page.

It is important that the form be completed properly. Incomplete or incorrect information on the form may delay payment.

If your doctor or supplier accepts assignment of the medical insurance claim, he or she completes the *Request for Medicare Payment* and sends it in.

If the doctor or supplier does not accept assignment, you must send in the form to receive payment. You fill in Part I of the form, and either have Part II completed by the doctor or supplier *or* attach itemized bills for the services you received.

This leaflet tells you how to complete a *Request for Medicare Payment* and where to send it. Page 6 lists the information that must be included on itemized bills if your doctor or supplier doesn't complete Part II of the form for you.

You should keep this leaflet handy so that you can refer to it whenever you have to fill out a *Request for Medicare Payment*.

If you ever need assistance in completing the form, the people in any social security office will be glad to help you. They can also answer any questions you have about Medicare.

2
HEW Publication No. (SSA) 76–10083

Print your health insurance number exactly as it's shown on your Medicare card. Be sure to include the letter at the end of the number.

Print your complete address—street, city, State, and ZIP code.

Briefly describe the condition (illness or injury) for which you were treated. If you were treated for different conditions, describe each.

If you have private health insurance or are covered under a State medical assistance program (such as Medicaid), print the name and address of the insurance company or State program.

Sign your name. (Do not print.)

If Part II (items 7 through 14) is completed by the doctor or supplier, you do not have to attach itemized bills. If your doctor or supplier does not complete Part II, you *must* attach itemized bills. See page 6 for a list of what must be included on an itemized bill.

3

Print your name *exactly* as it's shown on your Medicare card.

Check the box next to male or female.

Print the telephone number where you can be reached.

Check the box marked "yes" or "no."

Print your private insurance policy number or State medical assistance number.

Check this box *only* if you do *not* want information about this Medicare claim given to your private insurance company or State medical assistance program.

Print the date you signed this form.

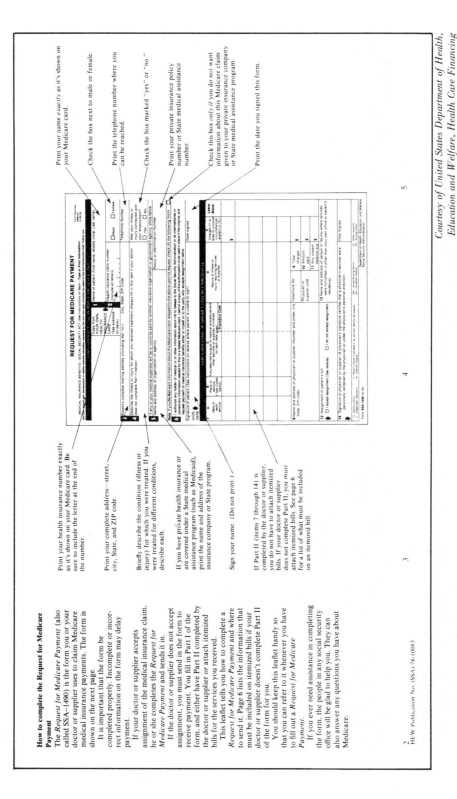

4

5

Courtesy of United States Department of Health, Education and Welfare, Health Care Financing Administration. Used by permission.

FIGURE 11-3A
HOW TO COMPLETE THE REQUEST FOR MEDICARE PAYMENT (HEW PUBLICATION NO. (SSA) 76-10083 JUNE 1976) (SIDE 1)

How to complete the Request for Medicare Payment

An itemized bill

If you are sending in itemized bills with your *Request for Medicare Payment*, they must contain specific information or your claim may be delayed. A bill which simply says "For professional services rendered" or "Balance forward" is not an itemized bill.

If the doctor or supplier gives you an itemized bill that does not show all of the following information, ask him or her to fill in what is missing. Each itemized bill you submit must show all of the following information:

▶ A complete description of each service or supply you received.

▶ The date you received each service or supply.

▶ The place where you received each service or supply.

▶ The charge for each service or supply.

▶ The name of the doctor or supplier who provided each service or supply.

▶ Your name and your complete health insurance number exactly as they are shown on your Medicare card. (If the doctor or supplier does not put your name and number on the bill, you can write them on it.)

▶ It is helpful, but not necessary, if the diagnosis is shown on the bill.

You can send in more than one itemized bill with a single *Request for Medicare Payment*. It doesn't matter whether all the bills are from one doctor or supplier, or from different doctors or suppliers. And, you can send in the bills either before or after you pay them.

Keep a record of your claim

It's a good idea for you to keep a record of your claim in case there is ever any need to inquire about it.

Before you send in a *Request for Medicare Payment*, you should write down the date you mail it, a description of the services or supplies you received, the date and charge for each service or supply, and the name of the doctor or supplier who provided the services or supplies.

Where to send your claim

Send the *Request for Medicare Payment* and itemized bills, if any, to your Medicare carrier. If the carrier's name and address are not shown in the upper left-hand block of the form, you can find the name and address in *Your Medicare Handbook.* Page 51 of the Medicare handbook tells you how to find the address. Or, you can call any social security office to get the carrier's name and address.

Be sure to include the word "Medicare" in the carrier's address when you write it on the envelope. Also, be sure to put your return address and the necessary postage on the envelope.

6

7

**U.S. Department of
Health, Education, and Welfare**
Social Security Administration
HEW Publication No. (SSA) 76-10083
June 1976

☆ U.S. GOVERNMENT PRINTING OFFICE 1976: 621-811/158

*Courtesy of United States Department of Health,
Education and Welfare, Health Care Financing
Administration. Used by permission.*

FIGURE 11-3B
HOW TO COMPLETE THE REQUEST FOR MEDICARE PAYMENT (HEW
PUBLICATION NO. (SSA) 76-10083 JUNE 1976) (SIDE 2)

Blue Cross Blue Shield
of Greater New York

PARTICIPATING PHYSICIAN'S STATEMENT OF SERVICES

P.O. Box 200
Murray Hill Station
New York, N.Y. 10016
Telephone (212) 490-4141

PLEASE MAKE CERTAIN YOU REPORT YOUR CURRENT IDENTIFICATION NUMBER ⟶

1. IDENTIFICATION NUMBER

PLEASE PRINT IN CAPITAL LETTERS

SUBSCRIBER COMPLETES

2. PATIENT'S NAME — First — Last   3. SEX   4. BIRTHDATE Mo. Day Yr.   5. GROUP NUMBER (if any)

6. CONTRACT HOLDER'S NAME — First — Last   7. SEX   8. RELATIONSHIP OF PATIENT TO CONTRACT HOLDER 1. ☐ self 2. ☐ spouse 3. ☐ child   9. CONTRACT HOLDER'S EMPLOYER

10. HOME ADDRESS — Number — Street   11. PATIENT'S OCCUPATION   12. IF PATIENT IS A FULL TIME STUDENT, GIVE NAME OF SCHOOL.

13. City — State — Zip Code   14. PATIENT'S PHONE NO.

15. IS ILLNESS OR INJURY CONNECTED TO YOUR EMPLOYMENT? ☐ Yes ☐ No   16. IS INJURY THE RESULT OF A MOTOR VEHICLE ACCIDENT? ☐ Yes ☐ No   17. IS PATIENT COVERED UNDER ANOTHER HEALTH BENEFIT GROUP PLAN? ☐ YES ☐ NO OR. MEDICARE PART B ☐ YES ☐ NO. IF YES GIVE NAME OF INSURANCE COMPANY.   18. MY FAMILY'S TOTAL YEARLY INCOME IS: 1 ☐ $2500-$4000 2 ☐ $4000-$6000 3 ☐ $6000-$7000 4 ☐ $7000-$8500 5 ☐ Over $8500

I certify that the above statements are correct and hereby authorize any doctor or organization to provide pertinent records to Blue Cross and Blue Shield of Greater New York upon request.

SUBSCRIBER'S SIGNATURE

ADDRESS

IDENTIFICATION NO.

DOCTOR COMPLETES

19. PLACE SERVICE RENDERED   1. ☐ Hosp. In-patient   2. ☐ Home Hospital   3. ☐ Office   4. ☐ Out-patient Dept.   5. ☐ Other   20. DATE OF ONSET OF ILLNESS   21. WAS SURGERY PERFORMED? ☐ Yes ☐ No

22. IF PATIENT WAS HOSPITALIZED GIVE HOSPITAL NAME AND LOCATION   23. DATE ADMITTED   24. DATE DISCHARGED   By whom? _____

25. DIAGNOSIS   26. NAME OF REFERRING DOCTOR (if any)   Type _____ Date _____

27. ADDRESS OF REFERRING DOCTOR   28. WAS THIS A WARD SERVICE PATIENT? ☐ Yes ☐ No

29. CALENDAR OF SERVICES C-Consultation O-Office Visits H-Hospital Visits R-Home Visits	Month	1	2	3	4	5	6	7	8	9	10	11	12	13	14	15	16	17	18	19	20	21	22	23	24	25	26	27	28	29	30	31

PLEASE DO NOT WRITE IN SHADED AREAS.		UNITS	PL	TY	PROCEDURE	CD	M	DATE(S) OF SERVICE						FEE CHARGED	I.F.C.
30. SERVICES RENDERED (List each service separately)								Mo.	Day	Yr.	Mo.	Day	Yr.	$	c
1															
2															
3															
4															
5															
6															
7															
8															

EXAMINER CHECK NOTATION	MISC. DATE	TOTAL CHARGES C.C.	MY FEE FOR THE SERVICES DESCRIBED ABOVE IS ⟹ $

DOCTOR'S NAME AND ADDRESS

31.   0. ☐ HAS   MY FEE   1. ☐ HAS NOT   BEEN PAID TO ME

I certify that I personally rendered the above services, and that the amounts shown as Fee Charged are the fees that I personally charged the Subscriber for the services. If the subscriber is eligible for Paid-in-full Benefits, I will accept, as full payment, the amount set forth in the applicable schedule of allowances.

TELEPHONE NO.   PROVIDER CODE NO.

FOR PLAN USE ONLY

DOCTOR'S SIGNATURE ▸ _____ DATE _____

Courtesy of Blue Cross Blue Shield of Greater New York. Used by permission.

FIGURE 11-4A
BLUE CROSS/BLUE SHIELD FORM (FRONT)

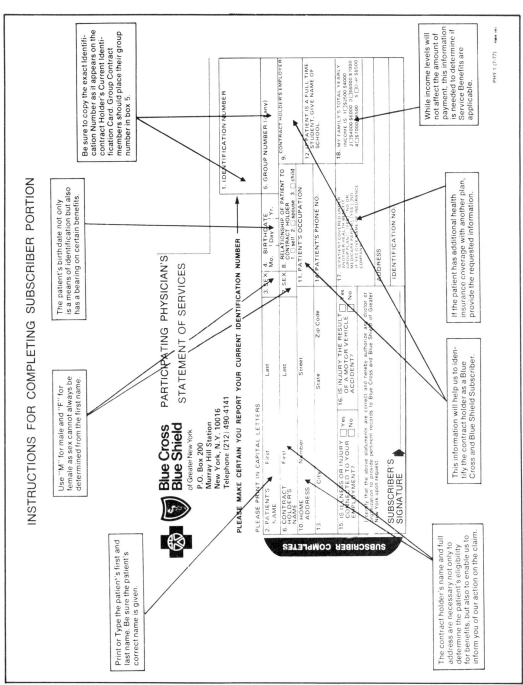

Courtesy of Blue Cross Blue Shield of Greater New York. Used by permission.

FIGURE 11-4B
BLUE CROSS/BLUE SHIELD FORM (BACK)

HAVE A BETTER UNDERSTANDING OF THE SECRETARY'S RESPONSIBILITIES

Since the doctor relies heavily upon you, the secretary, to fill out all insurance forms, care should be taken to fill them out completely and accurately. One of your important functions is the responsibility for processing insurance forms. Try to maintain a good supply of forms from the various companies and public agencies with which you deal most often. To obtain these forms, write or call the company or agency involved. (See Figures 11-5 and 11-6.)

Medical insurance is often complicated by changing rules and regulations. To keep up with these changes you should have available current instruction manuals from each company or agency. These can be obtained by writing or calling the nearest office. The address is always on the form, usually on the back. Any specific problems not covered in the handbooks can be answered by calling or writing the main office. Many insurance companies have specialists who conduct regular seminars explaining the correct way to fill out and process these forms.

Remember that an important point in handling medical insurance forms is not to let them pile up. Some doctors prefer to have the patients file their own form. In this case the diagnosis is filled in immediately and the patient will take the form when leaving the office. But if the doctor prefers to send in the form from the office, then a good policy is to attach the forms to the patient's record as soon as they are received and either fill them in immediately or set aside certain hours or days to take care of the forms. Unless a certain time is set aside as often as necessary, the backlog of work that builds up becomes impossible to cope with. If a routine is established, it is much easier to get the work done and you will not fall behind. There are no set ways of handling insurance forms; each secretary must find the system that best suits the routine of the particular office.

STREAMLINING THE PROCESSING OF FORMS

Knowing what has to be filled out, when it has to be submitted, and where or to whom it is submitted, will aid the secretary in processing forms quickly. Have special files set up with all standard information such as the doctor's name and address pre-stamped on the forms for the various companies (private) and government agencies.

A separate form is filed for each series of visits for a particular illness, or in prolonged illness a form is filed once every month or two. You or the doctor fill in the data about the office visit or the diagnosis and treatment, but the patient

**HEALTH INSURANCE
CLAIM FORM**

READ INSTRUCTIONS BEFORE COMPLETING OR SIGNING THIS FORM

TYPE OR PRINT   ☐ MEDICARE   ☐ MEDICAID   ☐ CHAMPUS   ☐ OTHER

PATIENT & INSURED (SUBSCRIBER) INFORMATION

1. PATIENT'S NAME *(First name, middle initial, last name)*	2. PATIENT'S DATE OF BIRTH	3. INSURED'S NAME *(First name, middle initial, last name)*
4. PATIENT'S ADDRESS *(Street, city, state, ZIP code)*	5. PATIENT'S SEX MALE ☐ FEMALE ☐	6. INSURED'S I.D. No. or **MEDICARE No.** *(Include any letters)*
	7. PATIENT'S RELATIONSHIP TO INSURED SELF SPOUSE CHILD OTHER	8. INSURED'S GROUP NO. *(Or Group Name)*
9. OTHER HEALTH INSURANCE COVERAGE - Enter Name of Policyholder and Plan Name and Address and Policy or Medical Assistance Number	10. WAS CONDITION RELATED TO: A. PATIENT'S EMPLOYMENT YES ☐ NO ☐ B. AN AUTO ACCIDENT YES ☐ NO ☐	11. INSURED'S ADDRESS *(Street, city, state, ZIP code)*
12. PATIENT'S OR AUTHORIZED PERSON'S SIGNATURE *(Read back before signing)* *I Authorize the Release of any Medical Information Necessary to Process this Claim and Request Payment of MEDICARE/CHAMPUS Benefits Either to Myself or to the Party Who Accepts Assignment Below* SIGNED DATE		13. *I AUTHORIZE PAYMENT OF MEDICAL BENEFITS TO UNDERSIGNED PHYSICIAN OR SUPPLIER FOR SERVICE DESCRIBED BELOW* SIGNED *(Insured or Authorized Person)*

PHYSICIAN OR SUPPLIER INFORMATION

14. DATE OF:	ILLNESS (FIRST SYMPTOM) OR INJURY (ACCIDENT) OR PREGNANCY (LMP)	15. DATE FIRST CONSULTED YOU FOR THIS CONDITION	16. HAS PATIENT EVER HAD SAME OR SIMILAR SYMPTOMS? YES ☐ NO ☐
17. DATE PATIENT ABLE TO RETURN TO WORK	18. DATES OF TOTAL DISABILITY FROM THROUGH		DATES OF PARTIAL DISABILITY FROM THROUGH
19. NAME OF REFERRING PHYSICIAN			20. FOR SERVICES RELATED TO HOSPITALIZATION GIVE HOSPITALIZATION DATES ADMITTED DISCHARGED
21. NAME & ADDRESS OF FACILITY WHERE SERVICES RENDERED *(If other than home or office)*			22. WAS LABORATORY WORK PERFORMED OUTSIDE YOUR OFFICE? YES ☐ NO ☐ CHARGES:

23. DIAGNOSIS OR NATURE OF ILLNESS OR INJURY. RELATE DIAGNOSIS TO PROCEDURE IN COLUMN D BY REFERENCE TO NUMBERS 1, 2, 3, ETC. OR DX CODE

1.
2.
3.
4.

24. A DATE OF SERVICE	B* PLACE OF SERV-ICE	C PROCEDURE CODE (IDENTIFY.) FULLY DESCRIBE PROCEDURES, MEDICAL SERVICES OR SUPPLIES FURNISHED FOR EACH DATE GIVEN *(EXPLAIN UNUSUAL SERVICES OR CIRCUMSTANCES)*		D DIAGNOSIS CODE	E CHARGES	F

25. SIGNATURE OF PHYSICIAN OR SUPPLIER *(Read back before signing)* SIGNED DATE	26. ACCEPT ASSIGNMENT *(GOVERNMENT CLAIMS ONLY) (SEE BACK)* YES ☐ NO ☐ 30. YOUR SOCIAL SECURITY NO.	27. TOTAL CHARGE	28. AMOUNT PAID	29. BALANCE DUE
32. YOUR PATIENT'S ACCOUNT NO.	33. YOUR EMPLOYER I.D. NO. I.D. NO.	31. PHYSICIAN'S OR SUPPLIER'S NAME, ADDRESS, ZIP CODE & *TELEPHONE NO.*		

* PLACE OF SERVICE CODES

1 — (IH) — INPATIENT HOSPITAL	4 — (H) — PATIENT'S HOME	7 — (NH) — NURSING HOME	O — (OL) — OTHER LOCATIONS
2 — (OH) — OUTPATIENT HOSPITAL	5 — DAY CARE FACILITY (PSY)	8 — (SNF) — SKILLED NURSING FACILITY	A — (IL) — INDEPENDENT LABORATORY
3 — (O) — DOCTOR'S OFFICE	6 — NIGHT CARE FACILITY (PSY)	9 — AMBULANCE	B — OTHER MEDICAL/SURGICAL FACILITY

APPROVED BY AMA COUNCIL ON MEDICAL SERVICE 6-74

*Courtesy of Histacount Corporation Subsidiary of
SCM Corporation. Used by permission.*

FIGURE 11-5A
HEALTH INSURANCE CLAIM FORM (FRONT)

MEDICARE PAYMENTS: If the patient cannot write, have him sign by mark (X) and have a witness sign in item 12. If the patient cannot sign by mark, another person may sign, showing his relationship and indicating on the reverse of the form why the patient could not sign. A patient's signature requests that payment be made and authorizes release of medical information necessary to pay the claim. If item 9 is completed, the patient's signature authorizes releasing of the information to the insurer or agency shown. In assigned cases, the physician agrees to accept the charge determination of the Medicare carrier as the full charge, and the patient is responsible only for the deductible, coinsurance, and noncovered services. Coinsurance and the deductible are based upon the charge determination of the carrier, if this is less than the charge submitted.

MEDICAID PAYMENTS: I hereby agree to keep such records as are necessary to disclose fully the extent of services provided to individuals under the state's Title XIX plan and to furnish information regarding any payments claimed for providing such services as the state agency may request. I further agree to accept, as payment in full, the amount paid by the Medicaid program for those claims submitted for payment under that program, with the exception of authorized deductibles and coinsurance.

SIGNATURE OF PHYSICIAN (OR SUPPLIER): I certify that the services listed above were medically indicated and necessary to the health of this patient and were personally rendered by me or under my personal direction.

NOTICE: Anyone who misrepresents or falsifies essential information to receive payment from federal funds requested by this form may upon conviction be subject to fine and imprisonment under applicable federal laws.

FORM 411   HISTACOUNT CORPORATION, MELVILLE, L. I., N. Y. 11746   HEALTH INSURANCE CLAIM FORM

Courtesy of Histacount Corporation Subsidiary of
SCM Corporation. Used by permission.

FIGURE 11-5B
HEALTH INSURANCE CLAIM FORM (BACK)

DATE	FAMILY PATIENT	PROFESSIONAL SERVICES	FEE	CHECK / CASH PAYMENT RECEIVED THANK YOU	CURRENT BALANCE	PRIOR BALANCE	N A M E	CONTROL NUMBER

PLEASE GIVE THIS SLIP TO RECEPTIONIST THANK YOU

ATTENDING PHYSICIAN'S STATEMENT

____ ACCIDENT $_____	____ INJECTION
____ BASAL METABOLISM	____ LABORATORY
____ BIOPSY	____ OBSTETRICAL
____ CAST	____ OFFICE CALL
____ COMPLETE BLOOD COUNT	____ OFFICE SURGERY
____ COMPLETE PHYSICAL	____ PHYSIOTHERAPY
____ DIAGNOSTIC SURVEY	____ RADIOLOGY
____ DRUGS	____ REDUCE FRACTURE
____ EKG	____ SKIN
____ EMERGENCY ROOM	____ SURGERY
____ ENDOSCOPY	____ SURGICAL ASSIST
____ FLUOROSCOPY	____ TONSILLECTOMY
____ FOLLOW-UP EXAM.	____ URINALYSIS
____ GASTRIC ANALYSIS	____ X-RAY
____ HEMATOLOGY	
____ HOSPITAL VISIT	
____ HOUSE CALL DAY	
____ HOUSE CALL NIGHT	

PATIENT   ☐ M ☐ F
☐ S   ☐ M   ☐ W   ☐ D   ☐ CHILD
ADDRESS
CITY   STATE   ZIP
PHONE NO.   DATE OF BIRTH
MO.   DAY   YR.
RELATIONSHIP TO INS'D.   RESPONS. PTY. OR POLICY HOLDER
EMPLOYER
MEDICARE NO.   MEDICAID NO.
INS. CO. CONTRACT GROUP NO.
DATE OF SYMPTOMS OR ACCIDENT: MO.   DAY   YR.
DISABILITY RELATED TO: ☐ ACC. ☐ IND'L. ☐ PREG. ☐ OTHER
DATES: FROM   OK TO RETURN TO WORK
TO
NEXT APPOINTMENT ON _____ AT _____ A.M. / P.M.
☐ OV   ☐ PX   ☐ EKG   NEXT CARD

RECORDS RELEASE AUTHORIZATION: I HEREBY AUTHORIZE & REQUEST THE UNDERSIGNED PHYSICIAN TO RELEASE ALL MEDICAL INFORMATION ACQUIRED FROM MY EXAMINATION, ILLNESS OR TREATMENT.

SIGNED (PATIENT, OR PARENT IF MINOR) _____ DATE _____

DIAGNOSIS OR SYMPTOMS _____

OTHER SERVICE RENDERED _____

PLACE OF SERVICE ____ OFFICE ____ HOSPITAL ____ EMERGENCY ROOM ____ HOME ____ NURSING HOME

DOCTOR'S SIGNATURE _____

ALVIN MYLES JONES, M. D.
965 WALT WHITMAN ROAD
MELVILLE, N. Y. 11749
HAMILTON 1-1200

SS No. 0000000
IRS No. 0000000   **0001**

FIGURE 11-6A
PEG-MASTER INSURANCE CLAIM FORM (FRONT)
(ALSO AVAILABLE NON PEG-MASTER)

PATIENT'S COPY

HEALTH INSURANCE

It is the policy of this practice to view the professional services provided as having been charged to the patient, not to an insurance company.

It is expected that patients who have health insurance will, in all instances, pay the appropriate fees when due, as services are rendered, unless other arrangements have been made in advance.

Even though a health insurance claim has been filed, a statement for the outstanding balance will be sent each month. This office cannot be responsible for collecting your health claims or for negotiating disputed claims. Your account is due in full for collection when the statement is rendered.

INSTRUCTIONS FOR CLAIM PROCESSING

1. Attach the "Insurance Copy" to the regular claim form of your insurance carrier, which may be obtained from them.

2. Fill in the patient's section of the insurance carrier's claim form and see that it is returned to the insurance carrier according to their instructions for processing.

3. The doctor's signature is not required on an insurance carrier's claim, as this form is sufficient. It is unnecessary for this office to fill out the insurance claim form, and our customary fee will be charged for additional itemization of services.

4. If you have any questions we will be happy to assist you, but your eventual reimbursement will be determined by your insurance carrier.

Courtesy of Histacount Corporation Subsidiary of SCM Corporation. Used by permission.

FIGURE 11-6B
PEG-MASTER INSURANCE CLAIM FORM (BACK)

FIGURE 11-7
BLUE CROSS/BLUE SHIELD FORM FILLED IN

must furnish the basic personal information and sometimes even furnish the form. If the patient furnishes the form, make sure that he does so immediately. If possible, complete the form on the day the patient comes in and have the doctor sign it immediately. Processing time is not only reduced, but also the form is filled out quickly and accurately because the information is fresh and you don't have to spend time trying to recall or look up the record.

The diagnosis and treatment is the most important part of the form. After you have filled in the forms, have the doctor check to see that the diagnosis and treatment are accurate, or if he prefers, leave the diagnosis and treatment portion blank for the doctor to fill in. (See Figure 11-7.)

Double-check each form before giving it to the patient to see that everything is filled in completely and accurately. Forms are often returned because one seemingly minor item was overlooked.

It is primarily the patient's obligation to complete and send in insurance claim forms for payment of his or her medical bills. Medical offices have fallen into this activity to facilitate third party payment, especially in the case of the confused elderly persons on Medicare.

If you submit the insurance form from your office to the company it is a necessity to keep a photocopy for your records. If space does not permit keeping a copy of the form, then a notation is entered on the patient's record or ledger sheet indicating the date of the claim and the office visits, laboratory tests, x-rays, or treatments that have been included on the claim form. If it is necessary to trace a form, the secretary may have to go back several months and fill out another form to be resubmitted.

Remember that the doctor depends upon you to process the records efficiently. Always keep careful, accurate records. A lost or misplaced record can mean hours of lost time and anxiety for the secretary, the patient, and the doctor. Handling insurance forms is an essential and important responsibility of the medical secretary. You can do this efficiently by being accurate and prompt in your processing of medical insurance forms.

Chapter 12

Keeping Better
Financial Records

Bookkeeping in a medical office is important. It is your duty as a medical secretary to maintain a well-functioning office. This is possible only if its financial records are in good shape. The degree to which you actually engage in the bookkeeping and accounting procedure will depend on the size of the doctor's practice. A bookkeeper or accountant may be employed if the office is very large, but the responsibility for seeing that the work has been completed will be yours.

It is your duty as the medical secretary to carry out whatever system of bookkeeping is adopted unless the doctor has a full-time bookkeeper. Even if this is the case, there are certain records that must be kept by you.

Among the financial record-keeping duties of the medical secretary are endorsing and recording checks received, preparing and making bank deposits, reconciling bank statements, preparing and maintaining employees' payroll records, keeping records for income tax purposes, writing receipts to patients for payment received, maintaining patients' ledger or account cards, and maintaining records on all doctor's personal bills.

In order to do this, an efficient bookkeeping system must be adopted and implemented. If the doctor does not collect fees, obviously the practice cannot continue; therefore, a great deal of emphasis must be placed on the business side of the practice. The medical profession is one of the most difficult in which to collect bills. Doctors usually do not like to use collection methods that are employed by large businesses. It becomes your job to see that bills are collected.

Remember, being an office manager is usually part of your job, so whether or not you do the actual bookkeeping, the responsibility will often be yours.

SELECTING THE RIGHT BOOKKEEPING SYSTEM

Selecting the proper bookkeeping system is very important. Several factors must be considered such as volume of business, type of patient seen, specialty of physician, location of office, one or more doctor office, whether or not house calls are made, hospital calls, how often a third party such as an insurance company is involved.

The bookkeeping system employed must be flexible enough to accommodate the wishes of the patient. Each patient will have different needs—for example, some will pay cash, some will need to settle through medical insurance, some by a welfare agency, and some will want to be billed monthly. The system should also show the doctor's income and expenses and should be relatively easy to maintain. The least complicated system of bookkeeping is desirable because of the time factor.

There are available, through commercial stationers who specialize in supplying hospitals and doctors, simple bookkeeping systems that will suit the needs of almost every type of doctor's office. These systems are set up to handle every aspect of bookkeeping right down to the monthly statement. Easy-to-follow instructions are furnished so that you can handle it on your own with efficiency. These pegboard accounting systems are called by brand names such as "The Posting Board," "Write-it-once," or "Peg Master." By using this method, the patient's visit is recorded on a ledger sheet and on a monthly statement at the same time. Another advantage is avoiding errors which occur with rewriting figures.

Many systems also include the bank deposit slips and checks. An added advantage of a system of this type is that the doctor can see at a glance the daily income, expenses, and outstanding accounts. (See Figure 12-1.)

This certainly speeds up the bookkeeping process for the secretary and at the same time furnishes current records of all patients seen.

Other types of bookkeeping systems are available—some that require a special bookkeeping machine. Information concerning the various systems available can be obtained by consulting salesmen and company representatives—use of periodicals advertising various record-keeping systems—and through other doctors. (See Figures 12-2 through 13.)

ADVANTAGES OF USING A BILLING SERVICE

Many doctors are turning to computer billing services, which have some very definite advantages over the conventional methods. The computer does not eliminate the responsibility the medical secretary has for bookkeeping. It is necessary to maintain certain records that cannot be automated.

Automated record-keeping systems are now available to doctors. Some of these systems maintain records of all the doctor's income and expenses, and take care of the billing. Others are designed only for handling the accounts receivable (income), which means that they will handle the patient billing and collections. The charge for this service varies—some firms base the charge on the number of statements sent out while others accept full responsibility for billing and collecting—charging a percentage of the doctor's net income. It has been found that through the use of automated billing and collections, slow-paying accounts are singled out and, in certain cases, a patient can be required to pay cash because his credit rating is not satisfactory. This, of course, helps to eliminate delinquent accounts.

Some advantages of utilizing an automated system are:

1. Doctor's overall income usually is increased.

2. Increased efficiency of operation of doctor's office.

3. Frees the secretary to assist the doctor more.

4. Records are more accurate and up-to-date.

5. Billing is prompt.

6. Past-due accounts are easily identifiable thus increasing effectiveness of follow-up.

7. Some automated systems will run a credit check on each patient and will accept responsibility for only those patients whose credit rating is favorable.

8. Furnishes 30-, 60 , or 90-day print-out of receivables indicating past-due accounts.

9. Especially good for doctors who specialize, for example, psychiatrist, obstetrician-gynecologist, pediatrician, dentist, or orthodontist.

Disadvantages:

1. System would not be suitable for all doctors.

2. Too costly if volume of business is small.

THE INCOME CONTROL SYSTEM

Illustrated below is an exploded view of the 5 basic parts of the **PEG-**Master Income Control System. The Pegboard **B** assures that the Daily Transaction Control Sheet **D** the Patient Account Card **D** and the Patient Transaction Slips **E** are in perfect alignment, so that one written entry will complete all forms. The Binder **A** will conveniently house the system. Both the Binder **A** and the Pegboard **B** are detailed on this page. The forms **C** **D** **E** are illustrated and further detailed on the next four pages.

NOTE: For best results use ballpoint pen and press hard.

Indicates how Daily Transaction Sheet and shingled Transaction Slips are attached to the **PEG-**Master Pegboard.

A The Three Ring Binder is 11'' x 11½'' and has a 1'' capacity with sturdy, easy-to-open metal rings. It is made of rugged binder board, covered in leather-like wolf grain finish. Two binders are available, in black for the Income Control System and in red for the Disbursements Control System. Both binders are gold stamped on the cover and on the spine.

B The Pegboard is 11⅜'' x 9⅞'' folded and when opened measures 11⅜'' x 18⅞''. It is sturdily constructed of aluminum and covered in colored vinyl for beauty. It has a smooth, grained finish writing surface. Corners are rounded; there are three large, metal eyelets positioned to fit the three-ring binder described above; and there are 11 sturdy brass pegs for holding record forms in position.

C The Daily Transaction Control Sheet is printed on 11'' x 17'' NCR (no carbon required) 20lb. white stock. When you lock the Daily Transaction Control Sheet onto the pegs of the pegboard, you are assured of perfect registration with other forms. The <u>second</u> hole from the top of the sheet must fit over the first peg from the top of the pegboard.

D The Patient Account Card is placed into position on the pegboard after the patient has seen the doctor. It is placed between the Daily Transaction Control Sheet **C** and the Patient Transaction Slip **E** aligned so that the entry on **E** will automatically record on the Patient Account Card and the Daily Transaction Control Sheet. The left edge of the Patient Account Card is placed against the right side of the brass pegs, with the horizontal lines aligned appropriately.

E Patient Transaction Slips: Lock a shingled sheet of 25 onto the pegboard, over the Daily Transaction Control Sheet. For perfect registration with Daily Transaction Control Sheet the first hole of the shingled Patient Transaction Slips is fitted over the first peg on the pegboard. This slip is the "master" form on which the original entry is made, and which reproduces on the other forms.

PEG-Master THREE RING BINDER

PEG-Master FOLDING PEGBOARD

PEG-Master DAILY TRANSACTION CONTROL SHEET

PEG-Master PATIENT TRANSACTION SLIP

PEG-Master PATIENT ACCOUNT CARD

FIGURE 12-1
PEG-MASTER INCOME CONTROL SYSTEM

Courtesy of Histacount Corporation Subsidiary of SCM Corporation. Used by permission.

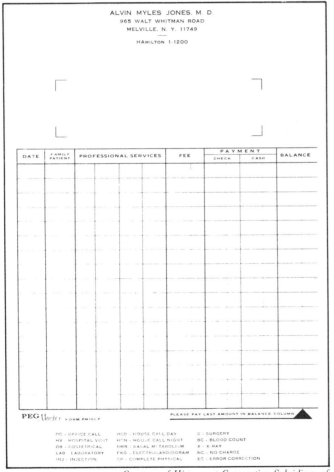

DATE	FAMILY PATIENT	PROFESSIONAL SERVICES	FEE	CHECK	CASH	CURRENT BALANCE	PRIOR BALANCE	NAME	CONTROL NUMBER
				PAYMENT RECEIVED THANK YOU				PLEASE GIVE THIS SLIP TO RECEPTIONIST. THANK YOU.	

HISTACOUNT CORPORATION
MELVILLE, N.Y. 11746

PEG Master FORM PM103P

ALVIN MYLES JONES, M. D.
965 WALT WHITMAN ROAD
MELVILLE, N. Y. 11749
—
HAMILTON 1-1200

OC - OFFICE CALL	HCD - HOUSE CALL DAY	S - SURGERY
HV - HOSPITAL VISIT	HCN - HOUSE CALL NIGHT	BC - BLOOD COUNT
OB - OBSTETRICAL	BMR - BASAL METABOLISM	X - X-RAY
LAB - LABORATORY	EKG - ELECTROCARDIOGRAM	NC - NO CHARGE
INJ - INJECTION	CP - COMPLETE PHYSICAL	EC - ERROR CORRECTION

OC - OFFICE CALL
HV - HOSPITAL VISIT
OB - OBSTETRICAL
LAB - LABORATORY
INJ - INJECTION
HCD - HOUSE CALL DAY
HCN - HOUSE CALL NIGHT
BMR - BASAL METABOLISM
EKG - ELECTROCARDIOGRAM
CP - COMPLETE PHYSICAL
S - SURGERY
BC - BLOOD COUNT
X - X-RAY
NC - NO CHARGE
EC - ERROR CORRECTION

NEXT APPOINTMENT	DAY	DATE	TIME	AM PM	Nº 0001	NEXT APP'T.	DAYS	WKS.	MOS.	TOTAL $

Courtesy of Histacount Corporation Subsidiary of SCM Corporation. Used by permission.

FIGURE 12-2
PEG-MASTER-PATIENT TRANSACTION SLIP

Courtesy of Histacount Corporation Subsidiary of SCM Corporation. Used by permission.

FIGURE 12-3
PEG-MASTER-PATIENT ACCOUNT CARD

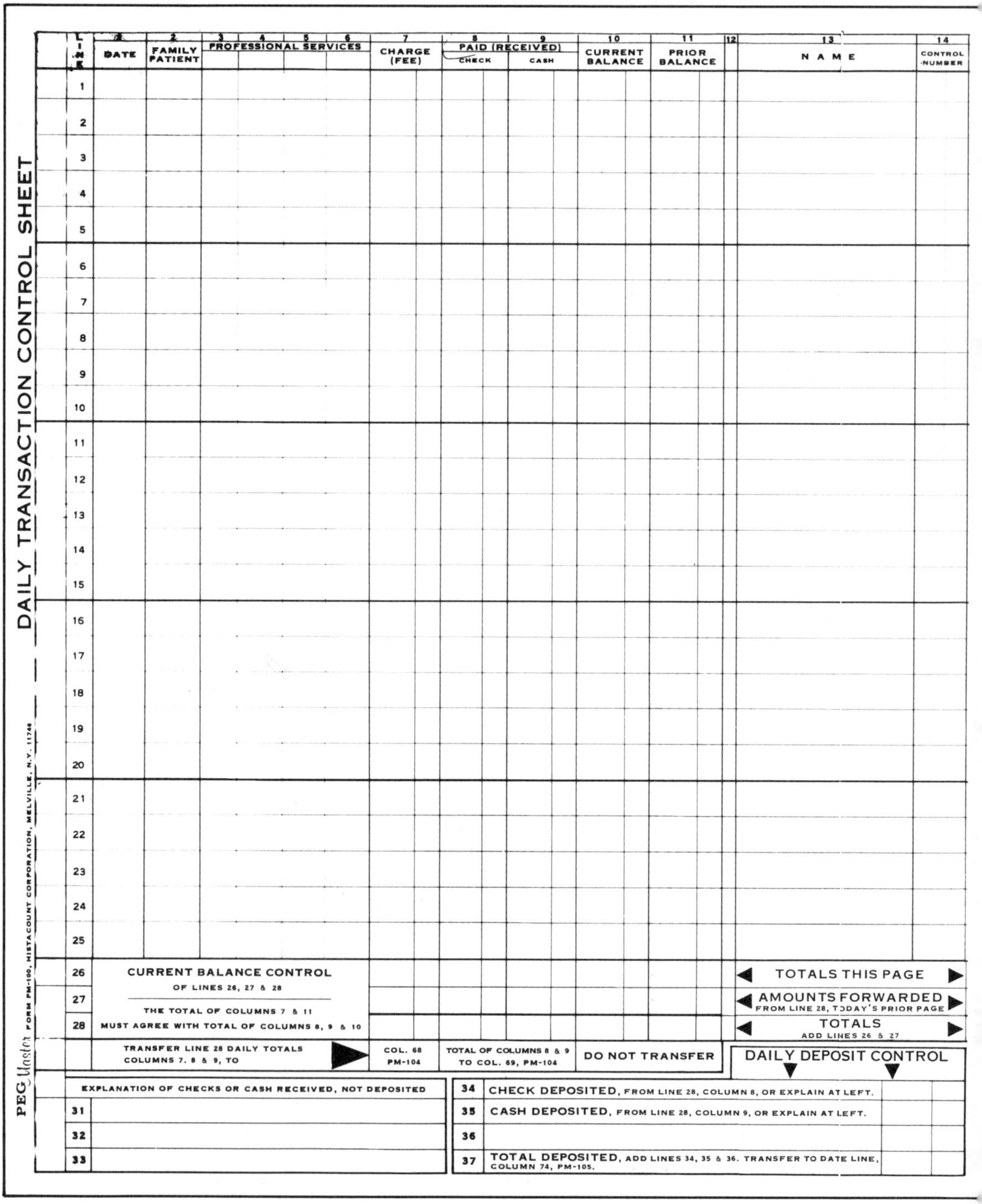

DAILY TRANSACTION CONTROL SHEET

LINE	1 DATE	2 FAMILY PATIENT	3 PROFESSIONAL SERVICES	4	5	6	7 CHARGE (FEE)	8 PAID (RECEIVED) CHECK	9 CASH	10 CURRENT BALANCE	11 PRIOR BALANCE	12	13 NAME	14 CONTROL NUMBER
1														
2														
3														
4														
5														
6														
7														
8														
9														
10														
11														
12														
13														
14														
15														
16														
17														
18														
19														
20														
21														
22														
23														
24														
25														
26	CURRENT BALANCE CONTROL OF LINES 26, 27 & 28												◀ TOTALS THIS PAGE ▶	
27	THE TOTAL OF COLUMNS 7 & 11												◀ AMOUNTS FORWARDED FROM LINE 28, TODAY'S PRIOR PAGE ▶	
28	MUST AGREE WITH TOTAL OF COLUMNS 8, 9 & 10												◀ TOTALS ADD LINES 26 & 27 ▶	
	TRANSFER LINE 28 DAILY TOTALS COLUMNS 7, 8 & 9, TO ▶						COL. 68 PM-104	TOTAL OF COLUMNS 8 & 9 TO COL. 69, PM-104		DO NOT TRANSFER			DAILY DEPOSIT CONTROL ▼ ▼	

	EXPLANATION OF CHECKS OR CASH RECEIVED, NOT DEPOSITED
31	
32	
33	

34	CHECK DEPOSITED, FROM LINE 28, COLUMN 8, OR EXPLAIN AT LEFT.		
35	CASH DEPOSITED, FROM LINE 28, COLUMN 9, OR EXPLAIN AT LEFT.		
36			
37	TOTAL DEPOSITED, ADD LINES 34, 35 & 36. TRANSFER TO DATE LINE, COLUMN 74, PM-105.		

PEG Master FORM PM-100, HISTACOUNT CORPORATION, MELVILLE, N.Y. 11746

FIGURE 12-4
PEG-MASTER - DAILY TRANSACTION CONTROL SHEET

LINE	15	16	17	18	19	20	21	22	23	24	LINE
	USE THESE COLUMNS TO ANALYZE INCOME BY SOURCE, BY GROUP MEMBER, BY INSURANCE CARRIER, OR AS DESIRED										
1											1
2											2
3											3
4											4
5											5
6											6
7											7
8											8
9											9
10											10
11											11
12											12
13											13
14											14
15											15
16											16
17											17
18											18
19											19
20											20
21											21
22											22
23											23
24											24
25											25
26											26
27											27
28											28
YESTERDAY'S LINE 30											29
MONTH TO DATE ADD LINES 28 & 29											30

IF DESIRED, MONTHLY ANALYSIS TOTALS MAY BE TRANSFERRED TO FORM PM—115 A, B OR C

PAGE_____OF_____PAGES   FOR   M   T   W   TH   F   S   S_____ 19_____

MONTH   DAY

Courtesy of Histacount Corporation Subsidiary of
SCM Corporation. Used by permission.

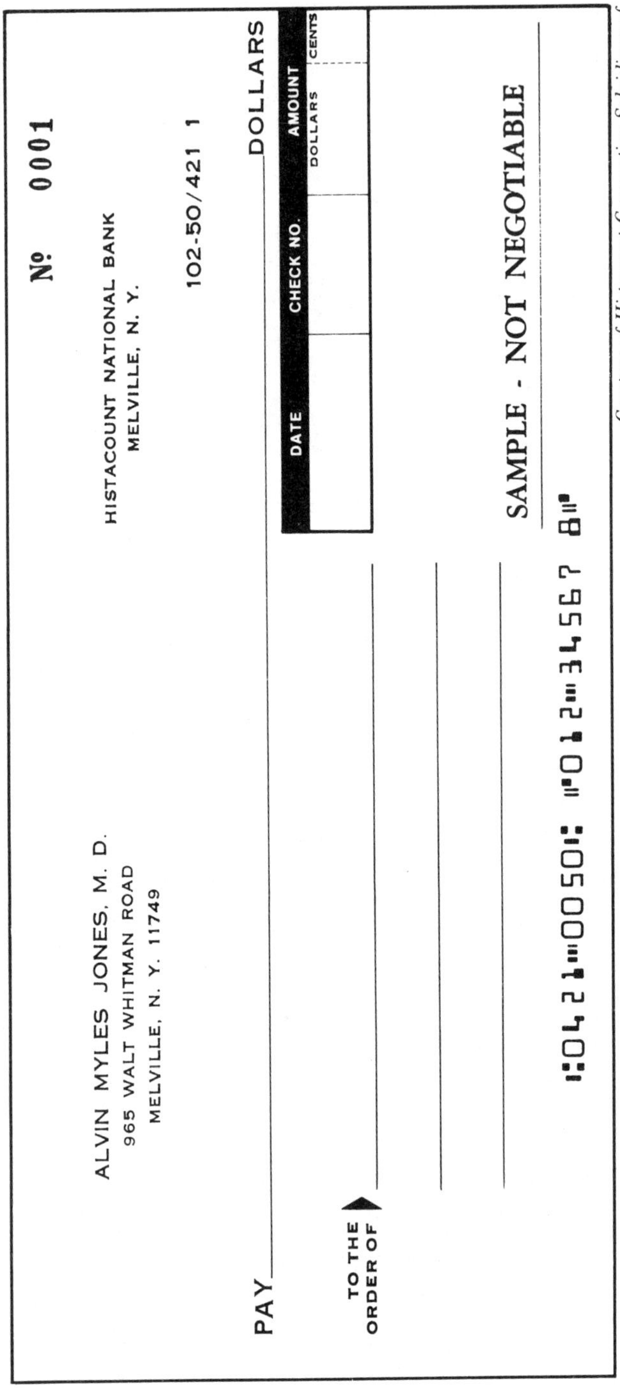

No. 0001

ALVIN MYLES JONES, M. D.
965 WALT WHITMAN ROAD
MELVILLE, N. Y. 11749

HISTACOUNT NATIONAL BANK
MELVILLE, N. Y.

102-50/421 1

PAY

TO THE
ORDER OF

DOLLARS

DATE	CHECK NO.	AMOUNT	
		DOLLARS	CENTS

SAMPLE - NOT NEGOTIABLE

⑆0421⑆0050⑆ ⑈012⑈34567⑈ 8⑈

Courtesy of Histacount Corporation Subsidiary of SCM Corporation. Used by permission.

FIGURE 12-5
PEG-MASTER - CHECK

ATTENDING PHYSICIAN'S STATEMENT

DATE	FAMILY PATIENT	PROFESSIONAL SERVICES	FEE	PAYMENT RECEIVED THANK YOU		CURRENT BALANCE
				CHECK	CASH	

PRIOR BALANCE

ACCIDENT $
BASAL METABOLISM
BIOPSY
CAST
COMPLETE BLOOD COUNT
COMPLETE PHYSICAL
DIAGNOSTIC SURVEY
DRUGS
EKG
EMERGENCY ROOM
ENDOSCOPY
FLUOROSCOPY
FOLLOW-UP EXAM
GASTRIC ANALYSIS
HEMATOLOGY
HOSPITAL VISIT
HOUSE CALL DAY
HOUSE CALL NIGHT

INJECTION
LABORATORY
OBSTETRICAL
OFFICE CALL
OFFICE SURGERY
PHYSIOTHERAPY
RADIOLOGY
REDUCE FRACTURE
SKIN
SURGERY
SURGICAL ASSIST
TONSILLECTOMY
URINALYSIS
X-RAY

RECORDS RELEASE AUTHORIZATION: I HEREBY AUTHORIZE & REQUEST THE UNDERSIGNED PHYSICIAN TO RELEASE ALL MEDICAL INFORMATION ACQUIRED FROM MY EXAMINATION, ILLNESS OR TREATMENT.

SIGNED (PATIENT, OR PARENT IF MINOR)_____ DATE _____

DIAGNOSIS OR SYMPTOMS_____

OTHER SERVICE RENDERED _____

PLACE OF SERVICE ____OFFICE ____HOSPITAL ____EMERGENCY ROOM ____HOME ____NURSING HOME

DOCTOR'S SIGNATURE _____

PATIENT
☐ S   ☐ M   ☐ W   ☐ D   ☐ M ☐ F
                                ☐ CHILD
ADDRESS
CITY   STATE   ZIP
PHONE NO.   DATE OF BIRTH
                    MO.   DAY   YR.
RELATIONSHIP TO INS'D. RESPONS. PTY. OR POLICY HOLDER
EMPLOYER
MEDICARE NO.   MEDICAID NO.
INS. CO. CONTRACT
GROUP NO.
DATE OF SYMPTOMS OR ACCIDENT: MO._____ DAY_____ YR._____
DISABILITY RELATED TO: ☐ ACC. ☐ IND'L. ☐ PREG. ☐ OTHER
DATES: FROM _____ OK TO RETURN TO WORK
       TO
NEXT
APPOINTMENT ON _____ AT _____ A.M. / P.M.
☐ OV   ☐ PX   ☐ EKG   NEXT CARD

NAME

CONTROL NUMBER

PLEASE GIVE THIS SLIP TO RECEPTIONIST

ALVIN MYLES JONES, M. D.
965 WALT WHITMAN ROAD
MELVILLE, N. Y. 11749
HAMILTON 1-1200

SS No. 0000000
IRS No. 0000000

0001

FIGURE 12-6
PEG-MASTER - ATTENDING PHYSICIAN'S STATEMENT

Courtesy of Histacount Corporation Subsidiary of SCM Corporation. Used by permission.

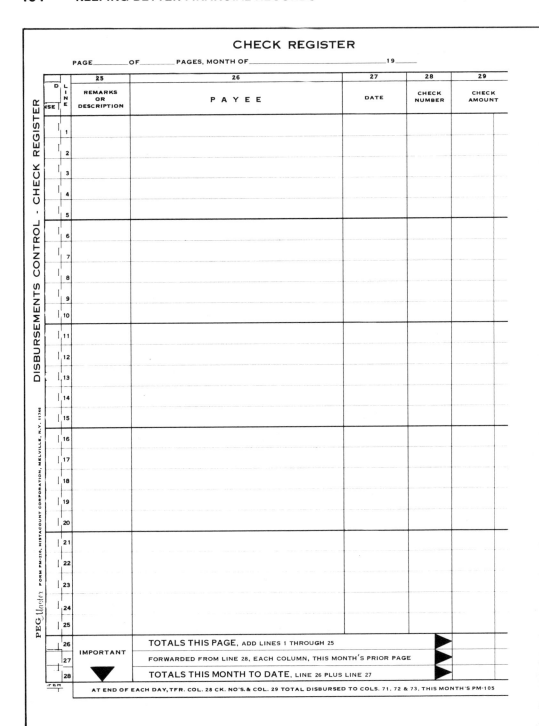

FIGURE 12-7
PEG-MASTER - CHECK REGISTER

PLEASE TURN SHEET FOR COLUMNS 42 TO 51 ➤

31 OFFICE EXPENSE	LINE	32 WAGES	33 AUTO & TRAVEL	34 MAINT.	35 MISC. EXPENSE	36 DRUGS & SUPPLIES	37 LABOR-ATORY	38 RENT	39 INTEREST PAID	40 INSTRU-MENTS	41 INSUR-ANCE	LINE
	DISTRIBUTION			OF	DEDUCTIBLE		DISBURSEMENTS					
	1											1
	2											2
	3											3
	4											4
	5											5
	6											6
	7											7
	8											8
	9											9
	10											10
	11											11
	12											12
	13											13
	14											14
	15											15
	16											16
	17											17
	18											18
	19											19
	20											20
	21											21
	22											22
	23											23
	24											24
	25											25
	26											26
	27											27
	28											28

TRANSFER MONTH END TOTALS, LINE 28, COLUMNS 31 TO 51, TO THIS MONTH'S COLUMN, FORM PM-115B OR C, LINE SHOWN BELOW

11		12	13	14	15	16	17	18	19	20	21

Courtesy of Histacount Corporation Subsidiary of
SCM Corporation. Used by permission.

MONTHLY CONTROL _____ 19 ____   FORM PM-104

ACCOUNTS RECEIVABLE CONTROL			
	68	69	70
DATE AND LINE	CHARGE (FEE)	PAID (RECEIVED)	CUMULATIVE CURRENT BALANCE YESTDY'S COL. 70 +TODAY'S COL. 68 -TODAY'S COL. 69
0	LAST MONTH'S CLOSING BALANCE LAST ENTRY COL. 70, PM-104 ▶		
1			
2			
3			
4			
5			
6			
7			
8			
9			
10			
11			
12			
13			
14			
15			
16			
17			
18			
19			
20			
21			
22			
23			
24			
25			
26			
27			
28			
29			
30			
31			
32	MONTHLY TOTALS (ADD LINES 1 THROUGH 31) TRANSFER LINE 32 TOTALS TO MONTHLY COLUMN LINES 6 AND 7, PM-115B OR PM-115C		
33	PRIOR TOTALS, FROM LINE 34 LAST MONTH'S PM-104		
34	YEAR TO DATE TOTALS, ADD LINES 32 & 33 TRANSFER TO LINE 33, NEXT MONTH'S PM-104		

MONTHLY NON-PRACTICE INCOME CONTROL		
65	66	67
DATE	DESCRIPTION	AMOUNT
35	TOTAL	

TRANSFER LINE 35, COL. 67 TO
THIS MONTH'S COLUMN, LINE 32, PM-115B OR PM-115C

MONTHLY NON-PRACTICE DEDUCTIBLE DISBURSEMENT CONTROL		
62	63	64
DATE	DESCRIPTION	AMOUNT
36	TOTAL	

TRANSFER LINE 36, COL. 64 TO
THIS MONTH'S COLUMN, LINE 34, PM-115B OR PM-115C

PEGMaster FORM PM-104, HISTACOUNT CORPORATION, MELVILLE, N.Y. 11746

Courtesy of Histacount Corporation Subsidiary of SCM Corporation. Used by permission.

FIGURE 12-8
PEG-MASTER - MONTHLY CONTROL

INDIVIDUAL PAYROLL RECORD   FROM_____19____TO_____19____   FORM PM-106A

NAME					SOC. SEC. NO.			FIXED DEDUCTIONS		
					HOURLY RATE:			F.I.C.A.		
ADDRESS					WEEKLY RATE:			FED. W/H		
					SEX:			STATE W/H		
					MARITAL STATUS:					
EMPLOYED AS			DATE		NO. OF EXEMP.:					
HOME PHONE								TOTAL		

PERIOD ENDING		HOURS WORKED		TOTAL EARNED	PAYROLL DEDUCTIONS						NET PAY
MO.	DAY	REG.	O/T		F.I.C.A.	FEDERAL W/H TAX	STATE W/H TAX				
1ST. MO. TOTALS											
2ND. MO. TOTALS											
3RD. MO. TOTALS											
1ST. QTR. TOTALS											
4TH. MO. TOTALS											
5TH. MO. TOTALS											
6TH. MO. TOTALS											
2ND. QTR. TOTALS											
TOTALS TO DATE											

TRANSFER MONTHLY TOTALS TO CORRESPONDING MONTH ON PAYROLL RECAPITULATION FORM PM-107A

PEGMaster FORM PM-106A, HISTACOUNT CORPORATION, MELVILLE, N.Y. 11746

Courtesy of Histacount Corporation Subsidiary of SCM Corporation. Used by permission.

FIGURE 12-9
PEG-MASTER - INDIVIDUAL PAYROLL RECORD

FORM PM-115A

MISCELLANEOUS ANALYSIS SUMMARY

USE THIS SUMMARY TO ANALYZE COLUMNS 15 THROUGH 24. FORM PM-100. IF NOT SUMMARIZED ON LINES 1 THROUGH 4, FORM PM-115B OR PM-115C.

MONTH	15	16	17	18	19	20	21	22	23	24	TOTALS
JAN											
FEB											
MAR											
APR											
MAY											
JUN											
JUL											
AUG											
SEP											
OCT											
NOV											
DEC											
TOTALS											

FINANCIAL STATEMENT

CURRENT ASSETS:			CURRENT LIABILITIES:		
CASH ON HAND			NOTES PAYABLE		
CASH IN BANKS			ACCOUNTS PAYABLE		
NOTES RECEIVABLE			NOTES RECEIVABLE DISCOUNTED		
ACCOUNTS RECEIVABLE					
INVESTMENT SECURITIES					
CASH VALUE LIFE INSURANCE			FIXED LIABILITIES:		
			MORTGAGES PAYABLE		
FIXED ASSETS:					
TOTAL COST					
LESS DEPRECIATION TO DATE			ACCRUED LIABILITIES:		
			ACCRUED TAXES		
NET VALUE			ACCRUED INTEREST		
PREPAID EXPENSES:					
PREPAID INSURANCE			TOTAL LIABILITIES:		
PREPAID TAXES			NET WORTH:		
OTHER ASSETS:			EXCESS OF ASSETS OVER LIABILITIES		
TOTAL ASSETS:			TOTAL LIABILITIES AND NET WORTH:		

PEGMaster FORM PM-115A, HISTACOUNT CORPORATION, MELVILLE, N.Y. 11746

*Courtesy of Histacount Corporation Subsidiary of
SCM Corporation. Used by permission.*

FIGURE 12-10
PEG-MASTER - MONTHLY AND YEARLY SUMMARY

MONTHLY & YEARLY SUMMARY FORM PM-115C

8 JUNE	9 JULY	10 AUGUST	11 SEPTEMBER	12 OCTOBER	13 NOVEMBER	14 DECEMBER	TOTALS	LINE
								1
								2
								3
								4
								5
								6
								7
								8
								9
								10
								11
								12
								13
								14
								15
								16
								17
								18
								19
								20
								21
								22
								23
								24
								25
								26
								27
								28
								29
								30
								31
								32
								33
								34
								35
								36
								37

NOTES

PEG-Master FORM PM-115C, HISTACOUNT CORPORATION, MELVILLE, N.Y. 11746

FIGURE 12-11
PEG-MASTER - MONTHLY AND YEARLY SUMMARY

PAYROLL RECAPITULATION SHEET FROM __________ 19____ TO __________ 19____ FORM PM-107A

1ST. QUARTER — TAKE FIGURES FROM INDIVIDUAL PAYROLL RECORD, FORM PM-106A

EMPLOYEE'S NAME	TOTAL EARNINGS	F.I.C.A.	FEDERAL W/H TAX	STATE W/H TAX				NET PAY
1ST. MONTH TOTALS								
2ND. MONTH TOTALS								
3RD. MONTH TOTALS								
1ST. QUARTER TOTALS								
TOTALS TO DATE								

2ND. QUARTER — TAKE FIGURES FROM INDIVIDUAL PAYROLL RECORD, FORM PM-106A

4TH. MONTH TOTALS								
5TH. MONTH TOTALS								
6TH. MONTH TOTALS								
2ND. QUARTER TOTALS								
TOTALS TO DATE								

ENTER RECORD OF PAYMENT OF WITHHELD PAYROLL TAXES AND EMPLOYER PAID F.I.C.A. ON FORM PM-107B, OTHER SIDE OF SHEET

MEMOS ______________________________

PEG*Master* FORM PM-107A, HISTACOUNT CORPORATION, MELVILLE, N.Y. 11746

Courtesy of Histacount Corporation Subsidiary of SCM Corporation. Used by permission.

FIGURE 12-12
PEG-MASTER - PAYROLL RECAPITULATION SHEET

ASSET DEPRECIATION RECORD FORM PM 150   SHEET NO.

25 ITEM				29 PURCHASE PRICE			
				30 LOSS OR GAIN ON TRADE IN			
				31 ACTUAL COST			
26 DATE PURCHASED	27 LIFE EXPECTANCY	28 METHOD (CIRCLE) SL = STRAIGHT LINE DB = DECLINING BALANCE SD = SUM OF THE DIGITS 20% = INITIAL 20%		32			
				33 DEPRECIABLE BALANCE			

DEPRECIATION SCHEDULE

NOTES:

INSTRUCTIONS FOR FORM PM-150
AT THE END OF THE YEAR BRING FORWARD INFORMATION FROM ITEMS 25 THROUGH 38 TO IDENTICALLY "KEYED" COLUMNS ON YEARLY DEPRECIATION SUMMARY, FORM PM-115D.

INSTRUCTIONS

25 ITEM – DESCRIBE ITEM WITH SERIAL NUMBERS, ETC.

26 DATE PURCHASED – WRITE DATE OF PURCHASE.

27 LIFE EXPECTANCY – THE SUGGESTED EXPECTED LIFE OF SOME ITEMS, AS LISTED IN INTERNAL REVENUE PUBLICATION "DEPRECIATION GUIDELINES AND RULES" ARE:

   AUTOMOBILE .... 3 YEARS
   INSTRUMENTS .... 5 YEARS
   FURNITURE & EQUIPMENT .... 10 YEARS
   BUILDING .... 45 YEARS

IF YOUR EXPERIENCE ON ANY ITEM DIFFERS FROM THE ABOVE YOU MAY USE YOUR OWN EXPERIENCE TO DETERMINE EXPECTED LIFE. FURTHER INFORMATION IS AVAILABLE FROM INTERNAL REVENUE SERVICE.

28 METHOD – CHOOSE THE DEPRECIATION METHOD MOST ADVANTAGEOUS TO YOU. SEE THE INTERNAL REVENUE CODE TO HELP YOU DETERMINE THIS, OR DISCUSS WITH A TAX CONSULTANT.

29 PURCHASE PRICE – THE SELLER'S PRICE TO YOU.

30 LOSS OR GAIN ON TRADE-IN – LOSS ON TRADE-IN RESULTS WHEN THE TRADE-IN ALLOWANCE IS LESS THAN THE NET VALUE OF THE ITEM TRADED. GAIN ON TRADE-IN RESULTS WHEN THE TRADE-IN ALLOWANCE EXCEEDS THE NET VALUE OF THE ITEM TRADED-IN.

31 ACTUAL COST – ACTUAL COST IS THE PURCHASE PRICE, PLUS ANY DELIVERY AND INSTALLATION COSTS, PLUS ANY LOSS ON TRADE-IN OR MINUS ANY GAIN ON TRADE-IN. ACTUAL COST BECOMES YOUR DEPRECIATION BASE UNLESS A TAX CREDIT IS APPLICABLE.

32 BLANK SPACE. DISREGARD OR USE FOR MISCELLANEOUS ADJUSTMENTS, WHEN APPLICABLE.

33 DEPRECIABLE BALANCE – SAME AS ACTUAL COST.

34 YEAR ENDING DATE – WRITE THE YEAR ENDING DATE.

35 PRIOR DEPRECIATION – EXCEPT FOR THE FIRST ENTRY WHEN THERE IS NO PRIOR DEPRECIATION FIGURE, THE FIGURE IN THIS COLUMN IS THE BALANCE IN COLUMN 37 DEPRECIATION TO DATE.

36 THIS YEARS DEPRECIATION – THE AMOUNT OF YEARLY DEPRECIATION ACCORDING TO THE DEPRECIATE METHOD YOU HAVE CHOSEN.

37 DEPRECIATION TO DATE – ADD THE LAST FIGURES IN COLUMNS 35 AND 36.

38 NET VALUE – LAST YEAR'S BALANCE IN COLUMN 38 MINUS THIS YEAR'S DEPRECIATION FROM COLUMN 36, GIVE YOU THIS YEAR'S CURRENT NET VALUE (VALUE REMAINING AFTER DEPRECIATION TO DATE).

34 YEAR ENDING DATE	35 PRIOR DEPRECIATION	36 THIS YEAR'S DEPRECIATION	37 DEPRECIATION TO DATE	38 NET VALUE

REMARKS: IF THE ITEM IS SOLD (NOT TRADED) FOR MORE THAN ITS NET VALUE (VALUE REMAINING AFTER DEPRECIATION TO DATE) THE RESULT IS A GAIN. DEPRECIATION FOR THE YEAR IN WHICH ITEM IS SOLD IS REDUCED BY THE AMOUNT OF GAIN. SEE INTERNAL REVENUE CODE FOR INSTRUCTIONS. IF IT IS SOLD FOR LESS THAN THE NET VALUE THE RESULT IS A LOSS. THE GAIN OR LOSS IS REPORTED ON YOUR TAX RETURN FOR THE YEAR.

IF THE ITEM ON THIS SHEET IS TRADED IN FOR ANOTHER ITEM THE GAIN OR LOSS ON THE TRADE-IN IS ENTERED ON LINE 30, FORM PM-150 FOR THE NEW ITEM.

NOTE: YOU MAY BE ENTITLED TO AN INVESTMENT CREDIT INCOME TAX ABATEMENT WHICH IS GRANTED TO TAXPAYERS ENGAGED IN BUSINESS OR WHO HOLD PROPERTY FOR THE PRODUCTION OF INCOME. TO DETERMINE IF YOU ARE ELIGIBLE FOR THIS TAX SAVINGS BENEFIT CONTACT THE INTERNAL REVENUE SERVICE OR DISCUSS WITH YOUR TAX CONSULTANT.

PEGMaster FORM PM-150, HISTACOUNT CORPORATION, MELVILLE, N.Y. 11746

Courtesy of Histacount Corporation Subsidiary of SCM Corporation. Used by permission.

FIGURE 12-13
PEG-MASTER - ASSET DEPRECIATION RECORD

KEEPING ACCURATE RECORDS OF PAYMENTS AND CHARGES

Whatever system is adopted, there are certain basic records that must be kept in any office where a fee is charged for professional services rendered. These are:

1. Record of all appointments and cancellations
2. Record of money collected
3. Record of bills paid
4. Record of charges
5. Record of all income
6. Record of all expenses

Each time a patient pays cash a receipt should be given. There are two reasons for this: 1. for the doctor's records and 2. for the patient's records for income tax purposes.

Each time the doctor sees a patient, charges should be entered on the patient's record. (See Figures 12-14A and B.) You should do this at the time the patient comes in or you should set aside a certain time every day for recording charges and payments. The books must be kept up to date at all times. If there is no time to enter charges at the time the patient comes in, it should be noted so that it can be properly recorded on the patient's permanent record later.

You may want to consider asking the doctor to use charge slips. You may find this makes record keeping easier. Charge slips are small forms that can be attached to the patient's chart with the patient's name, date, and a list of treatments that might be performed. The doctor checks the treatment rendered, indicates in space provided at the bottom whether the patient is to be seen again and when. This would provide you with an added record that you could use at the end of the day to double-check your own records, and it also is a good way for the doctor to communicate to you the reason for seeing the patient, any special medication or tests administered, the fee to be charged, and whether the patient is to come in again. (See Figures 12-15 and 12-16.)

Home and hospital calls have to be recorded also. You and the doctor should work out some convenient arrangement whereby the doctor can write down the names of the patients visited and give them to you immediately upon coming into the office. Charge slips might be an efficient means of handling this. You must be careful to form the habit of asking the doctor regularly for the names of the patients called on so that it will become routine for the doctor to report this information to you. If the doctor is very forgetful, try to devise ways of helping him remember. You could include in the medical bag a special sheet or note pad. Make it as convenient as possible to fill in the necessary information.

CASE NO.		PATIENT'S NAME	
ADDRESS		INSURANCE	DATE
TEL. NO.	REFERRED BY	OCCUPATION	AGE _____ SEX _____ S. M. W. D.

FAMILY HISTORY: FATHER _____ MOTHER _____ BROTHERS _____ SISTERS _____

CANCER _____ TUBERCULOSIS _____ INSANITY _____ DIABETES _____ HEART DISEASE _____ RHEUMATISM _____

GOUT _____ GOITER _____ OBESITY _____ NEPHRITIS _____ EPILEPSY _____ OTHER _____

PAST HISTORY: DIPHTHERIA _____ MEASLES _____ MUMPS _____ SCARLET FEVER _____ SMALL POX _____ INFANTILE PARALYSIS _____

TYPHOID _____ PNEUMONIA _____ INFECTIONS _____ GONORRHEA _____ SYPHILIS _____ TONSILLITIS _____ OPERATIONS _____

MENSTRUAL: ONSET _____ PERIODICITY _____ TYPE _____ DURATION _____ PAIN _____ L. M. P. _____

MARITAL: MISCARRIAGES _____ ABORTIONS _____ CHILDREN _____ STERILITY _____

HABITS: ALCOHOL _____ TOBACCO _____ DRUGS _____ COFFEE _____ TEA _____ MEALS _____ WATER _____

SLEEP _____ BOWEL MOVEMENTS _____ EXERCISE _____ AMUSEMENTS _____

PRESENT AILMENT _____

PHYSICAL EXAMINATION: TEMP. _____ PULSE _____ RESP. _____ B. P. _____ HEIGHT _____ WEIGHT _____

SKIN _____ MUCOUS MEMBRANE _____ EYES _____ EARS _____ NOSE _____ MOUTH _____

NECK _____ CHEST _____ LUNGS _____ HEART _____ ABDOMEN _____ RECTUM _____

VAGINA _____ GENITALS _____ EXTREMITIES _____ OTHER _____

LABORATORY FINDINGS: _____

DIAGNOSIS: _____

TREATMENT: _____

REMARKS: _____

HISTACOUNT® GENERAL PRACTICE FORM NO. 1400   HISTACOUNT CORPORATION, MELVILLE, L. I., N. Y.

FIGURE 12-14A
PATIENT PERMANENT RECORD CARD SHOWING SPACE FOR CHARGE AND
CREDIT (FRONT)

DATE			SUBSEQUENT VISITS AND FINDINGS	CHARGE	PAID	BALANCE
MO	DAY	YR				

Courtesy of Histacount Corporation Subsidiary of
SCM Corporation. Used by permission.

FIGURE 12-14B
PATIENT PERMANENT RECORD CARD SHOWING SPACE FOR CHARGE AND
CREDIT (BACK)

ALVIN M. JONES, M. D.
965 WALT WHITMAN ROAD
MELVILLE, N. Y. 11746
HAMILTON 1-1200

№ 0559

DATE_____

PATIENT'S NAME _____

ADDRESS _____

SERVICES RENDERED	FEE	√
CONSULTATION		
X-RAY		
INJECTION		
SURGERY		
DIATHERMY		
LABORATORY		
DRUGS		
TOTAL		

NEXT APPOINTMENT _____

PLEASE LEAVE WITH RECEPTIONIST

FIGURE 12-15
CHARGE SLIP

PLEASE LEAVE WITH RECEPTIONIST

DATE_____

PATIENT'S NAME _____

ADDRESS _____

SERVICES RENDERED	FEE	√
CONSULTATION		
X-RAY		
INJECTION		
SURGERY		
DIATHERMY		
LABORATORY		
DRUGS		
TOTAL		

NEXT APPOINTMENT _____

DATE_____

RECEIVED OF _____ $_____

_____DOLLARS

OFFICE OF _____

SIGNED _____

FORM No. 114   HISTACOUNT CORPORATION, MELVILLE, L. I., N. Y.

FIGURE 12-16
CHARGE SLIP

*Courtesy of Histacount Corporation Subsidiary of
SCM Corporation. Used by permission.*

FINDING THE TIME TO DO THE BOOKKEEPING

Establishing a routine for recording charges and payments assures a more efficient system of record keeping. This is especially important for the doctor's office because things can become very hectic when the office is full of patients. Everyone wants his particular needs met instantly including the doctor. To avoid such interruptions, it is best to set aside a specific time for record-keeping, perhaps in the mornings before the doctor comes into the office, so that the work can be accomplished with more speed and greater accuracy.

PRACTICAL TIPS ON COLLECTING FEES

The task of collecting unpaid bills will likely become a part of your duties. It is often true that people pay their doctor's bill last. Some of the following suggestions will be helpful in speeding up collections.

1. A billing pattern should be established from the very beginning and adhered to with regularity.

2. Any special arrangements about terms of payment should be worked out in advance if at all possible.

3. It is quite helpful to itemize bills. Most people want to know what they are being billed for.

4. Send follow-up bills promptly.

5. The majority of accounts can be collected within 90 days. They should not be allowed to run past this unless special arrangements have been made.

6. Maintain contact with the patient. It is important that the assistant be familiar with the Statute of Limitations governing the state. Every state has laws that declare a bill uncollectible if it is not collected within a certain period of time.

7. Use tactfulness in collecting past-due accounts.

8. Letters are a good means of collecting past-due accounts.

9. A friendly but firm telephone conversation may be a very effective means of collecting an account.

10. Threatening a patient must be avoided.

11. Only when all other methods have been tried should an account be turned over to an attorney or a collection agency and then only after careful consideration. Sometimes it is better to just forget a long over-due account. More money is sometimes spent trying to collect such an account than it is worth. (See Figures 12-17 through 12-21.)

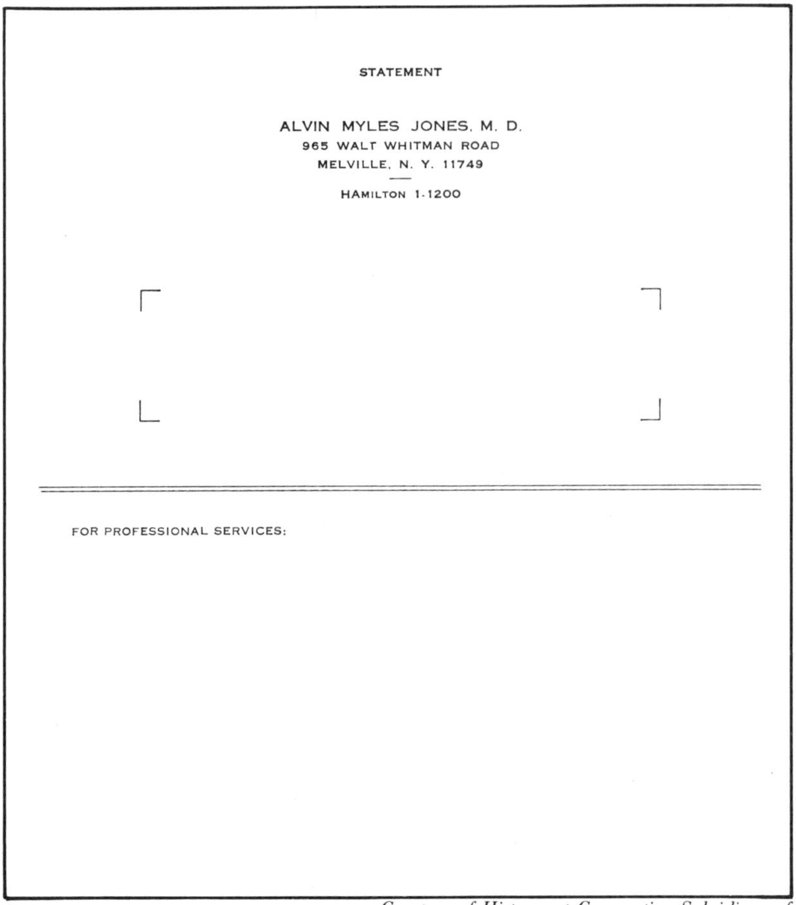

STATEMENT

ALVIN MYLES JONES, M. D.
965 WALT WHITMAN ROAD
MELVILLE, N. Y. 11749

HAMILTON 1-1200

FOR PROFESSIONAL SERVICES:

*Courtesy of Histacount Corporation Subsidiary of
SCM Corporation. Used by permission.*

FIGURE 12-17
STATEMENT FORM - CONTINUOUS

PLANNING IS THE KEY TO MORE EFFICIENT
RECORD KEEPING

Organization and planning are the keys in the efficient operation of the doctor's office. In order to plan the work efficiently, first write down each job that must be done and second, decide the most convenient times for doing the work. Actually make a schedule to follow in the preparing and mailing of the statements. Remember that the schedule can be altered if it does not work out satisfactorily, but the important thing is that once a plan is set up and actually written down, the job is more likely to be completed.

ALVIN MYLES JONES, M. D.
965 WALT WHITMAN ROAD
MELVILLE, N. Y. 11746

HAMILTON 1-1200

DATE	PROFESSIONAL SERVICE	CHARGE	PAID	BALANCE

Pay Last Amount In Balance Column ◀━

OC - OFFICE CALL	HCD - HOUSE CALL DAY	S - SURGERY
HV - HOSPITAL VISIT	HCN - HOUSE CALL NIGHT	BC - BLOOD COUNT
OB - OBSTETRICAL	BMR - BASAL METABOLISM	X - X-RAY
LAB - LABORATORY	EKG - ELECTROCARDIOGRAM	NC - NO CHARGE
INJ - INJECTION	CP - COMPLETE PHYSICAL	EC - ERROR CORRECTION

Courtesy of Histacount Corporation Subsidiary of
SCM Corporation. Used by permission.

FIGURE 12-18
ITEMIZED TRI-STATEMENT FORM NCR
(3 MONTHLY STATEMENTS AND 1 LEDGER CARD)

GUIDELINES FOR USING TIME MORE EFFECTIVELY

Stay on top of the work at all times. Never allow the work to get ahead of you. Working overtime occasionally may pay dividends later.

Emphasis upon keeping accurate records is necessary. Records should be checked and double-checked for correctness. When there are two people

ALVIN MYLES JONES, M. D.
965 WALT WHITMAN ROAD
MELVILLE, N. Y. 11746

HAMILTON 1-1200

DATE	PROFESSIONAL SERVICE	CHARGE	PAID	BALANCE	
					C A S E N O.
					N A M E

Pay Last Amount In Balance Column ◄

OC - OFFICE CALL	HCD - HOUSE CALL DAY	S - SURGERY
HV - HOSPITAL VISIT	HCN - HOUSE CALL NIGHT	BC - BLOOD COUNT
OB - OBSTETRICAL	BMR - BASAL METABOLISM	X - X-RAY
LAB - LABORATORY	EKG - ELECTROCARDIOGRAM	NC - NO CHARGE
INJ - INJECTION	CP - COMPLETE PHYSICAL	EC - ERROR CORRECTION

*Courtesy of Histacount Corporation Subsidiary of
SCM Corporation. Used by permission.*

FIGURE 12-19
STATEMENT FORM FOR PHOTOCOPYING

handling the billing they can check each other's work, but when one person is responsible for all the billing, everything must be double-checked.

Charges and payments must be recorded each day while the information is fresh. Each item must be recorded: the examination, special tests, medication, or x-ray. Here again, the charge slip is a big help and can act as a means of double-checking. Do not allow a day to elapse before recording charges, because the likelihood of an error is increased.

At the end of each day, all charges and payments received are recorded

STATEMENT OF OVERDUE ACCOUNT

_____ _____19

M_____

_____

Your attention is respectfully called to your account which has become overdue. The amount is $_____ and you are requested to send your remittance to cover this amount at the earliest possible moment.

Your promptness will be appreciated.

CC 1

_____

FIGURE 12-20A

REMINDER ON OVERDUE ACCOUNT

_____19

M_____

_____

It has become necessary to remind you again of your account in the amount of $_____which is now very much overdue. Payment in full is desired and will be appreciated. If, however, you cannot send the full amount, you should send at least a partial payment AT ONCE.

CC 2

_____

FIGURE 12-20B

REMINDER ON DELINQUENT ACCOUNT

. _____19

M_____

_____

Your account in the amount of $_____is now LONG PAST DUE and immediate payment is required. Several requests for payment have been made without results. So far the whole matter has been handled in a very lenient way. It is hoped that you will not make other (and vigorous) action necessary by sending a remittance AT ONCE.

CC 3

_____

Courtesy of Histacount Corporation Subsidiary of
SCM Corporation. Used by permission.

FIGURE 12-20C
REMINDER CARDS

LEGAL DEMAND FOR PAYMENT
OF PROFESSIONAL SERVICES RENDERED

_____19

M_____

_____

     In accordance with the laws governing professional services, pay-
ment of your account which is VERY MUCH PAST DUE, in the
amount of $_____is hereby demanded.

     It is imperative that you make IMMEDIATE PAYMENT in
this matter or make suitable arrangements with the undersigned.

cc 4

_____

FIGURE 12-20D

FIVE DAY NOTICE

_____19

M_____

_____

You are hereby notified that M_____
Attorney at Law will be authorized by the undersigned to proceed to
the fullest extent of the law in any way he may deem necessary and
proper to obtain immediate payment of your long past due account
amounting to $_____unless payment, or suitable arrangement
to pay, is made with the undersigned.

cc 5

_____

*Courtesy of Histacount Corporation Subsidiary of
SCM Corporation. Used by permission.*

FIGURE 12-20E
REMINDER CARDS

while still fresh in mind. It is much easier to recall special requests from
patients with regard to billing such as when to send statements, change of
address, or filling out insurance forms.

    Set aside certain time periods to prepare statements for mailing. You may
want to send out the statements on a staggered basis—A-E, the first week of the
month, F-I, the second week, and so on. Or you may prefer to do it all the last
week of the month. Use the system that best suits your schedule.

    At least twice a month, review the patients' accounts to determine the
slow-paying or delinquent accounts. Do not allow more than three months to
elapse without receiving payment or communicating with the patient to
arrange terms of payment. After three-months' time, send some type of

HAmilton 1-1200 ————————————19——

ALVIN M. JONES, M.D.
965 WALT WHITMAN ROAD
MELVILLE, N.Y. 11749

TO _____

_____

_____

PERHAPS YOU FORGOT

If so, please consider this a friendly reminder that your account has become past due. The amount owed is $_____. This envelope is for your convenience. Just insert your check and mail it. Won't you do this now? Thank you.

1C _____

USE THIS ENVELOPE FOR YOUR REMITTANCE

FIGURE 12-21A

HAmilton 1-1200 ————————————19——

ALVIN M. JONES, M.D.
965 WALT WHITMAN ROAD
MELVILLE, N.Y. 11749

TO _____

_____

_____

IS ANYTHING WRONG?

Perhaps there is a good reason why you haven't paid us the $_____, considerably overdue on your account. We try to be understanding and lenient but this requires your cooperation too. Won't you mail this envelope back to us promptly? Thank you.

☐ I am sending full payment in this envelope.
☐ Wish I could pay it all — but the enclosed check is the best I can do right now.
☐ I'll send you a check not later than_____

2 _____

USE THIS ENVELOPE FOR YOUR REMITTANCE

*Courtesy of Histacount Corporation Subsidiary of
SCM Corporation. Used by permission.*

**FIGURE 12-21B
REMINDER ENVELOPES**

HAmilton 1-1200 _____ 19___

ALVIN M. JONES, M. D.
965 WALT WHITMAN ROAD
MELVILLE, N. Y. 11749

TO _____

_____

_____

WON'T YOU COOPERATE?

We've tried hard, in a friendly way, to obtain payment of your long past due account amounting to $_____. We still want to be friendly and we hope you do too. But we must now firmly request prompt payment. This envelope is for your convenience. Please mail it back to us now, with your check enclosed, so that this can be settled just between ourselves. Thank you.

3C

USE THIS ENVELOPE FOR YOUR REMITTANCE

FIGURE 12-21C

HAmilton 1-1200 _____ 19___

ALVIN M. JONES, M. D.
965 WALT WHITMAN ROAD
MELVILLE, N. Y. 11749

TO _____

_____

_____

WE'VE TRIED HARD

We've gone as far as friendly methods will take us to obtain payment of your delinquent account for $_____. You've left us no choice. Unless this account is paid by_____, it will be given to our attorney for collection by whatever means the law provides. Why not avoid this by using this envelope to send us your check. Thank you.

4

USE THIS ENVELOPE FOR YOUR REMITTANCE

Courtesy of Histacount Corporation Subsidiary of SCM Corporation. Used by permission.

FIGURE 12-21D
REMINDER ENVELOPES

HAmilton 1·1200

_____19__

ALVIN M JONES, M D.
965 WALT WHITMAN ROAD
MELVILLE, N Y 11749

TO _____

_____ _____

_____

FIVE DAY NOTICE

You are hereby notified that M _____ ,
Attorney at Law will be authorized by the undersigned to proceed to
the fullest extent of the law in any way he may deem necessary and
proper to obtain immediate payment of your long past due account
amounting to $ _____ unless payment, or suitable arrangement
to pay, is made with the undersigned.

5C

USE THIS ENVELOPE FOR YOUR REMITTANCE

Courtesy of Histacount Corporation Subsidiary of
SCM Corporation. Used by permission.

FIGURE 12-21E
REMINDER ENVELOPE

persuasive letter. This should be continued regularly until payment is received. Should the account remain unpaid after several persuasive letters have been sent, further steps must be taken according to a plan. This will vary with the doctor and with the type of practice. (See Chapter 6.)

Schedule some time each month to update names and addresses if you do not follow the practice of changing addresses immediately when posting a charge or credit. Patients may request that statements be sent to their business address. Honor all such requests without fail, because the patient may want to keep confidential the fact that he is under medical treatment. This is the patient's privilege and right, and you have a responsibility to abide by this preference.

ITEMIZING STATEMENTS IS GOOD HUMAN RELATIONS

Patients prefer itemized statements whenever possible. Generally, people want to know what they are being billed for. This is another reason for maintaining accurate, up-to-date records. Every time a statement is rendered, those items included on the statement should be checked off to eliminate any future duplication in billing.

When statements are carefully rendered, goodwill among patients is enhanced. Patients sense that you and the doctor are interested, and there is the feeling of an effective relationship with the patients. Statements rendered with regularity not only let the patient know that their doctor's office keeps up with each patient, but gives an impression of a well-run office.

GUIDELINES FOR DETERMINING AND QUOTING FEES

A very important part of keeping financial records is the determination and quoting of fees. Who determines fees and who quotes fees? These two questions are very important because so many things hinge upon how they are carried out.

Creating good patient relations pays off in the long run. Ill feelings incurred through error, carelessness, or lack of tact on the part of the medical secretary could be severely damaging to the doctor's practice. The long-range effects of such acts are difficult to predict, but we do know from experience how important it is to handle money matters delicately.

People become excessively wary when their bank accounts are involved. With the rising cost of medical expenses, special care must be exercised in the discussion of financial matters.

A great many complaints are directed against the medical profession today because of high fees. Much of this criticism could be eliminated through careful planning. From the very first visit to the doctor's office, the patient should be informed about what to expect with regard to the fee.

It is generally known that doctors do not like to have anything to do with the handling of the financial arrangements of their patients. For this reason, your effectiveness as the medical secretary will be greatly enhanced if you are able to take a responsible part in quoting and explaining fees. This, however, is determined by your doctor. Usually after you have been on the job for a while and proven your ability, the doctor is only too glad to allow you more and more responsibility in this area if you show yourself willing to accept it. By doing so you will increase your value to your employer.

DETERMINING THE FEE

The fee schedule should be set by the doctor before any discussion with the patient takes place. Of necessity, the secretary and the doctor must discuss in detail every aspect of quoting fees. They must agree on a plan of action in situations where the secretary is required to quote the fee. The lines of authority should be clearly defined for the good of all involved.

Generally, it is up to the doctor to determine the fee, but in certain instances the secretary will probably have to assume a portion of this responsibility. In accepting such responsibility, some freedom should be allowed in the exercise of good judgment.

HELPFUL HINTS ON QUOTING FEES TO PATIENTS

The secretary must first be authorized by the doctor to explain or quote fees. Before any mention is made of charges, put the patient at ease. Establish a good relationship using the following suggestions.

1. Show a genuine interest and concern in the patient.
2. Treat each person the same. Make each feel his importance and worth.
3. People are naturally very concerned about themselves if they are seeing a doctor; therefore, do not *minimize* the patient in any way.

If the patient can be made to see how valuable the doctor's time is, there will be no anxiety about being overcharged. Explain as fully as possible the services that the doctor is rendering so that the patient will have a better understanding of the reasons behind the various charges.

Patients often call the office to inquire about the fee. *Never* quote fees before the patient has been seen by the doctor. Explain very politely and tactfully that until an examination is made, the fee cannot be determined because there may be additional charges for tests, x-rays, or medicine. Most of the time, people just do not stop to think, and once it is explained, they are satisfied.

The ability to negotiate fees successfully with patients is one quality through which the medical secretary can prove to be indispensable to the doctor.

Mrs. Farmer called to make an appointment for her son, Timmy. Dr. Jones has been treating him for a chronic sore throat and had mentioned to her that a tonsillectomy may be necessary if the condition continues. Mrs. Farmer asked how much this would cost. Naturally, you would be unable to quote her a fee until she sees the doctor and it is determined whether or not the tonsillectomy is necessary and whether or not the adenoids are involved. This must be explained to Mrs. Farmer.

KNOWING THE PATIENT'S ABILITY TO PAY

If a patient is concerned about the bill, you will usually know. There are certain questions that can be asked at this point that will give additional clues.

1. Are you covered by medical insurance?

2. If yes, what is the name of the company, type of coverage, and number?

3. Who is responsible for your bills? (Who should be billed?)

By this time, the interview will have taken a definite direction and you can decide the best direction to follow. Other factors influencing the discussion might be: the type of illness, the type of treatment, the time period involved in the treatment, the type of medication (cost), and whether or not hospitalization is required. Arrangements should, as nearly as possible, be suited to the desires of the patient. In some instances, the patient is unable to make a decision because of age or worry. In such cases, the secretary must help make the decisions. This is where experience becomes a valuable part of your training.

ARRANGEMENTS FOR PATIENTS TO PAY FEES

First, find out the patients' wishes. It will not always be possible to meet their exact desires, but usually some mutual agreement can be reached. If the charges are quite high, payments may be extended over several months or longer if need be. This may be the appropriate time to reduce the fee if the secretary sees that the patient is unable to afford the treatment. Never do this without the approval of the doctor. Care should be taken not to exert pressure on the patient. Again, good judgment on the part of the secretary is a key factor.

Some alternative plan should be available if the secretary encounters difficulty in negotiating billing arrangements with a patient. It may be necessary to have the doctor talk with the patient personally. Anxiety brought on by the discussion of finances may hinder the patient's recovery. It is the secretary's responsibility to handle things in a manner that will put the patient at ease.

Discussion of finances may not be pleasant. An open and honest approach is always best. The personality and attitude of the medical secretary are extremely important in dealing with the public. Although knowledge of the subject is important, experience and good judgment are valuable assets.

Chapter 13

Building Human Relations Through a Practical Approach

The importance of human relations in a doctor's office is obvious when we think of the constant personal contact between the medical secretary and patient, doctor and patient, and, of course, between the doctor and the secretary. Actually, the old "bedside manner" of the typical doctor of storybooks was nothing more or less than human relations.

Human relations are simply the ways in which people interact with each other. In the field of human relations, people concentrate on finding better means of getting along with each other both individually and collectively. The study of human relations is based upon the idea that every person has certain needs and that people differ in what they consider to be important. A very basic concept of the study of human relations is that every individual has the right to be treated with dignity and respect.

HOW TO INCREASE YOUR KNOWLEDGE AND UNDERSTANDING

In an ever-changing, fast-moving, competitive society such as ours, the need for building good human relations is increasing in importance. Where there is more competition, there is naturally more pressure put on the secretary and the doctor to be the very best in their field and to make sure that the public knows this. The doctor and his staff must project a good image.

Generally speaking, it is important to remember that every individual has the right to be treated as you would expect to be treated yourself. In short, practice the golden rule: "Do unto others as you would have them do unto you."

The basis of human relations in medicine is the individual relationship between the physician and the patient. The medical secretary plays a major role in establishing a good relationship that will continue as long as the patient is seeing the doctor. This relationship has a definite effect upon the physician's reputation whether it be a small community, large town, or huge city. Although the secretary is not the only one responsible for building good patient relations, it is a vital part of her duties, and having the right personality for the job can be very important.

PROJECT AN ATTITUDE OF CONCERNED GRACIOUSNESS

People generally do not look forward to coming to the doctor's office. They feel sick, they are concerned about their own or a relative's condition, or at the very least they may be a little annoyed at having to give up time to have a routine physical examination. Therefore, the medical secretary is dealing with people who may not be acting the way they do under normal circumstances.

Being able to deal with people in a pleasant, tactful way both face-to-face and over the telephone is a quality which is an absolute necessity for the medical secretary. For example, a patient has been trying to get the doctor on the telephone for hours and because of some mix-up with the answering service, the message did not get to the doctor. A common mistake is that people say "I would be nice to him, but he did not treat me right." After all, it is not the fault of the patient. This is an excellent test of one's ability to practice good human relations.

You as a medical secretary should not be influenced in your responses by the actions of others. In the foregoing example rudeness on the part of a patient requires that you respond with tact and politeness. First, calm the patient and then deal with the patient's attitude by suggesting that perhaps he should be willing to excuse such an error this time. By using a positive approach, the individual will usually respond accordingly.

Being a medical secretary puts a severe strain on the ability to be consistently able to practice good human relations. It may be that today is not your best day, you have a headache, there are some family problems that must be resolved, or you are waiting anxiously for news of the results of your brother's operation. You cannot allow this to influence the way you deal with

Reproduced with permission of A.T.&T. Co.

FIGURE 13-1
MEDICAL SECRETARY TALKING WITH PATIENT -
CALL DIRECTOR TOUCH-TONE PHONE ON DESK

the patients. The important thing to remember in building good human relationships with people is that a person can only direct his or her *own* actions; and in so doing, act in a manner that can reflect only good will for the doctor. (See Figure 13-1.)

TIPS ON HOW TO ACHIEVE GOOD HUMAN RELATIONS

To achieve good human relations, you must treat everyone fairly and equally. An essential part of the doctor-secretary-patient relationship is the patient's desire for continuity in his relationship with his doctor. You play a major role in building and maintaining such an ongoing relationship so that the patient will feel comfortable and accepted.

Coming into a pleasant, cheery office and being greeted by a secretary who shows that she is genuinely interested in the patient can change a person's whole attitude. One way to foster such a relationship is to greet the patients by name and inquire about some event in their lives such as a recent trip or a new grandchild. Always remember to smile warmly and spend a few moments with each patient individually. The time is well spent and will certainly be rewarded. Although this is not possible every time a patient comes into the office, try to make this a regular practice except when you are absolutely swamped with more pressing duties.

TIPS ON GREETING THE PATIENT

A patient needs and desires to feel that the doctor and the medical secretary care about him and his problem. Although it is not your specific duty to show affection to the patients, it is important that you demonstrate a sincere, active, and concerned interest in the patient's well-being. You, as the secretary, can aid the doctor in building this feeling of continuity with patients by reminding the doctor that "Mrs. Jones isn't feeling well today; she seems a bit depressed." Take a few extra minutes to talk with that patient just to let her know you care. In a busy office, with a full schedule ahead, there is always the temptation to cut corners, but what may seem trivial to you may be of major concern to the patient. Exchanging a few words with each patient, giving them a warm smile, a cordial greeting, or saying an unhurried goodbye will go a long way toward improving doctor-patient relations.

TIPS ON DEALING WITH THE UNEXPECTED

You, of course, will have available the telephone number of another physician for referral of patients should the doctor be called away on an emergency or have to be out of town. The patient must always feel confident that he will be able to contact a doctor if the need arises. This is part of the continuity that the patient must feel—that the doctor has a personal interest and that good medical care is of constant concern to the doctors.

It is a part of your responsibility to guard against the possibility of dissatisfaction with any services, fees, or other aspects of medical care that can result in complaints that will undermine the confidence of the public. Even though most complaints are unjustified or stem from misunderstandings, their existence can create serious problems.

It has been said that "foresight is better than hindsight." Much can be learned from the mistakes of others if we will heed their advice. In a sense, this is what education is all about: being forewarned about possible areas that may create problems. There are many areas in the medical office where problems can be avoided or at least minimized by being prepared. Some of these situations are as follows:

SCHEDULING MORE EFFICIENTLY

Discrepancies between the time the patient is told to come in and the time actually seen by the doctor cause a great deal of discontent on the part of the patient. Hurrying to arrive for a 1:15 appointment, then finding out that the doctor is not available and cannot see him until 2:30 will cause the patient to be annoyed and upset. There is generally no need to have these long waits if a little time and foresight are put into the setting up of appointment schedules. Most people are very understanding about emergency situations which delay appointments, but when the doctor makes a practice of being late, the feeling may be that he is not organized well enough or concerned enough about his patients to arrange his time properly. The fact that a doctor's waiting room is very busy does not by itself make the patient feel that he is going to be a good doctor.

MAXIMIZING TELEPHONE EFFECTIVENESS

Another area that can cause strain is when the doctor receives a telephone call during office hours. Sometimes it is very difficult for the doctor to take

Reproduced with permission of A.T.&T. Co.

FIGURE 13-2
MEDICAL SECRETARY ON TELEPHONE

these calls and it is important for the medical secretary to tactfully be able to get the patient to agree to having the doctor call back. Not being able to speak to the doctor is always difficult for a patient to understand, but if the proper rapport has been built up and the patient believes that the medical secretary is caring and interested, then the feeling of strain will be minimized. (See Figure 13-2.)

DISCUSSING FEES

The amount of the fee often causes difficulties in the relationship between doctor and patient. A patient often feels that the doctor is charging too much for what he feels is not enough service, so it is important that the doctor explain the fees to the patients. The medical secretary does not take this responsibility unless specifically instructed by the doctor. Doctors keep available a list of standard fees that you, as the secretary, consult upon request of a patient. This is usually sufficient explanation for minor charges such as injections or office visits. When the charge covers a more involved treatment, the doctor should explain it personally to the patient.

In the same general area are the monthly statements. People often forget what charges they had during the month, so an important safeguard against misunderstanding is to itemize end-of-month statements.

As a medical secretary, you should be constantly aware of the patient's desires, putting yourself in the patient's place, and treating the patient as you would want to be treated yourself. All of us want to be treated fairly and courteously, and if this is done consistently, the results will be shown in excellent human relations.

Human relations cannot be taught as stenography, typewriting, and bookkeeping are taught. It is the total of daily relationships with other people. Be careful not to prejudge people. Put your own feelings aside; think of the patient's concerns; a word of understanding, a smile when greeting and saying good-by, and better human relations will result.

Chapter 14

Outlining Your Legal and Ethical Responsibilities

Webster defines ethics as "the science of ideal human character." Medical ethics is the practice of ideal behavior on the part of those in that profession. Through the years the standards of the medical profession have been maintained on a very high level. From as far back as Greek times the medical profession has had a code of ethics based on the Oath of Hippocrates, which is largely concerned with the welfare of the patient. The American Medical Association has arrived at its own code of ethics based upon the Hippocratic Oath. The chief purpose of the American Medical Association's *Principles of Medical Ethics* is to keep the conduct of the members of the medical profession on a high level at all times.

You as a medical secretary should be familiar with the Oath of Hippocrates and the medical code of ethics. These will give you a general picture of the scope of the doctor's responsibility to his patients which in turn becomes your responsibility, too. Your conduct is governed by the same principles as those that guide the doctor. (See Figures 14-1 and 14-2.)

GUIDELINES FOR THE SECRETARY'S ETHICAL RESPONSIBILITIES

Even though you are guided by the same principles as the doctor, there are

The Oath of Hippocrates

You do solemnly swear by whatever each of you holds most sacred

That you will be loyal to the Profession of Medicine & just & generous to its members

That you will lead your lives & practice your art in uprightness & honor

That into whatsoever house you shall enter, it shall be for the good of the sick to the utmost of your power, your holding yourselves far aloof from wrong, from corruption, from the tempting of others to vice

That you will exercise your art solely for the cure of your patients & will give no drug, perform no operation, for a criminal purpose, even if solicited, far less suggest it

That whatsoever you shall see or hear of the lives of your patients which is not fitting to be spoken, you will keep inviolably secret.

These things do you swear. Let each of you bow the head in sign of acquiescence

And now, if you will be true to this, your oath, may prosperity & good repute be ever yours; the opposite, if you shall prove yourselves forsworn.

FIGURE 14-1
HIPPOCRATIC OATH

Principles of
Medical
Ethics

AMERICAN MEDICAL ASSOCIATION

Preamble These principles are intended to aid physicians individually and collectively in maintaining a high level of ethical conduct. They are not laws but standards by which a physician may determine the propriety of his conduct in his relationship with patients, with colleagues, with members of allied professions, and with the public.

Section 1 The principal objective of the medical profession is to render service to humanity with full respect for the dignity of man. Physicians should merit the confidence of patients entrusted to their care, rendering to each a full measure of service and devotion.

Section 2 Physicians should strive continually to improve medical knowledge and skill, and should make available to their patients and colleagues the benefits of their professional attainments.

Section 3 A physician should practice a method of healing founded on a scientific basis; and he should not voluntarily associate professionally with anyone who violates this principle.

Section 4 The medical profession should safeguard the public and itself against physicians deficient in moral character or professional competence. Physicians should observe all laws, uphold the dignity and honor of the profession and accept its self-imposed disciplines. They should expose, without hesitation, illegal or unethical conduct of fellow members of the profession.

Section 5 A physician may choose whom he will serve. In an emergency, however, he should render service to the best of his ability. Having undertaken the care of a patient, he may not neglect him; and unless he has been discharged he may discontinue his services only after giving adequate notice. He should not solicit patients.

Section 6 A physician should not dispose of his services under terms or conditions which tend to interfere with or impair the free and complete exercise of his medical judgment and skill or tend to cause a deterioration of the quality of medical care.

Section 7 In the practice of medicine a physician should limit the source of his professional income to medical services actually rendered by him, or under his supervision, to his patients. His fee should be commensurate with the services rendered and the patient's ability to pay. He should neither pay nor receive a commission for referral of patients. Drugs, remedies or appliances may be dispensed or supplied by the physician provided it is in the best interests of the patient.

Section 8 A physician should seek consultation upon request; in doubtful or difficult cases; or whenever it appears that the quality of medical service may be enhanced thereby.

Section 9 A physician may not reveal the confidences entrusted to him in the course of medical attendance, or the deficiencies he may observe in the character of patients, unless he is required to do so by law or unless it becomes necessary in order to protect the welfare of the individual or of the community.

Section 10 The honored ideals of the medical profession imply that the responsibilities of the physician extend not only to the individual, but also to society where these responsibilities deserve his interest and participation in activities which have the purpose of improving both the health and the well-being of the individual and the community.

Reprinted with permission from the American Medical Association.

FIGURE 14-2
MEDICAL CODE OF ETHICS

specific duties and responsibilities that the doctor outlines. There are certain things that you *never* undertake unless your employer instructs you.

Never diagnose or prescribe to a patient. Always refer the patient to the doctor for answers to medical questions, no matter how trivial. Many times you may know the answers but it is *not* your place to become involved in any medical question unless particularly instructed by the doctor.

You must be very careful in what you say and do, never forgetting that you act for your employer—whatever you say reflects back on the doctor. The position of a medical secretary assumes that you are prepared to accept a certain amount of responsibility. If you are a newcomer to the field, it is very important that ethical conduct is clearly understood.

HOW TO MAINTAIN PROFESSIONAL CONFIDENTIALITY

The key word describing the secretary's policy toward discussing work outside the office is "confidential." Everything that occurs in the office is necessarily confidential because people regard their relationship with their doctor as extremely personal. Your role as secretary is always to maintain strict control over what you say about your job to those outside the office. Even when tempted to discuss your work with your family, you must resist the urge. The rule of secrecy applies equally when talking with patients and their families. Patients will often try to obtain further information from you. Constantly be on the alert because it is easy to let some small bit of information out that the doctor did not want the patient to know or something that could be misconstrued as advice or instruction. Never give out advice or instruction unless specifically instructed by the doctor. The best policy for an assistant is to suggest that "the doctor will be glad to answer that question or discuss this with you," and then steer the conversation to a safe topic such as the weather or a coming vacation.

Develop skill and tact in talking with the doctor's patients. Never be surprised by any question that may arise and don't be thrown off your guard. Situations constantly arise to challenge your ability to handle people. The idea is to keep them happy without divulging confidential information. This may be very difficult at times but you will find that as you become more accustomed to your job and your patients you will develop little techniques that are helpful.

Keep papers away from prying eyes. If your desk is in a place where patients can see it easily, do not leave medical records lying out. Have a place to keep those being used out of sight. People are naturally curious and can't help looking if the opportunity presents itself.

The degree of tact and diplomacy needed often depends on your doctor's practice. More tact and diplomacy is required of the secretary of a psychiatrist or a doctor who specializes in venereal diseases. Very often the patients are sensitive about anyone knowing that they are seeing such a doctor. Under such circumstances you are called upon to develop an even stricter sense of what is confidential.

Under the law, doctors must have a *written* release from the patient to forward information. Guarding confidential information concerning the doctor's practice and patients is one of the most important responsibilities you as a medical secretary have. (See Figure 14-3.)

RECORDS RELEASE AUTHORIZATION

TO_____
DOCTOR OR HOSPITAL

_____
ADDRESS

I HEREBY AUTHORIZE AND REQUEST YOU TO RELEASE TO:

ALVIN   MYLES   JONES,   M. D.
965 WALT WHITMAN ROAD
MELVILLE, N. Y. 11749
—
HAMILTON 1-1200

THE COMPLETE MEDICAL RECORDS IN YOUR POSSESSION, CONCERNING MY ILLNESS

AND/OR TREATMENT DURING THE PERIOD FROM_____TO_____

NAME_____DATE_____

ADDRESS_____

SIGNATURE_____WITNESS_____
(IF RELATIVE, STATE RELATIONSHIP)

Courtesy of Histacount Corporation Subsidiary of
SCM Corporation. Used by permission.

FIGURE 14-3
RECORDS RELEASE AUTHORIZATION

MAINTAINING PROFESSIONAL COURTESY

Usually doctors do not charge other doctors or their families. Check with your doctor about his particular policy on this. Doctors and their families are also often given preferential treatment when making appointments. This, also, is up to the preference of the individual doctor.

TIPS ON KEEPING UP WITH THE DOCTOR'S LEGAL RESPONSIBILITIES

Since the doctor has legal responsibilities to the patients, you should also be aware of what they are. The guidelines are provided by the Medical Practice Act of the state in which the doctor practices. This act gives the limitations that govern the doctor's practice and the penalties for not complying with these rules. Most physicians are alert to avoid any conflict with the law so as to rule out the possibility of court proceedings which would be costly and time-consuming. A medical secretary assumes the same responsibility as the doctor in adhering to the Medical Practice Act.

The relationship among the doctor, patient, and secretary is one of complete honesty and confidence. You and the doctor try to put the patient at ease so that there will be easy and full communication about the symptoms and illness. This atmosphere of confidence is very reassuring to the patient. In creating such an atmosphere, you should not become overconfident and fail to take the necessary legal precautions to prevent any possibility of allowing a situation to arise whereby the patient will have cause to sue the doctor. It is the duty of the doctor to inform the patient of the diagnosis and the treatment. You as the secretary are never responsible for communicating information about a case to the patient unless specifically authorized by the doctor. You perform a duty that comes under the general classification of a medical secretary's duties. If you stay within these bounds, you will be doing what is expected of you.

Generally speaking, if the doctor, aided by a conscientious secretary, adheres to the laws of the state and the guidelines of the American Medical Association, there will be no danger of suit by a patient. Unfortunately, there are always exceptions to the rule. Some people actually look for an excuse to sue someone and will grasp at the slightest sign of laxity on the part of the doctor or the secretary. That is why the doctor is constantly on the alert to guard against any possibility of becoming involved in a suit resulting from a charge of malpractice, negligence, or lack of consent.

KEY TO PROTECTING THE DOCTOR FROM MALPRACTICE PROCEEDINGS

Malpractice is defined by *Black's Law Dictionary* as "a failure on the part of the physician to properly perform the duties which devolve upon him in his professional relationship to his patient; failure which results in some injury to the patient."

Recently there has been a rise in the number of malpractice suits. The doctor is, therefore, doubly careful in performing any treatment that involves risk of injury to the patient. This puts an equal amount of pressure on you as the assistant to be constantly alert to perform all the duties carefully and along certain set guidelines to avoid even the very appearance of neglect.

Malpractice suits usually are the result of negligence, failure to fulfill the contract, incompetence, and use of treatment not yet proven for use. Any careless act on the part of the doctor or an assistant that can be construed as incompetence or neglect should be carefully guarded against. A secretary who shows good judgment and skill in handling people will be able to help protect the doctor against involvement in malpractice suits.

Most doctors carry malpractice insurance. It has become a necessity. It is a secretary's duty to see that premiums are paid on time.

INFORMED CONSENT

If an operation, certain x-ray examinations, or special treatment is to be performed, written consent from the patient is required. The doctor carefully explains about the operation, x-rays, or treatment indicating any complications or side effects that may occur. If the patient for some reason is unable to sign the form, only an authorized person can sign for the patient. The doctor will have consent forms that you will prepare. (See Figure 14-4.) It is important that they be kept on hand at all times and not forgotten when the need arises.

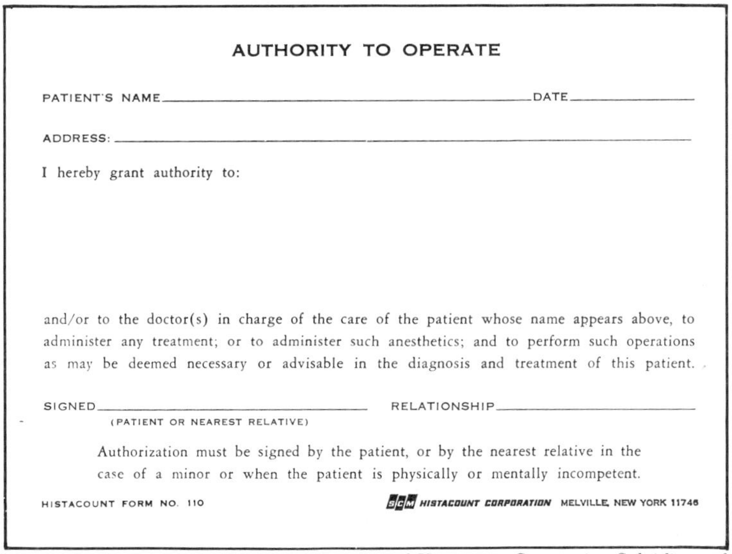

AUTHORITY TO OPERATE

PATIENT'S NAME_____DATE_____

ADDRESS: _____

I hereby grant authority to:

and/or to the doctor(s) in charge of the care of the patient whose name appears above, to administer any treatment; or to administer such anesthetics; and to perform such operations as may be deemed necessary or advisable in the diagnosis and treatment of this patient.

SIGNED_____ RELATIONSHIP_____
    (PATIENT OR NEAREST RELATIVE)

Authorization must be signed by the patient, or by the nearest relative in the case of a minor or when the patient is physically or mentally incompetent.

HISTACOUNT FORM NO. 110   *SCM* HISTACOUNT CORPORATION MELVILLE, NEW YORK 11746

Courtesy of Histacount Corporation Subsidiary of SCM Corporation. Used by permission.

FIGURE 14-4
AUTHORITY TO OPERATE

HOW THE LAW AFFECTS THE MEDICAL SECRETARY

Generally speaking, the doctor is responsible for all actions of the secretary. It is the doctor's responsibility to set up guidelines for the secretary to follow. The duties include reporting to the proper authorities births, deaths, and contagious diseases. Death resulting from violence or unexplained causes should be reported to the coroner or medical examiner. The assistant should find out what reports to file and obtain forms by contacting the police and the local health department.

Certain drugs are governed by federal legislation. The doctor is required to keep up with the law regarding these drugs. You as the secretary are required to follow the doctor's policies in such matters.

Legal and ethical responsibilities of the physician must naturally be important considerations of a medical secretary. You share in this responsibility to abide by the same laws and principles of ethical conduct governing the doctor's practice. Without your help, the doctor will be handicapped in adhering to these laws and principles. Whenever in doubt about what action to take, you should always ask rather than risk making a serious error.

The laws that govern medical practice and the code of ethics emphasize the highest ideals possible. You as the secretary should try to follow these ideals to the best of your ability and in so doing will help your employer. If you sincerely try to uphold the high principles that govern the medical profession, then problems that might arise will be minimized or even eliminated. The greatest asset that a medical secretary can bring to the job is a willingness to learn and to abide by the doctor's wishes.

Chapter 15

Checklist of Key Factors

There are few jobs where one's duties are as diversified as the medical office assistant. You are the receptionist, secretary, bookkeeper, insurance clerk, mediator, and doctor's assistant. Being the doctor's assistant may add several more duties such as assisting the doctor with patients in whatever capacity is required whether it be draping a patient or assisting with minor surgery.

ORGANIZATION IS THE KEY TO EFFICIENCY

Know-how in efficiently scheduling appointments is extremely important to the smooth running of a doctor's office. Everything revolves around the coming and going of the patients. It is necessary to have a clear picture of the way the doctor wants the office run. You and the doctor need to discuss his preferences very carefully.

You have the responsibility of organizing the schedule so that each patient has enough time, but not too much. Patients should come and go without confusion. Disruptions should be kept to a minimum. Part of the art of scheduling is being thoroughly familiar with the doctor's routine and getting to know the patients so well that any variation in the schedule will not disrupt the smooth running of the office.

Seeing that the reception room, doctor's office, and examining rooms are ready at the beginning of each day must become an automatic part of your duties. Even though you do no cleaning, you still have the last inspection before admitting patients. The doctor depends upon you to take care of these routine duties. It is important that the doctor is confident that you can be relied upon to do these things without supervision.

There is a great deal of paper work connected with the efficient operation of the doctor's office. In the last few years, it has grown and now consumes a great deal of the secretary's time. Just having the charts and patients' records ready each day is important. The charts should be in order according to the appointment schedule. A list of patients should be prepared for the doctor early in the morning or at the end of the day in readiness for the next day so that at a glance it can be seen who is due in the office. The doctor needs to feel prepared for the day ahead to aid in the smooth flow of patients. Even though emergencies will occur, they can be handled with a minimum of confusion if the office is already functioning smoothly.

Insurance forms should be in readiness—partially filled in if necessary. In some cases, the patients furnish their own forms. They should be informed by you as the secretary what information is expected of them regarding the filling out of the insurance forms and payment of bills.

You should be ready with the appointment book to schedule future visits. When it is possible to anticipate that the doctor will want to see that patient again, it will certainly speed up things to have the appointment book ready along with an appointment card for the patient.

Anticipating the patient's movements from arrival in examining room to dismissal by the doctor can greatly speed things up. Having everything possible in readiness for the patients and the doctor will always make for more efficient operation of the office.

EFFECTIVE COMMUNICATION IS VITAL

The telephone demands a great deal of the secretary's time. You must thoroughly familiarize yourself with the patients' names and something about each one so that you will feel prepared to answer questions quickly, tactfully, and without losing time in having to ask the doctor about everything.

Skill in handling patients in the office is an important aspect of your responsibilities. You are constantly in contact with the patients as they arrive and while they are waiting to see the doctor. They will have many questions and you must be able to talk with them courteously in an unhurried manner, yet without devoting too much time, because every minute counts in a busy office.

The doctor's friends and professional associates will be calling or contacting him—other doctors, businessmen, and acquaintances. It would be wise to keep a list of the people with whom the doctor would want to speak without delay. Find out what the preference is regarding them.

Salesmen and drug detail men will be constantly calling on the doctor. There are certain ones who will be seen, but obviously, not all can be seen. Find out which ones the doctor wants to see and what to tell the ones that cannot be seen. It is very important to be tactful, especially to those whom the doctor cannot see. Arrange with the doctor when it is convenient to see them— perhaps a few minutes could be set aside on a certain day each week.

Coordinating the doctor's day so that as many people as possible can be seen requires a great deal of cooperation between the doctor and you, the secretary. Although it can become complicated, with foresight and discussion with the doctor, the day's activities can be managed quite smoothly.

BECOME A BETTER OFFICE MANAGER

The degree to which you actually manage the office depends upon several things: the size of the office, the type of office, the number of nurses and other medical secretaries working.

Allowing time to prepare for each day is very important to the efficient operation of the office. Preparation for each day's activities should be planned. All the paper work for that day should be in readiness. Leftover work from the previous day should be completed. Keeping things up-to-date is important. There may be a certain time each day before the doctor comes in that the secretary can plan the day's work and also prepare the necessary paper work. If several office employees are involved, it may become your responsibility to delegate tasks and coordinate various jobs. The major task involved in planning the day's schedule may include: scheduling days off or vacations, keeping tabs on the custodial staff, keeping up with supplies and drugs, bookkeeping duties, filling out health insurance forms, dealing with delinquent accounts, and maintaining patients' charts. Acceptance of these responsibilities is a gradual process that grows with the job. As you gain experience in the office, you see things that must be done and organize the work accordingly. There is a great deal to be done, but learning about the various tasks is just part of learning the job.

Whatever the task or duty though, the medical secretary must exercise skill in dealing with people. You must show good judgment and maturity in handling difficult situations. Realize that every situation and every individual is different.

EVALUATE YOUR PERSONAL QUALITIES

Take stock of your own personality, skills, and interests. Do you possess those personal qualities needed by a top-notch medical secretary? Practicing good human relations, flexibility, willingness to accept responsibility, and being a self-starter are necessary characteristics. To help you evaluate yourself, make a personal evaluation checklist including such items as:

Do I show:
    Cheerfulness
    Tactfulness
    Courtesy
    Calmness
    Patience
    Sympathy
    Cooperation
    Consideration

Am I:
    Dependable
    Punctual
    Responsible

Is my work:
    Accurate
    Neat
    Efficient
    Thorough

How do I rate on:
    Initiative
    Motivation
    Organization
    Efficiency

Am I:
    Well-groomed
    Appropriately dressed

UPDATE YOUR KNOWLEDGE OF MEDICAL SPECIALTIES

Medicine has become highly specialized, and although we still have the general practitioner, many medical secretaries are working with a specialist or are involved in a specialized field of medicine. The secretary is not expected to be an expert on all the medical specialties, but should be able to intelligently assist the doctor. This necessitates a recognition of specialized terminology when taking instructions from the doctor, transcribing dictation, making referrals to other doctors, and answering the telephone.

There are approximately twenty major areas of specialization in the medical profession today that are recognized by the American Medical Association.

EXPAND YOUR MEDICAL VOCABULARY

A basic knowledge of medical terminology which includes definitions of the various medical specialties is necessary for the medical secretary, but it would be impractical to try to learn and remember all the terminology connected with all the different specialties. It is wiser to keep a medical dictionary close at hand and be continually aware of the type of terminology used by the doctor. Listen for often repeated words and phrases and keep a list in a stenography pad. The words will soon become an automatic part of your vocabulary without your realizing it.

You may write to the particular society that relates to the doctor's specialty or in which you have an interest for further information. Most doctors have reference material available to which you can refer. Do not forget that public, college, and hospital libraries are excellent sources of information. Also, the doctor himself will help you obtain information.

There are numerous medical specialties and the list continues to grow. Some of the major fields are mentioned here but the medical secretary must continue to keep up-to-date because with all the advancement in medicine, new specialties continually appear or old ones undergo changes.

The following is a list of many of the major medical specialties:

Anesthesiology	administration of anesthesia during surgery or diagnosis.
Dermatology	diagnosis and treatment of diseases of the skin.
Cardiology	study and treatment of heart and the cardiovascular system and its diseases.
Dentistry	care of the teeth and related problems.
Endocrinology	study and treatment of the glands of internal secretion.
Family Practice	treatment and care of a patient's or family's overall medical needs or prescribing other health care needed.
Geriatrics	treatment and care of people advanced in years.
Internal Medicine	deals with diagnosis and treatment of diseases of the internal organs such as

the heart and lungs. Or, for example, an internist might specialize in the treatment of a particular disease such as diabetes.

Neurology	diagnosis and treatment of diseases of the brain, spinal cord, and nervous system.
Nuclear Medicine	treatment of cancer, and other diseases, with radioactive isotopes.
Obstetrics and Gynecology	treatment of diseases of the female reproductive organs and the care and treatment of women during and immediately following pregnancy.
Oncology	treatment of tumors.
Ophthalmology	care and treatment of the eyes, including surgery.
Orthopedic Surgery	treatment, including surgery, of diseases, fractures, and deformities of the bones and joints.
Otolaryngology	treatment of diseases of the ear, nose, and throat.
Orthodontics	specialized branch of dentistry dealing with the straightening of the teeth.
Pathology	study of changes in the body organs, tissues, and cells as a result of disease.
Proctology	diagnosis and treatment of diseases of the anus, rectum, and colon.
Pediatrics	diagnosis and treatment of children's diseases.
Physical Medicine and Rehabilitation (Physiatrics)	diagnosis and treatment of diseases by physical therapy. It is sometimes used in treating the convalescent and physically handicapped.
Plastic Surgery	corrective surgery to restore and repair mutilated or deformed parts of the body. It is also used to change or improve one's appearance.
Preventive Medicine	deals with the prevention of diseases and improvement of health through

	the study of epidemiology and through public health.
Psychiatry and Neurology	diagnosis and treatment of mental disorders and diseases. The physical disorders may be due to organic injury, disease, or infection.
Radiology	diagnosis and treatment of disease by radioactive substances. These may include x-rays, radium, and cobalt.
Surgery	diagnosis and treatment by operative means of physical disorders caused by diseases, injury, or deformity. A surgeon may be either a general surgeon performing all types of operations or he may choose to specialize in a particular branch.
Thoracic Surgery	diagnosis and operative treatment of diseases of the chest. This involves the heart and lungs. This is an example of a specialized type of surgery.
Urology	diagnosis and treatment of diseases and disorders of the bladder, kidneys, ureters, urethra, and the male reproductive organs.

These definitions are brief, but the secretary can easily find more detailed information. Remember the need to have a good medical dictionary and to be continually aware of the type of terminology used by the doctor.

The doctor's vocabulary may include such specialized terms as "diplomates" (a physican who has received a diploma of the American Specialty Boards) or "fellows" (a doctor who is qualified in a particular medical specialty; i.e., he is a "fellow" in the American College of Physicians). Another example would be the use of the abbreviation of F.A.C.C. meaning a Fellow of the American College of Cardiology.

There is plenty of material available for the medical office assistant explaining the many branches of medicine. Most of the medical secretarial handbooks give a brief description of the major areas of specialization. There is also a booklet published by the American Medical Association entitled *Horizons Unlimited* which gives, in capsule form, information about various specialties and the addresses of societies to which one can write.

LOOKING TO THE FUTURE

Opportunity for employment in the health field is wide and varied. It is growing rapidly due to the advances in medicine and growth in better health care facilities everywhere. Medicare and health insurance benefits through employers have added to this awareness.

If you are not satisfied in your present position, look around and explore all the possibilities in the medical field that would be open to someone with your skills and knowledge. You will be surprised at the variety of jobs that are closely allied to medicine and health care.

The American Medical Association is an excellent source of information on careers in medicine and allied health fields. Another good source would be the American Association of Medical Assistants. These organizations publish up-to-date materials that give a broad view of what is available.

For instance, you normally think of a medical secretary as working in a doctor's office for one or two doctors. As you become more involved in your career, you begin to realize that medicine is closely allied to many areas both public and private. Public health facilities such as clinics and hospitals all need office workers. These facilities vary in size as to number of staff and office personnel needed. Size of the office or organization is one important factor that you will want to consider before making a decision.

People have various reasons for choosing a position. Some want to work close to their homes because of their children and families. Others want to be able to drive to work because the thought of commuting is distasteful. These people might choose a local one-doctor's office or a nearby hospital.

On the other hand, one who is looking for something different, perhaps in a larger medical facility with better pay, should look to the cities for more demanding and challenging work—for example, a secretarial position in a large medical center or health insurance company.

Other possibilities could be in a medical school, working for a doctor or doctors in a medical research institute. If there is a particular area of medicine in which you are interested, you should seek employment with a specialist— such as nuclear medicine, speech and hearing, or neurology.

You may not be interested in working in a doctor's office, but there are other possibilities such as a large airline that has its own medical department where doctors care for the employees. There would be additional benefits working for an airline such as flying privileges.

Perhaps you could work for the various government health offices such as national, state, or local—for instance, the World Health Organization, that is international in scope.

Animal lovers consider a veterinary—or animal hospital; people interested in scientific things look for opportunities with organizations which do research in such areas as environmental health, ecology, and engineering that is allied with medicine. Tropical diseases comprise another area where much research is being conducted.

Some people might have a feel for a particular career but do not know enough about it. Social workers require office assistants in rehabilitation centers. Perhaps your interest in medicine is very general. Medical organizations such as AMA or nursing associations require office staff.

Perhaps you are interested in part-time employment. Many doctors and hospitals want someone who can do part-time typing or medical transcribing either at home or in an office. Some companies furnish medical transcribers with typewriters and transcribing machines to be used at home.

Read newspaper ads to see what jobs are available. Follow through on some of the ads with a phone call. Even if the job is not exactly what you are looking for, it will give you some ideas about salary, type of work, and fringe benefits that you might expect. (See Figure 15-1.)

Medical Secretary/Receptionist

Busy, multi-staffed specialist's office, knowledge of medical terminology, typing, dictaphone, handle busy phone, process insurance forms, willing to train. Good salary.
Call 765-2245

FIGURE 15-1
WANT AD

Discuss the situation with friends who are employed in the medical field. Just by talking casually you can learn and broaden your knowledge about what employment opportunities are like and what you can look for when you are actually making a change in jobs. Any fears you may have because you lack self-confidence will begin to diminish. Give some thought to moving up the career ladder.

GROWING PROFESSIONALLY

Learning, growing, and developing on the job are important to your overall enjoyment of your work. Some people consider their jobs as "work," while others look forward to going to their jobs. They like what they do, because it is a meaningful and rewarding experience.

What can you, the medical secretary, do to make your job one that is more than "just a job"?

Learn all you can about your job. Enter into it with the attitude that you are going to like it. Be open to every possible way of adding to your knowledge and skills. Even though you may have specialized or college training, there is always more to learn.

Listen to your boss and try to be sensitive to particular needs and preferences. Talk with other medical secretaries. The mutual discussion can often provide answers to what may have seemed to be an impossible situation. Through this sharing with others of similar experiences, you are able to learn and develop much more rapidly.

How do you find those who have similar interests and are doing the same type of work? There are national professional organizations with local chapters all over the country. These organizations provide the opportunity to meet with others who are doing the same or similar type work as you. Regular meetings are held, usually monthly. Officers are elected by the group to lead, plan, and direct the activities of the organization. Although each local organization is free to plan and organize its own activities, it does have some guidelines from the national headquarters to follow such as paying dues, conducting a certain number of meetings a year, and planning programs.

Organizations of this type are beneficial in many ways. You begin to think of yourself as a professional. You enjoy meeting and discussing your work in a relaxed and casual setting. Besides providing an opportunity for professional growth, the organization furnishes a social outlet.

Activities are planned for the regular meetings. Programs may consist of guest lecturers, visits to offices, films, panel discussions, and meetings with nearby chapters of the organization. Social activities such as trips, dinners and parties, or bowling leagues are scheduled. The activities, of course, are determined by the members.

For the medical secretary, there is the American Association of Medical Assistants. This professional group has its national headquarters in Chicago. It is fully supported by the American Medical Association which has a Physician-Advisory Board to the AAMA and also a special liaison representative from the AMA Board of Trustees.

The AAMA was originally established to encourage the education and the opportunities for further training for the medical office assistant. In addition, it provides the assistant with more of a professional attitude toward medical assisting careers.

To become a member, locate the chapter nearest you. If you are unable to find one, write to the national office at:

American Association of Medical Assistants
One East Wacker Drive
Chicago, IL 60601

They will gladly send you information about joining and where to find the chapter nearest you.

CERTIFYING EXAMINATION

The AAMA encourages its members to improve themselves through further study and training by offering the assistants an opportunity to take a qualifying examination giving them the title of Certified Medical Assistant.

The purpose of the certification examination is to establish professional standards and goals for medical assistants and to help doctors identify those who are well qualified. The examination qualifies you to become a Certified Medical Assistant—Clinical or a Certified Medical Assistant—Administrative; or, you can take the entire examination consisting of four divisions—general, administrative, clinical and pediatric—and become a Certified Medical Assistant. (See Figure 15-2.)

In order to qualify for the examination, you must meet certain education and/or experience requirements. Membership in the AAMA is not a requirement for taking the certifying examination. There are application fees and fees for taking the examination depending upon which sections you take. Members of AAMA get a reduced rate. To obtain current information on eligibility requirements and fees, contact:

American Association of Medical Assistants
One East Wacker Drive, Suite 2110
Chicago, IL 60601

There are other organizations for secretaries or office assistants. The National Secretaries Association (International) is open to all secretaries regardless of specialty. Like the AAMA, it promotes professionalism among its members, offers opportunity for further training and study, and opportunity to meet people socially.

The National Secretaries Association also offers secretaries an opportunity to take a qualifying examination that would give them the title of CPS—Certified Professional Secretary. To find out more about the organization and the certifying examination, write to:

Institute for Certifying Secretaries
2440 Pershing Road
Suite G 10 Crown Center
Kansas City, MO 64108

Some other professional organizations are:

The Certifying Board
of the
American Association of Medical Assistants, Inc.
created in 1962 for the certification of medical assistants,
hereby certifies that

has met certain standards and qualifications, has passed the examination prepared and administered under the authority of the Certifying Board, and has been found to be fully qualified

as a

CERTIFIED MEDICAL ASSISTANT

Chicago, Illinois

________________ Certifying Board Chairman

________________ Date

________________ AAMA President

Certificate No. __________

Courtesy of American Association of Medical Assistants, Inc. Used by permission.

FIGURE 15-2
CMA CERTIFICATE

The Business and Professional Women's Clubs

National Association of Bank Women, Inc.

National Association of Educational Secretaries

National Association of Legal Secretaries

Your job can become more than just a job. Through further training, study, and membership in professional organizations such as the ones mentioned, your opportunities for advancement will be enhanced. Your interest in the job will be stimulated with the result that you will be a top-notch secretary.

Appendix I

The following is a glossary of some of the most commonly used medical word parts and illustrations of how they are combined to form complete words.

a, an — word part meaning without or not

anesthesia — lack of sensitivity or feeling

aphonia — a loss of voice

ab — word part meaning from or out from

aberration — to deviate from what is normal

acr (o) — word part meaning extreme or extremity

acromegaly — abnormal enlargement of the extremities of body—nose, jaws, hands, and feet

ad — to or toward

addiction — becoming physically or psychologically dependent upon something (such as drugs) that tends to increase with use

aden (o) — word part meaning gland

adenoid — resembling a gland

ambi — word part meaning both

ambidextrous — able to use both hands equally well

angi (o) — word part meaning pertaining to lymph and blood vessels

angioma — a tumor containing lymph and blood vessels

angiectasia — stretching of a vessel

ante — word part meaning before

anterior — toward the front

anti — word part meaning against

    anticoagulant — substance that prevents or delays clotting of blood

anus — surface opening of the rectum

arteri (o) — word part meaning artery

    arteriosclerosis — hardening of the arteries

arthr (o) — word part meaning joint

    arthritis — inflammation of the joints

bi — word part meaning two

    biarticular — affecting two joints

bio — word part meaning life

    biology — scientific study of life

    biopsy — removal of living tissue for study or to examine

blast (o) — word part meaning the early stages of cell development

brachi (o) — word part meaning arm

    brachial — pertaining to the arm

    brachiocephalic — pertaining to the arm and head

bronchi (o) — plural of bronchus or word part meaning tubes

    bronchioles — the smaller tubes branching from the bronchi

    bronchus — the larger tubes carrying air to the lungs

carcin (o) — word part meaning cancer

    carcinoma — a cancerous tumor

cardi (o) — word part meaning heart

    cardiogram — the record of heart activity

    cardiograph — an instrument used to chart heart activity

    cardiomegaly — an enlarged heart

    carditis — inflammation of the heart

carpus — wrist

    carpal — pertaining to the wrist

cele — a herniation or protrusion through an opening or a break

cephal (o) — word part meaning head

    cephalgia — headache

cerebr (o) — word part meaning cerebrum

    cerebral — pertaining to the cerebrum

    cerebrum — main part of the brain located in the upper part of the cranial cavity

cheil (o) — lips

cheiloplasty — surgical repair of the lips

chir (o) — word part meaning hand

chiroplasty — plastic surgery on the hand

chole — word part meaning gall or bile

cholecyst — gallbladder

cholelith — gallstone

chondr (o) — word part meaning cartilage

chondrogenesis — formation of cartilage

colp (o) — word part meaning vagina

colpopexy — surgical fixation of the vagina

contra — word part meaning against

contraindicate — any condition that indicates that a particular type of treatment is inadequate or improper

core (o) — word part meaning pupil

coreoplasty — surgical repair of the pupil

crani (o) — word part meaning skull

craniotomy — any operation on the cranium

cyst (o) — word part meaning a sac or bladder

cystitis — inflammation of the bladder

cyte — a cell

dacry (o) — word part meaning tears or lacrimal parts of the eye

dacryocyst — tear or lacrimal sac

dactyl (o) — finger or toe (can be used as word part)

dent (o) — word part meaning tooth

dental — pertaining to the teeth

derma (dermo) — skin (also a word part for skin)

dermatitis — inflammation of the skin

dilation — stretching

dys — word part meaning bad or difficult

dyspepsia — difficult or poor digestion

ectasia — word part meaning stretching

ectomy — word part meaning excision or cutting out

electr (o) — word part meaning electricity

electrocardiograph — the machine used to record the electric currents produced by the action of the heart muscles

encephal (o) — word part meaning brain

encephalocele — protrusion of brain tissue through an opening in the skull

encephaloma — tumor of the brain

enter (o) — word part meaning intestine

enterogastritis — inflammation of the stomach and small intestine

epithelium — tissue covering internal and external body surfaces

erythr (o) — word part meaning red

erythrocyte — red blood cell

extra — word part meaning outside of or beyond

extrahepatic — outside of or beyond the liver

femor (o) — word part meaning thigh

femorocele — herniation of the femur

fibr (o) — word part meaning fibers or fibrous tissue

fibroblast — a cell from which fibrous tissue develops

gingiva (o) — gums (also word part)

gingivoglossitis — inflammation of the gums and tongue

gloss (o) — word part meaning tongue

globin — the protein element of hemoglobin

hemi — word part meaning half

hemiplegia — paralysis of one half or one side of the body

hem (o) or hemat (o) — word part meaning blood

hemorrhage — excessive flow of blood from the vessels

hidr (o) — word part meaning sweat or perspiration

hidrorrhea — excessive perspiration

hist (o) — word part meaning tissue

histologist — one who specializes in the study of tissues

hyper — word part meaning more than normal

hypertension — high blood pressure

hypertrophy — overdevelopment

hyp (o) — word part meaning less than normal or below normal hypotension — reduction in tension; lowered blood pressure

hypothyroidism — deficient thyroid activity

hyster (o) — word part meaning uterus

hysterectomy — removal of the uterus by surgery

in — word part meaning within; into; indicates a negative connotation

incompetence — not able to function properly

infra — word part meaning below or under

infraclavicular — below the clavicle

inter — word part meaning between

intercostal — between the ribs

intra — word part meaning inside of or within

intravenous — within a vein

ir (o) or irid (o) — word part meaning iris

iridoptosis — prolapse of the iris

jejun (o) — word part meaning jejunum which is the second portion of the small intestine

jejunostomy — creation of an opening into the jejunum by surgery, usually permanent

kerat (o) — word part meaning cornea

keratalgia — pain in the cornea

laryng (o) — word part meaning larynx

laryngitis — inflammation of the larynx affecting the voice and breathing

larynx — the structure located at the top of the trachea through which air passes to the lungs

leuk (o) — word part meaning white

leukocyte — white blood cell

ligature — material (thread or wire) used to tie off vessels or make repairs after an injury or during surgery

lip (o) — word part meaning fat or fatty

lipoid — resembling fat

lymph (o) — word part meaning lymph

lymphoma — a tumor composed of lymphatic tissue

macr (o) — word part meaning large

macrocyte — large cell

mal — illness; disease; bad

malignancy — a condition that usually gets progressively worse and results in death

malpractice — unprofessional, illegal, or immoral conduct, or lack of skill or negligence in carrying out professional duties

mening (o) word part meaning membrane; the three membranes that are part of the brain and the spinal cord

meningitis — inflammation of the meninges

meningocele — herniation of the meninges through a break in the skull or vertebral column

mes (o) — word part meaning middle

mesoderm — during the embryo stage of development the mesoderm is the middle of the three primary germ layers

meta — word part meaning change or after

metabolism — those changes that occur within the body (both physical and chemical) related to bodily handling of nutrients

metr (o) — word part meaning uterus

metritis — inflammation of the uterus

micr (o) — word part meaning small

microcyst — a cyst that can only be seen with a microscope

Muc (o) word part meaning mucous (mucus)

mucous (adjective) — pertaining to mucus

mucus (noun) — secretion of the mucous membrane

my (o) — word part meaning muscle

myocarditis — inflammation of the muscular walls of the heart

myel (o) — word part meaning bone marrow

myeloid — resembling bone marrow

necr (o) — word part meaning death

necropsy — examination of a body after death

nephr (o) — word part meaning kidney

nephropexy — surgical repair of a kidney

nephritis — inflammation of the kidney

neur (o) — word part meaning nerve

neuroblast — embryonic cell from which nerve tissue is formed

neuralgia — pain in a nerve or around one or more nerves

odont (o) — word part meaning tooth

odontalgia — toothache

oma — a word part meaning tumor or a new growth

oo — word part meaning egg or ovum

oophor (o) — word part meaning ovary

oophorectomy — surgical removal of one or both ovaries

ophthalm (o) — word part meaning eye(s)

ophthalmologist — the doctor who is a specialist in treating the eyes and performing surgery

ophthalmorrhexis — rupture of an eyeball

orth (o) — word part meaning straight; correct

orthodontist — a dentist who specializes in irregularities of the teeth and associated facial problems

osis — word part meaning a condition; used in many words, such as neurosis

oste (o) — word part meaning bone

osteomalacia — softening of the bones

ot (o) — word part meaning ear

otalgia — pain in the ear

pancreat (o) — word part meaning pancreas

pancreatectomy — surgical removal of part or all of the pancreas

para — word part meaning beside; beyond; a part of

paraneural — beside a nerve

path (o) — disease

pathology — the study of diseases

ped (o) — word part meaning foot or child

pedodontics — the dental specialty that deals with the teeth and mouth of children

pedal — pertaining to the foot or feet

per — word part meaning throughout; completely

perforation — a break in a wall or membrane of a body organ

peri — word part meaning around; near

perivaginal — around the vagina

peritoneum — the thin membrane lighing the walls of the abdomen and pelvic space

pharyng (o) — word part meaning pharynx

pharyngocele — a herniation of the throat

pharynx — throat

phleb (o) — word part meaning vein

phlebitis — inflammation of a vein

pneum (o) — word part meaning air or lung

pneumonia — inflammation of the lung

pneumon (o) — word part meaning lung

pneumonectomy — surgical removal of lung tissue, a small part or an entire lobe

poly — word part meaning many

polydipsia — excessive thirst

post — word part meaning after

postoperative — after surgery

posterior — toward the back

proct (o) — word part meaning rectum

proctoscope — an instrument for examining the rectum

psych (o) — word part meaning mind

psychoanalysis — a form of treatment of mental illness developed by Sigmund Freud

psychoneurosis — a mental disorder that occurs when a person is governed by emotion rather than reason

py (o) — word part meaning pus

pyocyst — a cyst containing pus

pyel (o) — word part meaning renal pelvis

pyelonephritis — inflammation of the kidney and the renal pelvis

quadrant — a fourth of a particular region, used in describing a fourth part of a whole, for example the abdomen

quadri; quadr — word part meaning something that consists of four

quadriplegia — paralysis of all four limbs

quinti — word part meaning fifth

quintuplet — one of five children born of the same mother during the same confinement

renal — kidneys

rhin (o) — word part meaning pertaining to the nose

rhinorrhagia — a nosebleed

salping (o) — word part meaning uterine tube (fallopian) or eustachian tube

    salpingo-oophorectomy — surgical removal of a uterine tube and ovary

schiz (o) or schist (o) — both are word parts meaning split or divided

    schizophrenia — a mental disturbance that can include multiple disorders affecting one's feelings, thoughts, and behavior

scler (o) — word part meaning hard

    sclerosis — a condition of hardening

semi — word part meaning half

    semicomatose — person who is partially conscious or can be aroused

splen (o) — word part meaning spleen

    splenomegaly — enlargement of the spleen

sub — word part meaning below or under

    subcutaneous — below the skin

super or supra — word part meaning over or above

    suprapubic — over or above the pubis

suture — stitching

symptom — any sign or indication of a disease that is used in diagnosis

syn — word part meaning with or together

    syndrome — a combination of symptoms occurring together

thorac (o) — word part meaning chest

    thoracocentesis — surgical puncture of the chest

thorax — chest

thromb (o) — word part meaning a blood clot

    thrombus — a blood clot

    thrombosis — presence of a blood clot

tonsillectomy — surgical removal of the tonsils

trachea — the tube leading from the larynx to the lungs

trache (o) — word part meaning trachea

    tracheotomy — an incision whereby a new opening is formed in the trachea

trans — word part meaning across, beyond, through

    transabdominal — across the abdomen

tri — word part meaning three

    triceps — a muscle having three heads

uni — word part meaning one

    unilateral — affecting only one side

ur (o) — word part meaning urine

    urodynia — pain during urination

    urinalysis — process of analyzing urine for diagnosis of disease

uter (o) — word part meaning uterus

    uteropexy — surgical repair of the uterus

uterus — the womb

vas (o) — word part meaning vessel

    vasospasm — contraction or constriction of a blood vessel

ven (o) — word part meaning vein

    venotomy — incision of a vein

    venous — pertaining to a vein

    (intra)venous — to put into a vein

vesic (o) — word part meaning bladder or a sac

    vesicocele — herniation of the bladder

wart — viral skin tumor

wheeze — respiratory sound that resembles whistling

xanth (o) — word part meaning yellow

    xanthosis — a condition of yellowness

x-ray — any radiations of very short wave length used in radiography due to their penetrating ability and use on photographic film

zoology — the study of living animals

zoophobia — abnormal fear of animals

zoophilia — abnormal attraction to animals

Appendix II

The following is a list of some commonly used medical abbreviations. Usage will vary among doctors and medical personnel as will the abbreviations themselves. Make sure that any abbreviation used is approved by your doctor and understood by your co-workers.

A

ā — morning
āā — equal part of each
abd — abdominal
a.c. — before meals
amt — amount
A.S.H.D. — arteriosclerotic heart disease
ad lib — as desired

B

Bid — twice a day
BMR — basal metabolism rate
BUN — blood, urea, and nitrogen
BP or B/P — blood pressure

C

c̄ — with
CA — chronological age
cap — capsule
CBC — complete blood count
cc — centimeter
C.C. — current complaint
cg — centigram
C.H.F. — congestive heart failure
C.O. — coronary occlusion
C/O — complains of
C.V.A. — cerebrovascular accident; blood is prevented from flowing to brain

247

D

d.c. — discontinue
D/W — dextrose and water
Dx — diagnosis

E

EEG — electroencephalogram
EKG — electrocardiogram
EMG — electromyogram
E.R. — emergency room

F

o — female
F.F. — force fluids
F.H. — family history
fl. — fluid ounce

G

GI — gastrointestinal
grs. — grains
gtts. — drops
GU — genito-urinary
Gyne — gynecology

H

Hb — hemoglobin
Hd — at bedtime
hr or h — hour
H.s. — hours of sleep
ht — height
H.V.D. — hypertensive vascular disease

I

in or " — inches
I.C.C. — intensive coronary (or cardiac) care for heart attack victims
I & D — intake and output
IV — intravenous

J

J or jt — joint
J or jour — journal
JAMA — Journal of the American Medical Association
jaund — jaundice

K

kg — kilogram
km — kilometer

L

lbs — pounds
LoNa — a diet with low salt content
LLQ — left lower quadrant
L.P.N. — licensed practical nurse
L & W — living and well

M

m — meter
M — mix
M.D. — doctor of medicine
mg — milligram
M.H. — marital history
ml — milliliter
mm — millimeter
Med/Surg. — medical and surgical service
/min — per minute
M.S.D.W. — married, single, divorced, widowed
M.S. — multiple sclerosis

N

NA — nursing assistant; nurse anesthetist; not applicable; not available
NB — new born
Neg. — negative
neuro — neurology
noct. — in the night
NPO — nothing by mouth
non rep. — do not repeat

O

O.B. — obstetrics
O.O.B. — out of bed
oz. — ounce
O.R. — operating room

P

$\overline{p}$ — after noon; p.m.
P. — pulse
p.c. — after meals
Peds. — pediatrics
P.I. — present illness
P.I.D. — pelvic inflammatory disease
per — through
prep. — readying the patient
p.r.n. — whenever necessary
PT — physical therapy; physical therapist
pvt. — private
Px — prognosis
pt. — pint
pt — patient
pts — patients

Q

q — every 4 hours
q.d. — every day
q.i.d. — 4 times a day
q.n. — every night

q.o.d. — every other day
q.s. — as much as required
qt. — quart

R

RBC — red blood cell count
R.H.D. — rheumatic heart disease
Rehab. — rehabilitation
R.N. — registered nurse
RLQ — right lower quadrant
R — respiration
RR — recovery room; respiratory rate
R & R — rate and rhythm of pulse
R.T. — radiologic technologist
R_x — take

S

$\bar{s}$ — without
$\bar{s}\bar{s}$ — one half
S or Sig. — label
S.O.B. — shortness of breath
s.o.s. — if necessary
stat. — at once

T

t.i.d. — three times a day
T. or Tbsp. — tablespoon
T. — temperature
T. & A. — tonsillectomy and adnoidectomy
tab. — tablet
tsp. — teaspoon

U

UA — urinalysis
URI — upper respiratory infection

V

V.D. — venereal disease
V.D.R.L. — venereal disease research laboratory
V.O. — verbal orders
v.s. — vital signs

W

WBC — white blood cell count
wks — weeks
wt. — weight

X

X — times
XRT — x-ray therapy

Y

yel — yellow
y/o — years old
yr — year

Z

Z — zero

Index

A

Abbreviations, medical, 247-250
"Annoyed" person, 32
Answering service, 35-36
Appearance, receptionist, 45-46
Appointments, scheduling, 13-25 (see also Scheduling appointments)
Atmosphere, 45-47
Automatic recording device, 36
Automation, filing, 136

B

Bibliography, manuscript, 126
Billing service, 177
Blue Cross/Blue Shield, 166-167, 172
Bookkeeping:
    automated, 177
    billing service, 177
    bookkeeper or accountant, 175
    collecting fees, 195-196, 206
    determining fees, 204-205
    duties, 175
    effective use of time, 197-203
    finances, patient's, 206
    finding time, 195
    itemizing statements, 203-204
    patient's ability to pay, 205-206
    planning, 196
    quoting fees, 204, 205
    records of payments and charges, 192-194
    selecting system, 176, 178-191

C

Cabinet, supply, 112
Cancellations, 15, 23, 24, 25
Cards:
    appointment, 21, 22, 23, 25
    professional, 21, 22
Catch-up time, 17, 23, 25
Certifying examination, 233, 235
Charges, records, 192-194
Charts, 50
Clerical work, 55
Color scheme, 52
Communication, 224-225
Compensation, worker's, 160
Computer billing service, 177
Confidential information, 29, 137, 216, 217-218
Consent, informed, 220
Correspondence:
    advertisements, 76
    bills and statements, 76
    certificate of health, 101
    circulars, 76
    dictation, 96
    envelopes, 95-96
    follow-up file, 76
    grammar, 84-86
        comma, 84-85
        spelling, word division, 85-86
    handling contents, 74-75
    incoming, 73
    innoculation certificate, 101
    instruction slip, 103
    letters, 78-83, 86-95, 99
        block, 93
        closings, 91
        corrected, 78
        excusing school absence, 79
        full block, 92
        incorrect, 78
        insurance company, 87
        negative, 89
        personal, 82-83
        points to emphasize, 86
        positive, 90
        professional, 79-82
        referral, 80, 99, 100
        salutations, 91
        semi-block, 94
        styles, 91-95
        thank you for referral, 81
        transmittal, 88
    mail register, 75
    outgoing, 77
    periodicals, 76-77

Correspondence *(cont'd)*
    personal mail, 75-76
    professional mail, 76
    professional publications, 76-77
    school note, 101
    short-kut note, 102
    stationery, 95
    telephone memo form, 82
    time-savers, 98
    transcribing, 97-98
    when doctor is away, 77
Custodial staff, 50

D

Decorator, 52
Desk, 45, 55
Dictation equipment:
    photocopying, 67-68
    secretary analyzes, 68-69
    transcription, 59-63, 69-71
    word processing, 63-67
Doctor:
    bag, 112-113
    informed consent, 220
    legal responsibilities, 218-219
    malpractice, 219
    Oath of Hippocrates, 214
    Principles of Medical Ethics, 215-216
    professional courtesy, 218
Doctors, other, 33, 218
Dress, style, 45, 46
Drug detail men, 31
Drugs *(see* Supplies)

E

Elderly patients, 42, 173
Electrocardiogram, record, 156-157
Emergencies:
    appointments, 15, 25
    receptionist, 41, 43-44
    telephone, 29
Equipment, 50, 56, 59-71, 107-109, 135-136
    (see also Dictation equipment)
Ethical responsibilities, 213-217
Examination, preparation, 38, 41
Examining rooms, 38, 41, 56

F

Fees:
    arranging for patients to pay, 206
    collecting, 195-196

Fees *(cont'd)*
    determining and quoting, 204-205
    discussing, 212
    itemized statements, 203-204
    patient's ability to pay, 205-206
Filing:
    alphabetic, 131
    alphabetize last names first, 128
    analyze various systems, 131-132
    arrange firm names as written, 129
    automation, 136
    charge card, 135
    choosing supplies and equipment, 135-136
    color coding, 132
    cross-referencing, 134, 135
    damage to patient, 128
    disregard "The," 129
    geographic, 132
    hyphenated names, 129
    inactive files, 134
    indexing names, 135
    information on particular subject, 127
    materials clearly visible, 134
    medical records librarian, 127
    medical school or hospital, 127
    neat and sloppy, 134
    nothing comes before something, 128
    numbers, 130
    numeric, 131-132
    one word is better than two, 129
    political divisions, 132
    prefixes are part of names, 129
    preparing materials, 132-135
    references and guides, 127, 128
    removing clips, 135
    size of office, 127
    sorting alphabetically, 135
    stapling, 135
    stored folders, 134
    subject, 132
    systems for every purpose, 128
    two-word geographical names, 130
    up to date, 127, 134
Floor covering, 52
Footnotes, manuscript, 124
Format, manuscript, 124, 126
Free time, 17, 23, 25
Furniture, 52
Future, 230-231

G

General practice, permanent record, 151-153

Glossary, medical word parts, 237-246
Graciousness, 208-209
Greeting patient, 210
Gynecology, permanent record, 149-150

H

Health insurance, 159-173 (*see also* Medical insurance forms)
Hippocratic oath, 214
Human relations:
  concerned graciousness, 208-209
  discussing fees, 212
  good, how to achieve, 209-210
  greeting patient, 210
  knowledge and understanding, 207-208
  scheduling efficiently, 211
  telephone, 211-212
  unexpected, dealing with, 210

I

Identification card, insurance, 163
Image, receptionist, 45
Informed consent, 220
Insurance forms, 159-173 (*see also* Medical insurance forms)
Interviewing patient, 38
Inventory, 109, 110, 111

J

Job description, 49, 50, 51

L

Languages, 42
Law, 220-221
Legal responsibilities, 218-219
Letters, 50, 73-103 (*see also* Correspondence)
Lighting, 52

M

Mail (*see* Correspondence)
Malpractice, 219
Management of office:
  assigning vacations, 50
  attractive office, 52-55, 56
    appropriate, 55
    color scheme, 52
    decorator, 52
    first impressions, 52

Management of office (*cont'd*)
    floor covering, 52
    furniture, 52
    ideas, 53, 55
    lighting, 52
    magazines, 55
    neatness, 56
    plants, 55
    smoking, 55
  custodial staff, 50
  duties, checklist, 56-58
  equipment, 50, 56
  examining room, 56
  immediate supervisor, 49
  job description, 49, 50, 51
  key factors, 225
  letters or charts, 50
  liaison, 50
  line of authority, 50
  medication, 56
  ordering items, 50
  paper work, 55
  preparing payroll, 50
  scheduling work hours, 49
  temporary or part-time help, 49
  uncluttered desk, 55
  vacation replacements, 49, 50
Manuscript:
  bibliography, 126
  edited rough draft with footnote, 121
  final corrected copy, 122
  finding information, 118-119
  footnotes, 124
  format, 124, 126
  gathering information, 120
  guide sheet, 125
  hints on producing, 120, 123-124
  margins, 124
  mid-page documentation, 122
  preparing, 119-124
  proofreaders' marks, 123
  quoted material, 124
  reference books, 116-118
  table of contents, 126
  title page, 126
  you can assist, 115-116
Margins, manuscripts, 124
Medicaid plans, 160
Medical Assistants, American Association of, 232, 233
Medical history, 38, 139
Medical insurance forms:
  accurate and prompt processing, 168, 173
  backlog of work, 168

Medical insurance forms *(cont'd)*
  Blue Cross/Blue Shield, 166-167, 172
  current manuals, 168
  diagnosis and treatment, 173
  elderly persons, 173
  fill out completely, 168
  firms hold seminars, 160
  good supply, 168
  government agencies, 159
  health insurance claim, 169-170
  how to find out about, 159-160
  identification card, 163
  lost or misplaced record, 173
  many different plans, 160
  Medicare, 159, 161-162
  patient's obligation, 173
  Peg-Master insurance claim forms, 171
  photocopy, 173
  pregnancy, 160
  private plans, 160
  prolonged illness, 168
  request for Medicare payment, 164-165
  rules change, 160, 168
  secretary must find system, 168
  seminars of insurance company, 168
  series of visits for an illness, 168
  Social Security Office, 159
  special files, 168
  streamlining processing, 168
  time limits, 160
  welfare or Medicaid plans, 160
  worker's compensation cases, 160
Medicare, 159, 161-162, 164-165
Medication, 56 *(see also* Supplies)
Messages, taking, 33-35
Mirror opposite desk, 46, 47
Mix-ups, appointments, 15

N

New patient, 37-38

O

Obstetrics, permanent record, 143-146
Office, management *(see* Management of
    office)
Ordering items, 50, 59-71, 106-107, 109 *(see
    also* Dictation equipment)
Organization, 223-224
Overstocking, 109

P

Paper work, 55
Part-time help, 49
Patient record card, 155
Patient registration form, 138
Patients' permanent records:
  basic statistics, 137-138
  doctor dictating, 139, 140
  electrocardiogram, 156-157
  general checklist of information, 154
  general practice, 151, 152, 153
  gynecology, 149, 150
  keep current, 139
  make entries immediately, 137
  medical history, 139
  medical secretary processing, 158
  obstetrics, 143-146
  patient registration form, 138
  processing in hospital, 138
  record card, 155
  record for electrocardiogram, 156-157
  responsibility, 137
  samples, 142-153
  secretary transcribing, 141
  surgical, 147, 148
  time, 154
  urgent, 154
Payments, records, 192-194
Payroll, preparing, 50
Pegboard bookkeeping, 16
Peg-Master insurance claim form, 171
Personal data, 38
Personal qualities, 225-226
Photocopying, 67-68
Pregnancy, insurance forms, 160
Privacy of patient, 29, 38, 41
Problems, telephone, 32-33
Professional courtesy, 218
Professional organizations, 232, 233, 235
Proofreaders' marks, 123

Q

Quoted material, 124

R

Rapport, television, 238
Receptionist:
  appearance, 45-46
  atmosphere, 45-47
  calm in times of stress, 42-45
  coffee, 47

Receptionist *(cont'd)*
  courteous and polite, 44
  desk, 45
  doctor unwell, 43
  easily seen, 45
  elderly patients, 42
  emergency, 41, 43-44
  examining rooms, 38, 41
  first person patient sees, 3
  greeting other callers, 45
  handbags, 42
  image, 45
  impersonal, but warm, 44-45
  impression you make, 37
  interviewing patient, 38
  languages, 42
  late doctor, 44
  medical history, 38
  mirror, 46, 47
  needs of patient, 41-42
  new patient, 37-38
  obstetrician's, 43
  pediatrician's, 43-44, 47
  personal data, 38
  physical aids, 47
  planning work, 43
  preparation for examination, 38, 41
  privacy of patient, 38, 41
  restless patients, 47
  running late, 41
  styles of dress, 45, 46
  tape recording voice, 47
  uniform, 45, 46
  waiting patient, 38, 41
  your personal problems, 42
Recording device, automatic, 36
Records:
  financial, 175-206 *(see also* Book-
    keeping)
  patients' permanent, 137-158 *(see also*
    Patients' permanent records)
Reference books, manuscripts, 116-118
Registration form, patient, 138
Restless patients, 47

S

Salesmen, 31
Scheduling appointments:
  appointment book, 16-21
    before giving card, 21
    catch-up time, 17, 23, 25
    15-minute intervals, 16
    legal evidence, 21, 25

Scheduling appointments *(cont'd)*
    legibility, 21
    necessity, 16, 21
    pegboard system, 16
    pen or pencil, 21
    single practice, 18
    spelling, 21
    two doctors, 19
    week at time, 20
  appointment card, 21, 22, 23, 25
  cancellations, 15, 23, 24, 25
  checklist, 16-25
  doctor's preferences, 14-15
  doctor wants to see patient again, 25
  emergencies, 15, 25
  human relations, 211
  knowing patients, 14
  mix-ups, 15
  needs of individual, 23
  patient's preference, 23
  professional card, 21, 22
  sensitivity to patient needs, 16
  telephone number of patient, 23
  telephone numbers, doctor's, 25
  timing and coordination, 13-14
Scheduling work hours, 49
Servicing equipment, record, 108
Smoking, 55
Specialties, medical, 226-227
Specialty, doctor's, 31
Storage, supplies and drugs, 110-111
Stressful times, 42-45
Supplies:
  cabinet, 112
  checking against purchase order, 110
  checklist, 106, 112, 113
  doctor's bag, 112-113
  inventory charts, 110, 111
  keeping up with, 105-106
  ordering, 106-107, 109
  overstocking, 109
  running inventory, 109
  shortcuts, 111
  storing, 110-111
  your responsibility, 107, 109
Surgical record, 147-148

T

Table of contents, manuscript, 126
Telephone:
  "annoyed" person, 32
  answering service, 35-36
  attitude, 29

Telephone *(cont'd)*
    automatic recording device, 36
    caller on hold, 29
    calls from other doctors, 33
    confidential information, 29
    drug detail men, 31
    emergencies, 29, 30
    first impression on caller, 27
    human relations, 211-212
    importance, 27
    kind of practice, 31
    listen carefully, 29
    more than one doctor, 28
    not rush patient, 28
    person insists on talking with doctor,
      32-33
    pick up on first ring, 28
    polite, 31
    problem calls, 32-33
    rapport, establish, 28
    taking messages, 33-35
      duplicates, 35
      follow-up action, 35
      forms, 34, 35
      record of calls taken, 35
    voice, diction and manners, 28-30

Temporary help, 49
Terminology, medical, 227-229
Title page, manuscript, 126
Transcription, 59-63, 69-71

U

Uniform, 45, 46

V

Vacations:
  assigning, 50
  replacements, 49
Vocabulary, medical, 227-229
Voice, 47

W

Welfare, 160
Word parts, medical, 237-246
Word processing, 63-67
Worker's compensation, 160
Writing *(see* Manuscript)
Written consent, 220